Indo-Russian Relations

Indo-Russian Relations

The Making of A Relationship: 1992–2002

Sreemati Ganguli

Maulana Abul Kalam Azad Institute of Asian Studies, Kolkata

SHIPRA

Views expressed are those of authors and not necessarily of the Institute.

ISBN: 978-81-7541-494-5

First Published in India in 2009

Indo-Russian Relations: The Making of A Relationship: 1992–2002

Published by :
SHIPRA PUBLICATIONS
115-A, Vikas Marg, Shakarpur, Delhi-110092 (India)
Tel. : 91-11-65277210, 22500954, Fax : 91-11-22458662
Email : info@shiprapublications.com
www.shiprapublications.com

For
My Father

Preface

This is a book, very dear to my heart, as this is my first book, but more so, as this was a part of my life, my academic endeavours as well as my creative pursuits for a long period of time.

I am immensely grateful, for the publication of this study, to the Executive Council of the Maulana Abul Kalam Azad Institute of Asian Studies, and to Prof. Jayanta Kumar Ray, the Chairman of the Executive Council.

I owe debts of a magnitude, which words of gratitude can hardly suffice, to numerable persons of stature for the preparation of this study. I must begin with Dr. Hari Vasudevan, Professor, Department of History, University of Calcutta, and presently, the Director of Maulana Abul Kalam Azad Institute of Asian Studies, who has encouraged me to look and think beyond the available literature on the subject with materials, hints and suggestions and to reach a standard, worthy of the meticulous scrutiny of his supervision; and Dr. Purusottam Bhattacharya, Professor, Department of International Relations, Jadavpur University who painstakingly has supervised this study through these years and has lent me invaluable advice.

I am also grateful to Prof. Suranjan Das, Vice-Chancellor, University of Calcutta, for his pertinent comments on this study, as the external examiner of the dissertation.

Interviews granted to me by the office–bearers of the government of India have been of crucial help in my understanding of the knotty bilateral issues from India's point of view. I should express my sincere gratitude to Dr. APJ Abdul Kalam, Hon'ble ex- President of India, for reasons of his ground level knowledge in related matters in his earlier capacity as the Director of the Defence Research and Development Organization (DRDO) and his written answers have been of immense help towards my understanding of the issues asked. I met hon'ble former Prime Minister of India, (late) Sri PV Narshima Rao at his New Delhi residence and he kindly sent me his written replies to my questionnaire, which reflected the postures and attitudes of the then Head of the Government of India (1991–96) towards teething problems confronting the relations. Also revealing have been the comments of Sri Pranab Mukherjee, the Minister for Commerce and Finance in the Indira Gandhi Cabinet and the Minister for Commerce and External Affairs in the Narshima Rao Cabinet, in his interview granted to me, particularly from his comprehensive grasp over every aspect of the bilateral relations since the Soviet era. Interviews of (late) JN Dixit, the former Foreign Secretary and of NN Vohra, the former Defence Secretary, have helped my understanding of the growth of this bilateral relation in its formative years. SK Lamba, the Indian Ambassador to Moscow (1998–2001) has immensely helped me to understand the significance of Russia to India during the period of his tenure.

My interviews of scholars, strategic analysts, and key personalities in the Indian private sector, engaged in bilateral trade, have helped me comprehend accurately the perspective of Indo–Russian relations and I am greatly indebted to all of them.

I am indebted to Professors of the Department of International Relations, Jadavpur University who taught me. I would also thank Prof. Dr. Madhavan K. Palat of the Centre for Historical Studies of Jawarharlal Nehru University, New Delhi.

I would like to personally thank all my friends and colleagues in this Institute for their encouragement and support.

I am grateful to my teacher Mrs. Susmita Bhattacharya for whatever knowledge I have of Russian language.

To me, this is an appropriate occasion to remember my mother, who saw the beginning but could not see the completion of this study. And this study, through all these years, has been a journey in which I have found a co-traveller in my father.

Contents

Introduction

The disintegration of the Soviet Union in late December 1991 and the eventual emergence of fifteen independent states, including the Russian Federation as the successor-state to the Union of Soviet Socialist Republics (USSR), had put an end, for all practical purposes, to the Indo-Soviet relationship, built carefully over forty years. The resultant concerns, from the Indian point of view, were the following disruptions in the flow of necessary spare parts for its military equipments that were overwhelmingly dependent on Soviet supplies, as well as in the continuation of bilateral economic relations – the cornerstone of the former relationship.

The study traces step by step how the Indo-Russian relations have evolved against this backdrop and will examine whether the relations have been necessarily upgraded to make a relationship in a new context of global configuration. The post-Cold War world has been characterized by two simultaneous trends: the bipolar world order has been replaced with largely unipolar tendencies; and it has been increasingly globalized and interdependent as the prevailing environment has required countries to connect, to include and to engage others despite their very different persisting conditions, which logically has suggested a trend towards a multipolar world order. The Indo-Russian relations have evolved under this context.

It examines whether the strong points of the earlier relationship have been made relevant against constraints, largely from Russia's end, of Russia's transitional difficulties from a command-economy to a market economy, as well as of Russia's foreign policy orientations, more inclined towards the West rather than to the East to include its traditional friends like India.

From India's point of view, the disintegration of the Soviet Union may be conceived as a crucial dividing line – a watershed – between relations with the Eurasia region, during the Soviet years and during the post-Soviet period. Among the consequences of the disintegration, India had to build relations with an altogether new state – the Russian Federation (RF). This new entity was often seen as a successor to the USSR – but the problems of such a categorization were evident in the description of the RF much later by its Foreign Minister and subsequently the Prime Minister, Yevgeny Primakov to Strobe Talbott, Deputy Secretary of State under President William Jefferson Clinton. Primakov spoke of the RF as "recovering from the loss of nearly half its land, the evaporation of its alliances, the precipitous decline of its military budget, the looming obsolescence of its strategic forces and, on top of all that, an upsurge in terrorism and secessionism on its territory."[1] The RF – as the successor-state to the Soviet Union – was only recognizable by the tokens of its inheritance – the permanent seat of the UN Security Council and the nuclear arsenal. It had to confront an uncertain geopolitical situation with an economic strength and military power that could not be compared with that of the USSR. The threats of the Cold War were no more, but the RF's perceptions of insecurity were evident.

For India, the catastrophic changes in the Soviet Union had a portentous significance in the context of its long-standing and enduring relations with that state. Its fragmentation into fifteen independent sovereign states meant that the process of dialogue would have to be conducted with a number of authorities and agencies, each with diverse concerns.

The RF assumed the role of a "state-continuator" – and took on responsibilities of all the agreements and commitments of the former USSR. This implied that the relations that had been developed with the erstwhile USSR, are to be continued with Russia, the status having been denied to other members of the Commonwealth of Independent States (CIS). Russia's status as the "State-Continuator" has been unanimously acknowledged by the international community, and it has inherited the permanent seat of the UN Security Council and other memberships of the international fora without objection from the global community.

The purpose of this study is to examine the patterns of change in Indo-Russian relations in the context of the radically altered global perspective, consequent on the Soviet disintegration. It deals with how far the continuity factor has been relevant in the growth of relations in the new perspective and how far "growth" of a relationship has been sustained in spite of the systemic and institutional changes in both countries' domestic environment. The study also sets out how far Russia has been responsive to India's urgency for a reciprocal approach to each other's needs; and whether the bilateral relations have found new areas for cultivation where each country's interests converge.

No theoretical approach, however, has been attempted in the study except on occasions as and when theories have come up as interesting reference points.

The present study seeks to examine the basic facts and evidence used in the standard literature, adding to it where possible. It also deals with indications of policy inclinations that await actualization but are realizable on valid grounds in the near-future. The material cumulatively can affirm or deny:

(a) that the continuity of the relationship between India and Russia has been more than a formal one;
(b) that both countries have been eager/prepared to salvage the essentials of the earlier relationship as are permitted by the new compulsions of the post-Cold War environment;
(c) that Russia, weakened through its disintegration, hardly promises to be a viable partner to make a relationship with; and
(d) that, alongwith the salvage of the essentials of the earlier relationship, new material grounds, objectively related to the new pattern of global arrangements, have been located and cultivated by the two countries to strengthen the chances for a relationship, since the strong points of the earlier relationship, developed under a different context of global configuration, can hardly be dragged on to get linked to a new gestalt of international relations.

This quest, for the answers to the questions raised, runs through the Chapters of the present study to develop the point of argument for or against the viability and sustainability of a meaningful relationship between India and Russia.

Chapter one, while providing an outline of Indo-Soviet relations pre-1992, serves as the background to the development of Indo-Russian relations. It views the dynamics of Indo-Soviet relations in perspective of their objective relations with other actors in the sub-continent in the Cold War context. It analyses how the Indo-Soviet relationship evolved from indifference to a near-strategic partnership and studies explicitly the compulsions of both countries to come close to each other in view of their respective national interests as well as to deter other actors' machinations in the sub-continent. It notes in the process the impact of subsequent Soviet foreign policy goal to radically alter the global Cold War milieu on Indo-Soviet relations alongwith its protracted reverberation on subsequent Indo-Russian relations.

Chapter two concentrates on the transitional phase of Russian economy in its restructuring process from a command-economy to a market economy; on its impact on Indo-Russian economic relations, marked by a precipitous decline to reach at its nadir in the initial years, elevated subsequently to a relatively stable stage; and on newer areas of cooperation, other than the traditional ones, identified and cultivated by both to ground the bilateral sluggish economic relations on a solid base.

Chapter three expatiates on the evolution of Russian foreign policy priorities from its preponderantly inclined orientation towards the West in the initial years to its belated realization of its vital stakes in the East to initiate reprioritization of its foreign policy orientations; on their impact on Indo-Russian relations over the decade; and on the objective circumstances under which defence relationship between the two countries as well as their common approach to political issues of regional and global dimensions were reinforced in the essentially altered environment of the post-Cold War period.

Chapter four delineates the interests and stakes of India in the Central Asian Region and convergence of the intertwined interests and stakes of these Republics with Russia and India, imparting it a trilateral dimension, while the region is increasingly becoming a crucial area for Russian and Indian foreign policy goals.

The Conclusion rounds-up the points of argument that have been developed through the four chapters in a resume to affirm or deny the viability as well as the meaningfulness of Indo-Russian relationship during the decade.

Notes and References

1. Strobe Talbott, *The Russia Hand: A Memoir of Presidential Diplomacy*, Random House, New York, 2003, p. 413.

Chapter 1

Indo-Soviet Relations: The Background

In early 1992, when the Union of Soviet Socialist Republics (USSR) had ceased to exist, Russia became the main successor-state to the erstwhile USSR, and an important relationship evolved between India and the Russian Federation in the decade that followed. Some of the aspects of this relationship were guided by the Indo-Soviet relationship of the past.

The Indo-Soviet relationship, as most bilateral relations, did not essentially preclude close interactions with others. It committed partner to bloc politics. And thereby permitted flexibility in strategy and behaviour. However, the Indo-Soviet relationship grew intimate out of compulsions of mutual need, and so came to deter other players from encroaching on their common interests. Hence, India had simultaneous good relations with the United States (US), the other and the predominant superpower and its good relations with countries of the so-called Soviet bloc or of the Western bloc did not earn for it the stigma of either of the bloc's identity. Again, India's identity as a leader of the Third World and the ablest exponent of Non-Alignment gave it a special status. The latter, it may be added, was one of the inducements for the Soviet Union to come close to India and the dominant inhibition, for the US, to be intimate with it, even while the status earned the country respect.

This chapter proposes:

(i) to view the dynamics of Indo-Soviet relations, bearing in mind Indo-United States relations, Indo-Pakistan relations, and Sino-Indian relations. A range of other issues form an important background: United States – Pakistan relations,

Soviet-Pakistan relations, Sino- Pakistan relations and a range of others;

(ii) to reveal the nature of the evolution of relations in their entire gamut-in political, economic and defence spheres; and

(iii) to note, the impact and reverberations of Soviet foreign policy goals to radically alter the global Cold War perspective, on Indo-Soviet relations, and ultimately on Indo-Russian relations.

Growth of Relations Before 1947

Indo-Soviet relations developed in the overall context of independent India's formation of nation-to-nation relations. Before this, tangible interactions between leading Indian political figures and the Soviet leadership came to be noticed in the immediate aftermath of the Revolution and with the participation of Manabendrathnath Roy, as leader of the Mexican Communist Party, in the Second Communist International (Comintern) of June 19-August 7 1920, in Petrograd, where Roy's thesis on colonies was submitted by V.I. Lenin, along with his own, to the Plenum. In October 1920, Roy founded the Indian Communist Party in Tashkent.

Under Stalin in the mid-1920's there was a rapid rise of Soviet interest in the "East" which concentrated on China. The 1927 visit of Indian nationalist leader Jawaharlal Nehru and his appreciation of Soviet achievements did do little to moderate Stalin's deep suspicions of the Indian National Congress. In the mid-1930's Stalin sought British support against the rise of Nazi Germany and Fascist Italy and could hardly support the anti-British nationalists. With the end of the World War II and the allied relationship with Britain sapped, the USSR established diplomatic relations with India in 1947.

Establishment of Indo-Soviet Relations: The Backdrop

The foreign policy of the interim Indian government formed in August 1946, the role of Indian diplomacy in establishing direct contact with the Soviet leadership and the British position on the issue received sufficient exposure in the Documents of the India Office, published in 1970–80 and through the opening of the British archives, related to the end of the 1940's and the beginning of the 1950's.[1]

The then international status of India had an uncertain character: As a colony, the country was denied an independent status in international fora and, simultaneously, it was having diplomatic representative offices in China and the US. India was invited to the San Francisco Conference in 1945 and the unofficial delegation led by Vijaya Lakshmi Pandit participated in it. Documentary evidence suggests that Pandit, as Head of the Indian delegation to the UN General Assembly, and K.P.S. Menon, a member of the delegation, initiated the talks with Soviet Foreign Minister V.M. Molotov at New York on establishing diplomatic ties between the two countries under near secrecy, bypassing the British authorities. Nehru, as the Head of the crucial foreign ministry of the interim Indian government, had an active interest in establishing diplomatic relations with the Soviet Union for strengthening of India's international position.

Principled agreement for establishing diplomatic relations between the two countries was confirmed in V.K. Krishna Menon's meeting with Molotov in New York on 31st October, 1946. All India Radio confirmed on 12th November, 1946, Nehru's assertions in the Constituent Assembly about both nations' intention to exchange diplomatic representatives. "Though such a development is undesirable for royal government of Great Britain, nevertheless, it is necessary to give concession", said one of the documents. This concession played a crucial role in later years. It was decided that public statements about both countries' intention to exchange diplomatic representatives at ambassador's level would be made at Delhi and Moscow at the same time on 13th April, 1947 at 20.00 hrs. Indian Standard Time and 17-30 hrs. Moscow time.

In 1945, British ruling circles, while offering dominion status to India, counted on signing an agreement with it as one of the pre-conditions and accordingly the Department of Foreign Affairs at Delhi was instructed to urgently prepare the provisions for inclusion in the agreement between Britain and India. The Department put forward its proposals, text of which was sent from Delhi to London on 27th October, 1945 in a telegram. Certain clauses of the proposal are worth noting:

— Indian federation would be a dominion, as part of the British Commonwealth that retains all rights including the right to conclude agreements, that would remain in force in all member-states of the Commonwealth.

— The Union will take all obligations and receive all rights of India as member of the UNO and as a founding member that signed the UN Charter at San Francisco.

— In case of war or emergency situation, Indian government will provide all kinds of support to Britain on *Indian territory*, including use of Indian ports, airports and other communication facilities, which requires corresponding legislative and administrative measures.

Thus the obligations, that were to be forced upon India as pre-conditions to obtain dominion status, would have made India's sovereignty and independence subservient to British interests. Establishment of Indo-Soviet bilateral diplomatic relations on equal terms – and the opening of Indian Embassy in Moscow – contradicted unequivocally this position for India, sending out a positive assertion of India's independent status to the world at large, essentially ruining the British plan. This backdrop is helpful to understand, in depth, Nehru's sense of urgency when he established relations with the Soviet Union – then deemed by Indian leaders as an epitome of anti-imperialism.

Andrei Zhdanov, a leading associate of Stalin, in a significant speech in September 1947 categorized India as one of the few exceptional states (others being Egypt and Syria) that posited themselves, though being non-socialist countries, outside the fold of the imperialist camp. The categorization itself was the earliest pointer to India's emerging non-aligned status. The Soviet stance towards India, with East-West Cold War positions inflexibly drawn by early 1948, underwent a sea change: India came to be viewed as a semi-colony of the British, its non-alignment as an "imperialist device." Nehru's visit to the US in 1949 portended a potential isolation for the Soviet Union. In the early 1950's, there was a perceptible softening of attitude: the Soviet Union transported much-needed shipments of wheat to India, Stalin consented to grant an interview to the departing Indian ambassador Dr. S. Radhakrishnan in 1952, his first in two years to a foreign diplomat, and to the new Indian ambassador K.P.S. Menon as a "gesture of goodwill" in 1953.[2]

US Relations with India and Pakistan: The Cold War Calculus

During this initial post-1947 period, it was widely believed that a close affinity would grow between India, the largest and Asia's first democracy and the US, the most celebrated one. But India's policy of non-alignment that fundamentally rejected the premises of the Cold War and coalesced with a group of newly-born independent states to resist incorporation either in the US-led or the Soviet-led bloc, ran counter to the US' interests. The initial western perceptions of Nehru that took him for a prototype of the Westminster tradition steeped in the western value system, had misread him. Nehru's preference for parliamentary democracy was qualified by a deep seated hatred of western colonialism, a commitment to socialism and an appreciation of the Soviet Union's rapid industrialization.

The eruption of hostilities in October 1947 leading to a war between the newly-born nations of India and Pakistan over the volatile issue of the strategically situated region of Kashmir, provided an important reference point for India as it established its position. In April 1948, the US and Britain sponsored a Security Council Resolution for setting up a UN Commission on Kashmir that established a cease-fire line between India and Pakistan. The fact that this Resolution treated the two countries as equal parties to a "dispute" and avoided branding Pakistan as the "aggressor" prompted Nehru to charge that "the motive of the United States was to get military and economic concessions in Pakistan."[3] The situation was specifically ripe for the perception that India and Pakistan were prone, because of their respective compulsions, to take opposing stances toward emergent Cold War.

Nehru's first visit to the US in October 1949 almost coincided with the United States' shocking realization that it no longer enjoyed a monopoly of the atomic bomb and with the news that mainland China had been brought to the Communist fold with the establishment of the People's Republic of China on October 1, 1949. Nehru's own "assessment" of the end result of the visit was that the US government had expected "acquiescence" from him on all issues and were unwilling to assist India for "anything less."[4]

The invasion of South Korea by Communist North Korea in 1950, the US intervention in that conflict under United Nations (UN) auspices in 1951, the eventual entry of China into the Korean War and their initial military successes against MacArthur-led UN forces prompted the US to a frenzied witch-hunt for alleged subversives at home. This culminated in McCarthyism and moves to install a cordon sanitaire around the Soviet Union and its allies in East Europe institutionalizing the policy of containment authored primarily by

George F. Kennan in 1947. India's refusal to contribute combat units and its token service of the medical team it lent to the UN force in Korea, its decision to accord diplomatic recognition to China against American pleadings, its insistence on the anti-colonialist, as contrasted with the Communist dimensions of the Chinese revolution, its support of mainland China's application for UN membership (even after its entry into the Korean Conflict), its role in moulding Geneva Accords and complicating the Japanese Peace Treaty by its refusal to sign it alongwith the USSR – fell into a certain pattern from the US point of view. All these went a long way to contribute to the US perception of India's non-alignment as equivalent to being pro-communist and the simultaneous Soviet perception of India's non-aligned stance as conducive to Soviet interests, further from being an "imperialist device", previously assumed.

The resultant impact of the fact that from 1950 both superpowers had atomic weaponry led to a nuclear deadlock and to ideologically driven power politics in the Third World where confrontation, without the high risk of nuclear escalation, seemed possible. As Barnet points out "… Under the nuclear 'umbrella' … a more aggressive strategy was developed for opposing political and economic changes in the Third World deemed threatening to US interests."[5]

The idea of US military aid to Pakistan was a strange concurrence of British Tory geopolitical thinking, as a follow-up to the partition of India, to fill the "power vacuum" left by the departure of the Raj, propounded by Sir Olaf Caroe and of the Cold War imperatives of the late Harry Truman and early – D. Eisenhower years. Sir Olaf argued for inclusion of Pakistan as part of the Middle East to be an obvious base for Middle-Eastern defence against the Soviet Union.[6] In Washington, the Caroe argument provided the needed rationale for supporters of a policy of "choosing" between India and Pakistan. By November 1953 Vice-President Richard Nixon, after his return from an India-Pakistan visit, made it clear that he favoured the alliance with Pakistan, not for its purported defence value against Soviet aggression, but "as a counter-force", in the words of one of his early biographers, "to the confirmed neutralism of Jawaharlal Nehru's India."[7]

Post-Stalin Era: Indo-Soviet Relations

In the post-Stalin era, a significant change, in essence, in Soviet perceptions of India was manifest in the address of G.M. Malenkov,

Chairman of the Council of Ministers to the USSR Supreme Soviet, in August 1953: he appreciated India's role in ending the Korean War and of the impact of its peace efforts on the "peace loving countries" and hoped that "relations between India and the Soviet Union will continue to develop and grow, with friendly cooperation as the keynote."[8] Indian ambassador in Moscow, K.P.S. Menon noted this as the first occasion on which so friendly a reference to India or indeed to any non-communist state had come from "so important a personage in the Soviet Union."[9]

In December 1953, the first Indo-Soviet trade agreement was signed. In June 1955 Nehru visited Moscow, his gesture was reciprocated by the visit of Nikita Khrushchev and Bulganin to India in November 1955. Nevertheless, the shifts and adjustments in Soviet perceptions of India must be noted in the context of a larger process of change in Soviet foreign policy. In the arena of the Third World alone, the Soviet leaders had concluded that the West seemed particularly vulnerable. The nationalist movements in the Afro-Asian countries were potentially positioned against western imperialism and neocolonialism, against their countries' economic dependence on the West and would be equally responsive to the Soviet appeal for Peace and Peaceful Coexistence – which they would need most for their countries' reconstruction. All this, expectedly, in conformity with Soviet goals, might be achieved through a pragmatic and flexible Soviet foreign policy, attuned to the emerging aspirations and inherited susceptibilities of the Third World, significantly with little risk. The West had already started the game through military pacts in the Middle East, in South and South-East Asia.

The essence of this viewpoint was stated in Nikita Khrushchev's Report of the Central Committee to the Twentieth Party Congress (1956) of the Communist Party of the Soviet Union (CPSU), deemed as a watershed in Soviet foreign and domestic policy. He stressed, in the context of the accelerated pace of disintegration of the world colonial system, upon "peaceful coexistence" of both socialist and non-socialist states in Europe and the East to establish a vast "zone of peace". He assured Soviet cooperation to those countries which "refused to be involved in military pacts" and also assured the under-developed countries of Soviet readiness to help with its "industrial development on terms of equality and mutual benefit", to neutralize economic pressure of the West.[10]

The Soviet policy change towards India recognized the US policy initiatives in the region and India's reaction to them. The US formed the anti-communist Southeast Asia Treaty Organisation and the Baghdad Pact in 1954 and 1955 respectively and US-armed Pakistan was taken in both as a member. India resented the initiative, as the Cold War was being brought into South Asia, military blocs were being formed and Pakistan being armed vis-à-vis India, the ultimate victim to the influx of US military aid to Pakistan. In spite of President Eisenhower's assurances to Nehru to the contrary in 1954, the Eisenhower administration by 1957, openly acknowledged that Pakistan wanted American weaponry for use against India, rather than against the Communist powers.

In March 1954, the USSR supported in the UN the Indian demand to recall Americans from the group supervising the Indo-Pak ceasefire line in Kashmir.[11] In February 1957, the USSR used its first veto to defeat a Security Council Resolution recommending the use of a temporary UN force to facilitate demilitarization in Kashmir. Consequent on India's liberation of Goa in December 1961, Soviet support for India including a Security Council veto at the UN, contrasted markedly with western hostility because of Portugal's status in NATO. In January 1962, the USSR vetoed the UN Security Council Resolution that called for a plebiscite in Kashmir.

1962 Sino-India Conflict: Differences in Postures of the Superpowers

The Sino-Indian border clashes at the end of 1959 summer brought to the fore a strained Sino-Indian relations that coincided with escalation of the Sino-Soviet antagonisms by the summer of 1959. The Soviet leaders announced a position of neutrality on the clash and called for talks between New Delhi and Beijing. The Soviet stance pleased the Indian leaders but infuriated the Chinese. The 1962 Sino-Indian border war started on October 20 at the height of the Cuban missile confrontation between the superpowers. Nehru wanted "to avoid irritating the Soviets as much as possible."[12] On October 27, Nehru sent an urgent appeal to all Heads of State requesting diplomatic and material support in the campaign against China. Two days after Nehru's appeal, J.K. Galbraith the US ambassador to New Delhi, met Nehru to find out what kind of foreign assistance India needed. American arms supplies, however, started arriving in India on November 3. At this juncture of Indian history, the Indo-US relations were closer than ever before but it was short-lived for other foreign policy objectives of both. The US was disinclined to shift its focus from its main contender, the USSR or to push Pakistan closer than desired to PRC. India, for its part, was anxious to preserve its non-aligned status and an amicable relationship with the USSR. Beijing declared a unilateral ceasefire and withdrawal of force on November 20.

In September 1963, the Soviet Union endorsed the Colombo Plan of December 1962 for the settlement of the Sino-Indian conflict, questioned the validity of the Chinese leaders' adage that "the Nehru government is an imperialist and expansionist government" and forwarded a question: "Did they perhaps wish to settle the border quarrel with India by military means and hope to obtain support from the Soviet Union?"[13] It was a clear statement of support for India that exposed the Sino-Soviet breach and warded off a certain degree of temporary coolness in Indo-Soviet relations. Interestingly, Nikhil Chakravarty, the founder editor of "Mainstream" reminisced. '...on the 23rd, Pravda came out with an editorial, 'Brothers and Friends, they are brothers, India is a friend',... So I wrote an open letter to Pravda by an "Indian Marxist" in *Mainstream* criticising that position quite strongly...on the sixth or seventh of November. *Pravda* came out with another editorial criticizing the Chinese position and supporting the Indian position. In the December meeting of the Supreme Soviet, Khrushchev in typical style abused the Chinese for committing aggression against India; that was the dividing line in the Sino-Soviet conflict over India'.[14]

Along with the primary Soviet goal to reduce and eliminate western influence in the Third World, the second one crept into Soviet perception since 1959 with the exacerbation of the Sino-Soviet split, to reduce or contain China's involvement in the Third World particularly in South Asia. The Soviet assistance to India in both military and economic spheres was to continue significantly. The Sino-Soviet-Indian relationship as well as the Soviet-US-Indian one developed into a pattern to play a crucial role in 1969 and throughout the 1970's. In the 1960's there were perceptible shifts, though of a temporary nature, in Soviet stance towards India and in US stance towards Pakistan. In May 1964, during the Kashmir debate in the Security Council, there came a perceptible shift in Soviet stance that stated that the "dispute" between India and Pakistan were to be resolved by "the two interested parties by peaceful means"[15] from its earlier position in 1962 that condemned Pakistan's "armed aggression" in

Kashmir and the "continued occupation of one third of the territory of Kashmir by Pakistan troops"[16] On the other hand, the refusal by the US and Britain to link military assistance to India to a settlement of the Kashmir dispute in John F. Kennedy – Harold Macmillan's joint statement on 30 June 1963, weakened substantially the US-Pak "alliance" – a significant development for the USSR and China.

The 1965 Indo-Pak War: Significant Soviet Mediation

Moscow took a neutral stance towards the Indo-Pak armed clash in the Rann of Kutch in April 1965. Pakistan's infiltration of guerilla forces into Kashmir in August led step by step, to the second Indo-Pak war in September. Backed by the US military aid relationship, Pakistan was emboldened to launch a war against India with overall qualitative superiority. In the view of Indian decision makers, Nehru's reservations about Eisenhower's decision for arms aid to Pakistan were thus confirmed. The US came to be seen as a tacit supporter of Pakistan's interests. The American unwillingness to criticize Pakistan and its apparent stance to equate the aggressor with the victim by clamping an embargo on arms sales to South Asia strengthened India's apprehensions about US intentions. This distrust widened (as evidenced by subsequent events) into more generalized versions of misgivings about US interests and intentions regarding India. Deep-seated distrust between India and Pakistan blocked America's long-term security hopes for the sub-continent. Contradictory pulls of the US policy to perceive India and Pakistan as countervailing powers at the same time and compulsions to improve relations with one at the cost of the other led it to a dilemma that persisted till the end of the Cold War.

The Soviet leaders were quick to recognize that neutrality would hardly be defensible in case of a prolonged war and they worked for a ceasefire in the UN. A ceasefire was finally agreed to on September 22. When no progress towards disengagement was noticed, the Soviet offer was repeated in November (Premier Kosygin made two offers of Soviet good offices earlier on September 4 and again on September 19) and was accepted by both the parties. Kosygin stuck to the letter and spirit of the offer of good offices at Tashkent during 4–11 January 1966. He used his powers of persuasion with much finesse and skill, while maintaining a low profile, to make the two leaders see each other's point of view in the interest of peace in the subcontinent.[17] Lack of

US concern about South Asia, with its preoccupations in Southeast Asia, provided the rationale behind the US acquiescence to the Soviet role and growing influence in the region.

Nixon Doctrine: US Disengagement from Asia

President Richard Nixon was anxious to find a way to disentangle the US from the Third World issue of Vietnam "with honor" and this was the foundation of the so-called "Nixon Doctrine." The USSR came to a near effective parity with the US in the strategic area and challenged its exclusive capabilities for distant operations through its own development of intercontinental ballistic missiles at this time. The deteriorating Sino-Soviet relations offered a potential opening for the US strategy in the three-sided conflictive relationship. Nixon and Henry Kissinger envisaged a restructuring of the international order that would create a balance of competition and interdependence among the five major powers: the US, Western Europe, Japan, the Soviet Union and China. The US interest in Asia was restricted to nations possessing power: China, presumably in politico-military and Japan, assuredly, in the economic sphere. The Asian agenda in the US foreign policy had a new and compelling focus – the opening to China.

Irritants in Indo-Soviet Relations

There were three possible irritants in the development of Indo-Soviet relations at this time – NPT, Soviet arms aid to Pakistan and the idea of Collective Security. The implicit requirement by those who signed the Nuclear Non-Proliferation Treaty (NPT) of July 1968 that non-nuclear states should sign and confine themselves to their prevailing status, might have posed an irritant in Indo-Soviet relations. India objected to the Treaty being implemented as it sought to discriminate against the "have nots" in the nuclear weapons field, while permitting the five so-called "haves" to develop and stockpile more weapons. However, as Arkadii Shevchenko[18] has pointed out, the USSR was remarkably flexible at this time in its concerns with the Treaty and other similar ones. Unlike the United States (which, incidentally, was also relatively down-played at this time concerning proliferation), NPT seldom formed a cardinal preoccupation of Soviet policy.

A possible major concern for Indian foreign policy was the Soviet decision to supply arms to Pakistan in 1968, following the US cutoff of aid in 1965. This arms deal of July 1968 was a one shot agreement and was never repeated. Significantly, in May 1968, Pakistan served the notice for the US to close down its surveillance station at Badaber near Peshawar that "proved to be a catalytic element in the Kremlin's policy review, leading it to recognize Pakistan's legitimate needs for Soviet arms assistance."[19]

Again, on 7 June 1969, Leonid Brezhnev advocated, at the Moscow International Meeting of Communist and Workers' Parties, a "system of Collective Security in Asia" in the context of a probable power vacuum consequent on the proposed withdrawal of Britain from the East of Suez by 1971. But Mrs. Gandhi's response to the Brezhnev proposal was cautious, as she objected to its "military overtones" and disagreed with its assumptions of a "power vacuum" in Asia, following the British withdrawal by 1971. She mooted a proposal, while on a visit to Tokyo and Jakarta in June, that envisaged mutual guarantees from both the US and the USSR for peace in Asia for an interim period following a Vietnam settlement.[20]

But, the tense Sino-Soviet relations in the post-Ussuri river conflict, the potential Sino-US rapproachement in the offing (as President Nixon secretly asked President Yahya "to explore the possibility of providing links between Washington and Peking"[21] during Nixon visit to Pakistan in mid 1969), the unreceptive stance of Pakistan towards Soviet overtures and growing closeness of Sino-Pak relations in view of their respective foreign policy goals in the region, necessitated a revision of Soviet policy of equidistance.

Bangladesh War: A Proximity in Relationship

The concurrent trends at the great power level running parallel to the trauma in the subcontinent (in the wake of the macabre human tragedy from March 25 in East Pakistan), which compelled an influx of nine million refugees in India, were viewed with trepidation in New Delhi. On his way to Islamabad, Henry Kissinger stopped at New Delhi in early July 1971 to caution India that "China would intervene on behalf of Yahya Khan if India intervened on behalf of Mujib," with the assurance that "Washington would support India in the event of a Chinese attack."[22] But on his return to Washington, Kissinger met the Indian ambassador and lent unequivocal substance to India's intense apprehensions: he reversed his earlier pledge through his assertion that the US would stay neutral in the event of China's intervention[23] in favour of Pakistan. The Indian overtures to China to ensure its non-involvement in case of a Indo-Pak conflict included Mrs. Gandhi's letter to Chou-En-lai, explaining India's position and offering to hold talks with China and sending of D.P. Dhar to Moscow to hold talks with Lin Hsinchinan, Chinese ambassador to Moscow. These efforts, however, led to no change in Sino-Indian relations. On 9th August Andrei Gromyko and Swaran Singh signed a significant bilateral Agreement – the Treaty of Peace, Friendship and Cooperation.

The Treaty: A Prelude

A prelude to the Treaty itself might be traced as far back as 1968. During 1968, President Zakir Hussein, and after him Swaran Singh as Foreign Minister and Dinesh Singh as Commerce Minister visited Moscow to reiterate the Indian argument against Soviet military aid to Pakistan that the Soviets could hardly "repeat the American style of influencing by giving arms" to Pakistan.[24] To extend further mutual cooperation in various fields, the Soviet leaders offered a treaty of peace and friendship in 1968. Mr. Kaul, the then Foreign Secretary, went to Moscow in mid-1968 and "exchanged drafts with them of the proposed treaty, without commitment on either side."[25] Then came the split in the Indian National Congress and Mrs. Gandhi was on the defensive. The Soviet leaders fully appreciated the problems on the Indian side and asserted that "whenever you feel like, we can take up this draft again."[26] To a question advanced by M.K. Palat, several years later, about what had prompted the Soviets to offer a treaty to India in 1968, A.K. Damodaran, Indian Minister in Moscow at the time of the signing of the Treaty, had this answer: "I think, it is due to the tradition of treaties in Soviet diplomacy. They had been more interested in the crucial clauses, promising support in case of trouble, than we had been."[27]

India got interested in the Treaty, following the Bangladesh crisis, apprehending the real danger of isolation. "Swaran Singh came over to Moscow and we went through all the Warsaw Pact Treaties."[28] Damodaran obviously referred to Swaran Singh's visit in June which the Indian Press had termed as a failure. We are privileged to have an access to the inner side of the story. Nikhil Chakravartty, had this to add: "The Indo-Soviet treaty, as Damodaran has said, was spurred not only by the Bangladesh development but by Kissinger going to Beijing via Pakistan"[29]

Hafeez Malik, the Pakistani analyst, however, denounced the Pakistani Foreign Office's assessment as less than "novice" and went on to recognize "...the Soviet Union had exploited a strategic opportunity in creating an Indo-Soviet counterweight to the emergence of a US-China entente, in which Pakistan played a subordinate role."[30] During Mrs. Gandhi's visit to Washington, President Nixon and Kissinger refused to persuade Yahya to yield, in Kissinger's words, to "India's determination to establish its pre-eminence in the sub-continent."[31] Though she succeeded in getting a US promise to hold back weapons to Pakistan already "in the pipeline," she, however, got no objective facts indicative of US intervention in South Asia. India was apprised of a US analysis that China probably would not intervene either.

Pakistan formally declared war on India on the morning of the 4th December, after bombarding airfields in North and West India the previous evening. TASS on December 5 strongly denounced Islamabad for the war and warned all outside powers to stay out to keep the conflict localized. On December 5, 6 and 13, the USSR vetoed a US-backed Resolution, in the Security Council, that supported Pakistan by way of calling for a ceasefire and the withdrawal of troops. Obviously, Moscow's support of India in the UN provided India the much-needed minimum required time to complete the "liberation" of Bangladesh. As the Indian operations in East Pakistan continued beyond the time-limit, set by Moscow (a week, as reported by *The Statesman*),[32] D.P. Dhar was sent to Moscow on 11th December and First Deputy Foreign Minister V.V. Kuznetsov arrived in New Delhi on the 12th "to co-ordinate strategies." Kuznetsov made it a point to Mrs. Gandhi that a threat to the integrity of West Pakistan would, in all probability, invite interventions from the US and China. He also pointed out that "Soviet opposition to a ceasefire became more untenable the longer the war goes on the east."[33] Kuznetsov's extended stay at New Delhi revealed that "India did not have carte blanche."[34] But it was explicit that full discretionary power of a single country was incompatible with the concerted approach of the two towards the problem of peace and stability.

Soviet naval deployment in response to Washington's despatch of the carrier "Enterprise" and a task force from the Seventh Fleet into the Bay of Bengal, deterred the US from intervening. The Soviet threat to China with diversionary action in Xinjiang was a key factor for Beijing's staying out of the conflict. Augmented Soviet arms deliveries dating from August also substantially added to India's edge over Pakistan. It supplied India advanced weaponry worth $500 million[35] between 9th August and 15th December.

On December 16, the "Pakistan forces in Bangladesh surrendered to the Joint Command of India and Bangladesh"[36] and the next day Mrs. Gandhi declared a unilateral ceasefire in the west, that was accepted by Pakistan a day later. An independent entity of Bangladesh, recognized by India earlier, on 6th December came into reality.

The Relationship: A Pointed Review

"A bargaining relationship" between the two countries, as an analyst observed, was involved during the Bangladesh crisis.[37] Cooperative accommodation would perhaps be a helpful phrase in discerning the interactions of India and the USSR during the crisis: each was essentially in a continuous process of accommodating the other on issues it regarded essential, while accommodating itself to its partner wherever it safely could. The Soviet policy was completely supportive of New Delhi until about the mid-way point of the on-going war when it advised restraint as regards the West Pakistan front.

The US Role During the Crisis: Its Rationale

The low-key level of Washington's official reactions to the Indo-Soviet treaty that would have been seen as a major blow to the international standing of the US a decade earlier, reflected in a way the low interest the US had towards India.

The incursion of the Enterprise taskforce into the Bay of Bengal on December 10, ostensibly to protect Americans in besieged Dhaka, was, in fact, meant to signal US concern about the integrity of Pakistan. The move was intended as a political gesture to a new partner, China, showing American support for a mutual friend, Pakistan.[38] An American analyst has assessed the net result of the Enterprise affair in India as "that the United States was seen as threatening but ineffective, as there is no convincing evidence that Indian politics were affected in any significant way by the cruise of the Enterprise."[39] It only revealed the reversal of the US role in sending the Enterprise in 1962 on a mission in support of India against China and a decade later, in sending the same supporting both China and Pakistan against India. This unjustifiable reversal of the role led India to question the credibility of the US as a friendly country. The impact of the Enterprise episode on Indian policy-makers, however, was that it was seen as an implicit nuclear threat since the Enterprise presumably carried nuclear weapons and the perception was instrumental in shaping Indian naval and nuclear strategy thereafter.

The Regional and Global Frame of Reference to the Relationship: A Change

With the emergence of Bangladesh, India earned for itself the recognition of its leadership role in South Asia and of its status as a major power in the region, as noted by Canadian – Indian scholar Baldev Raj Nayar: "The war in South Asia in 1971 resulted in a major restructuring of power in the region, raising India to a position of preeminence in the subcontinent and consequently making it an important middle power."[40] The international milieu of the bilateral relationship was also experiencing transposition: détente between the US and the USSR was being promoted that culminated in President Nixon's visit to Moscow in May 1972. Moreover, Nixon's significant visit to China in early 1972 substantiated the commencement of Sino-US normalization process. On May 18, 1974 India detonated an underground nuclear device at Pokhran, and Mrs. Gandhi was quick to reassure other states that the explosion was meant for peaceful purposes and not for making nuclear weapons. Moscow reported the news routinely, but its dilemma was manifest in its dispassionate response and in its reported offence implied in the temporary recall of the Soviet ambassador from New Delhi for "consultations."[41] The Indian move was suggestive of its intended reduced dependence on the Soviet Union. On the other hand, it typified further proliferation of nuclear weapons – opposite to what the USSR had advocated for long.

New Power Alignment

Indo-US Relations: Towards "Maturity"

Deputy Assistant Secretary of Defence, James Noyes stated in a Congressional hearing that "(a) new power alignment in South Asia has emerged from the (1971) Crisis. India is now unquestionably the major power in the area .... Its potential for exercising influence or being dominant in the entire – not the entire, but over much of the Indian Ocean area, I think the potential is there."[42] This statement went beyond noting India's pre-eminence in South Asia and indicated a wider trans-regional role for it. Another US attitude towards India was revealed in its repeated statements of the period to build the bilateral relationship on the basis of "maturity."[43] To rebuild the relationship, the US settled the rupee problem, generated from food imports of many previous years under the PL-480 programme: it retained access to one third of the amount for embassy expenses and the remaining $2 billion was written off.[44] Two other events – the Indian nuclear explosion and the imposition of a state of emergency in India in 1975 – also gave out significant signals about the new "maturity" of the relationship. The US administration chose in both the cases to play the matter in a low key.

India's Overtures for Normalization of Sino-Indian Relations

India signaled in 1976 several gestures of goodwill towards China – again a show of new power-alignments in South Asia. India supported China's candidature for the Asian Development Bank and restored its diplomatic representation to Beijing to the ambassadorial level and new Chinese ambassador to New Delhi Chen Chao-yuan declared that "full normalization of Sino-Indian relations through joint efforts" was in the interests of the peoples of both countries.[45] Also, a change in Beijing's attitude towards India was noticeable in its downplaying the October border clash with India in 1975, presumably India's opposition to the Asian Collective Security idea might have played a role in changing, to a certain extent, Beijing's perception of India. India's positive initiatives to the normalization of its relations with China broadened its potential options in foreign policy. Mrs. Gandhi's remark in her address at the banquet on the first night of her visit to Moscow in June 1976 was particularly suggestive of India's independent policy postures vis-à-vis China in a broad perspective of its commitment to non-alignment: "Darkness is not dispelled by cursing but by lighting lamps. Alongwith international efforts for peace, each country must act on its own to reduce areas of suspicion and to enlarge areas of goodwill."[46]

Soviet Armed Intervention in Afghanistan: An Ordeal for the Relationship

The high expectations of superpower détente by this time in the global arena had started eroding well before Moscow's armed intervention in Afghanistan on December 27, 1979. By April 1979, notions of naval arms limitation in the Indian Ocean had been scrapped, and a buildup had recurred there in the forces of both superpowers, including the despatch by both of aircraft carriers in the area.[47] Pakistan almost immediately, following the intervention, gained an elevated status in Washington's calculations as a frontline state and a potential block to further southern advance of Soviet power and influence. It was assured of Washington's commitment of support under the bilateral Defence Treaty of 1959.

India's trying dilemma was that, on the one hand, the USSR was its most important and dependable major power ally. The Soviet action in 1978 had pushed back the possibility of a fanatic Islamic state in Afghanistan, as in Iran, to India's relief and had reduced the US' meddling in Afghanistan's internal situation to India's interest. On the other hand, most of the non-aligned states were opposed to the Soviet move. Furthermore, the deployment of Soviet forces on the soil of Afghanistan, a non-aligned country, was a situation that was repugnant for India's consistent foreign policy principles. The dilemma was between the choices of opposition to the Soviet move to maintain its stature and leading role in the NAM as well as to be consistent with its foreign policy principle and avoidance of any resultant erosion in Indo-Soviet relations, while opposing the Soviet move. The problem with India was how to fit itself in the texture – as a participant player or a non-participant victim. India was the second country after the USSR to recognize the new Marxist regime in Afghanistan after the April 1978 coup that indicated India's keen interest in the return of stability there. As a consequence of the events in Kabul in late December, India's reactions centred round two themes and these, with shifting grades of relative stress, were persistently prevailing in Indian stance. First, India was opposed to outside interference in the internal affairs of one country by another. Second, a major fall-out of the invasion was that arms race in the region was likely to be restored and accelerated.

Policy preferences for India were focused in a series of Mrs. Gandhi's interviews with foreign press. She scoffed at suggestions that she was pro-Russian. "Not a bit" she said," "I am pro-Indian." She insisted, "Our problem here is not to take sides. We are only concerned with India. We are not in one bloc or the other."[48] On the question that India would feel pushed towards Russia, with China as well as the US apparently helping Pakistan, she retorted, "No, No, No. We do not need any support from whomsoever. We feel to be strong enough ourselves ... It is a front against Moscow, and it will force Moscow to counteract. The Russians will have to strengthen their presence in this region ... all over Southeast Asia. And that will be a great danger."[49] The concerted efforts of the US and China to increase military aid to Pakistan as they reached an agreement consequent on the early January visit of the US Defence Secretary Brown to Beijing, evoked sharp criticism from Mrs. Gandhi, as it would pose a danger to India and the rest of the Third World.[50]

India's position on the Afghan issue (given India's stature within the Non-Aligned Movement and the Third World) came to be viewed in Moscow's perception as unquestionably crucial, since its isolation in the General Assembly vote on the Afghan issue, where 17 non-aligned nations sponsored a Resolution on Afghanistan, calling for an "*immediate*, *unconditional* and *total* withdrawal of foreign troops from Afghanistan.[51] Foreign Minister Gromyko visited New Delhi in February 1980 to assess the new government's policy preferences and to seek India's support for Moscow's military intervention to forestall interferences from Washington, Islamabad and Beijing.[52] At the end of the visit, J.N. Dixit, the spokesman of the External Affairs Ministry, stated that Moscow's armed intervention could not be looked at out of context, as "many things are happening in the world which impinge on the situation in Afghanistan" like American use of Indian Ocean-Persian Gulf military facilities, massive build-up of US naval forces in the region, strengthening of Diego Garcia and reports that "certain countries are openly saying" that they were training Afghan rebel fighters.[53]

Though Gromyko felt assured that India's perceptions "held the United States as much to blame as the Soviet Union for the tensions gripping the region",[54] he was unsuccessful in getting India's unqualified support on Afghanistan, while India failed in its persuasion to get a timetable for Soviet withdrawal. A kind of a concerted effort by visiting Soviet Deputy Foreign Minister Firyubin, the Cuban Foreign Minister and the Vietnamese Prime minister Pham Van Dong during April 1980 ostensibly to convert India's view to their own perceptions on the Afghan issue, brought forward the fact that the USSR needed India's cooperation and friendship in its trying time much in the same way as India needed the USSR in 1971.

Gorbachev Era: Radical Changes in Soviet Foreign Policy Goals

The Backdrop: Compulsions for Change

From the beginning of the first term, the US administration under

President Ronald Reagan followed a well-chalked out strategy vis-à-vis the USSR:

(a) Through tightening controls on technology transfer and lowering the price of oil[55] – Moscow's prime source of hard currency – Washington raised the cost to Moscow of its continued acquisitions;
(b) The Reagan administration raised the state of US-Soviet competition to a new and advanced variety of an unprecedented technological competition with the introduction of space-based defence, the Strategic Defence Initiative (SDI);
(c) Additionally, the US increased the cost to the Soviets of far-flung and over-extended involvements through its support of resistance movements in Angola, Afghanistan, Kampuchea, Nicaragua and elsewhere;
(d) The Reagan administration proceeded to disrupt Soviet power internally, stimulating resistance to Communist rule, prominently, in Poland;[56]
(e) The US proceeded to rebuild containment systematically, strengthening relations with its European and Asian allies and China; NATO deployed a modernized intermediate range missile force, Japan conceded in assuming greater responsibility for defence of the sea-lanes; China after 1982 increasingly changed its position towards the US, particularly in economic relations; relations with Pakistan got a boost after the Afghan crisis; and
(f) The US initiated its forward move towards a second-strike capability, based upon sea-based mobile MIRV (Multiple Independently-Targeted Re-entry Vehicle) that would substantially neutralize Moscow's very expensive and fixed land-based first strike threat.

The qualitative changes initiated by President Mikhail Gorbachev in the Soviet foreign policy goals transformed the global perspective of the Cold War we were familiar with. We, now, need to concentrate on the backdrop to ascertain the compulsions for the change from the Soviet point of view. President Reagan's SDI announcement in March 1983 boded a strategic crisis for Moscow. The debate within the Soviet military establishment between General NV Ogarkov and V. Kulikov focused on the need to get the necessary resources to meet the challenge within the context of the Brezhnev strategy, i.e., "to change by military means the global correlation of forces to Soviet advantage."[57] The Soviet political leadership, on the other hand, concluded that any attempt to confront the American challenge would eventually drain out an already overblown economic capacity. Precisely, the Soviet leadership decided that Brezhnev strategy would hardly succeed in the face of the perceived American counteraction and needed a change.

The decision to change strategy was represented by the appointment of Mikhail Gorbachev as the General Secretary of the CPSU in March 1985. For him, the idea underlying the change of strategy was to make the USSR competitive – the sole hope to provide for resources needed to revitalize the country, modernize its forces, restore the economy and elevate its geopolitical position. In foreign policy, under the rubric of "new political thinking," he chose to take up earlier offers of détente from the US, West Germany, Japan, China and Iran.

In the first rough draft of "new political thinking", Gorbachev told the 27th Congress of the Communist Party of the Soviet Union (CPSU) in 1986: "Never, perhaps in the postwar decades, was the situation in the world as explosive and hence more difficult and unfavourable, as in the first half of the 1980s."[58] In February 1987, while addressing the Moscow International Peace Forum, he emphasized the necessity to concentrate Russian constructive endeavours to improve the quality of life in the domestic arena: "This is why we need lasting peace, predictability and constructiveness in international relations."[59] When Gorbachev assumed power, the Soviet economy was mired in a decade-long slump: for the period 1976–85, the average GNP growth rate was just over 2 per cent per year, including less than 1.5 per cent in 1984 and zero growth in the first quarter of 1985.[60] Détente with the US was the essential prerequisite for the Soviet domestic and foreign policy reform. The reversal of Soviet strategy signifying termination of hostile relationship with the West, led Gorbachev to come to terms with West Germany, thus slowing the process of European unification; to return to détente with China, with the offer of significant leverage on Northeast Asian Affairs, including Japan; to end the Afghan crisis and to improve relations with Iran – a Soviet objective for long. Détente with Beijing was the chosen means for Gorbachev to avert both its marginalization in North-east Asia and a Sino-Japan détente. Notably, Soviet disengagement from

Afghanistan was also prompted by the economic costs of the Soviet involvement there as well as by the Soviet eagerness to improve relations with countries in South Asia and the Middle East that viewed the Soviet intrusion as a long-term threat to their countries' security.

To relieve the gathered tensions in US-Soviet relations, President Gorbachev signed Intermediate Range Nuclear Forces (INF) Treaty, the first nuclear arms reduction accord in 1987. On 8 May, he initiated the process of withdrawing Soviet forces from Afghanistan. In December 1988, while addressing the UN General Assembly, he abdicated class warfare as the basis of Soviet foreign policy, welcomed "pan-humanist values" and "global interdependence" and undertook to alter an "economy of armaments into an economy of disarmament." The New York Times extolled President Gorbachev and placed him at the stature of President Woodrow Wilson and President Franklin Roosevelt.[61] Divergent views were reflected in the US National Intelligence Estimate: some analysts saw the current policy changes as "largely tactical, driven by the need for a breathing space from the competition"; other analysts believed that Gorbachev's policies reflected a fundamental rethinking of national interests and ideology, namely, "the withdrawal from Afghanistan and the shift toward tolerance of power sharing in Eastern Europe to be historic shifts in the Soviet definition of national interest."[62] The Conventional Forces in Europe (CFE) Treaty was concluded in 1990 and the Strategic Arms Reduction Talks substantially advanced in 1991.

President Gorbachev made a series of concessions in these treaties: To get the INF Agreement, he made major concessions, that President Brezhnev and his two successors had rejected, which included asymmetrical reductions and intrusive on-site inspections. Regarding the CFE Treaty, the USSR accepted in May 1989 NATO's proposal for equal force ceilings which meant that the Warsaw Pact would have to destroy far more weapons than NATO. And in the START-1 Treaty, President Gorbachev made three major concessions – he agreed to conclude the Treaty, without insisting on restrictions on the US Strategic Defence Initiative (SDI); he accepted a 50 per cent reduction in "heavy" SS-18 missiles – the backbone of the Soviet nuclear deterrent; and he also accepted a 50 per cent reduction in "throw weight" for its ICBMs and SLBMs.[63]

The decisive moment of the unification of the two Germanies came at the White House on 31 May 1990 during the second Soviet-American summit. When US President George Bush (Senior) asked whether the Germans had a right to choose their own alliance, President Gorbachev unexpectedly agreed.[64] The Soviet Union lost virtually all its allies in Eastern Europe in the process of the "silent revolution" that followed and the lines of its defence moved directly to the lines of its state borders. The collapse of communist power in Eastern Europe was a windfall for the US, specifically in the military – strategic area. The withdrawal of Soviet troops from East Europe resulted in a tremendous burden on the already overblown Soviet economy. Soviet Foreign Minister Aleksandr Bessmertnykh, who succeeded Eduard Shevardnadze and sided with the diehards during the August coup of 1991, remarked that the unification of Germany was "one of the most hated developments in the history of Soviet foreign policy, and it will remain so for decades."[65] In response, the then Soviet Foreign Minister, Shevardnadze held his ground: "No matter how strong an ideological mortar has cemented the bricks in this wall (the Berlin wall), the popular will is stronger and can break down any barriers .... If a policy cannot respond to these feelings it is doomed.... The most disturbing thing about the (domestic) criticism... was rather the lack of a rational alternative .... A columnist I greatly respect remarked that history creates opportunities, while politics takes advantage of them. I would add: or else politics does not take advantage of them, but instead tries to "arrange" history according to preferred ideological patterns."[66]

Between Iraq's invasion of Kuwait on August 2, 1990 and the US air strikes on Iraq, started in January 1991, there were hurried interactions between the US and the Soviet Union: both published a joint statement denouncing the invasion and Presidents of both countries attended a special meeting on the issue in Helsinki on September 9. The then Soviet Foreign Minister Eduard Shevardnadze recalled "The aggression against Kuwait was aggression against the tendency toward positive change introduced into international life by the policy of new thinking .... All through those days we worked extremely hard to promote the formation of an international consensus and an appropriate reaction by the world community to the events in the Persian Gulf."[67] US-Soviet joint opposition to Iraq's occupation of Kuwait was heralded in Washington as the first test of a new post-Cold War relationship – the so-called "new world order." Sovetskaya Rossiya, however, remarked that cooperation with the US "had ended the USSR's existence as superpower."[68] The Soviet military withdrawal from Eastern Europe and the CFE Treaty made it possible for the US to redeploy troops and material from Germany to the Middle East for

Operation Desert Storm. Soviet Defence Minister Dmitri Yazov commented that the Gulf war and the CFE Treaty taken together signalled a basic shift in the "correlation of forces" between the NATO and the USSR in the West's favour.[69] The 1991 August coup in the Soviet Union posed a dilemma for the US Intelligence Community. The first post-coup assessment of September 1991 spelled out three possible scenarios for the post-Soviet future: one was political and economic "confederation" in which the republics would coordinate economic, defence and foreign policies, while continuing to pursue economic reform; the second one was a "loose association," in which several key republics would break away but maintain a common market; and the third one was "disintegration and collapse of the centre."[70] The Special National Intelligence Estimate (SNIE), cited above, concluded that the second scenario was the most likely and the third the least likely over the coming year.

Reverberations on Indo-Soviet Relations

The radical changes in the milieu of international relations following major shifts in Soviet foreign policy goals had their logical reverberations on Indo-Soviet relations during Gorbachev regime. The Joint Communiqué after Rajiv Gandhi's Moscow visit in May 1985, revealed no movement of the Indian side towards the Soviet position on either Afghanistan or the Collective Security in Asia and both issues were not mentioned in the Joint Communiqué of May 1985. The Soviets referred to China in friendly terms for the first time since the Sino-Soviet split. Gorbachev broached his Asia-Pacific strategy first with Rajiv Gandhi, and projected the USSR as a leading power in Asia and beyond the Pacific.

On July 28, 1986 in his Vladivostok speech, Gorbachev embraced a whole range of issues from the Afghan conflict to Soviet relations with China and Japan and announced a basic framework of his Asia-Pacific strategy. His reflections on security in the Asia-Pacific region took into account that "the five principles of peaceful coexistence and the ten principles of Bandung have not disappeared into oblivion."[71] The purposeful citation of the principles, on which India built its non-aligned foreign policy, was aimed at accommodating India in the Asia-Pacific strategy.

The Delhi Declaration "on the Principles of a Nuclear Weapon-Free and Non-Violent World" of 26 November 1986, by Prime

Minister Rajiv Gandhi and President Gorbachev emphasized both countries' unique commonness of approach to the vision of a world, free from nuclear weapons and violence. The Declaration was Perestroika's first international document on "New-Thinking", carved out of the Indo-Soviet exchanges, as noted by the Soviet Ministry of Foreign Affairs.[72] Gorbachev revealed, in hindsight, the importance he attached to the Declaration, in an interview with Dev Murarka: "I have just completed my memoires where, among the top achievements of new thinking and Soviet foreign policy, I have listed the signing of the Delhi Declaration. This Declaration is no less actual today than at the time it was signed." He referred, in the interview, to his address in New Delhi animatedly: "It is said in the Vedas: the path is won by he who is walking it ... And I had thought that it was something novel pertaining to the new age, the *pronouncing* it to *end my address.* I had something fresh, that we had embarked on a *new path, a new stage of coming closer.*"[73]

The Soviet decision to start withdrawing troops from Afghanistan in May 1988 met India's long-expressed wishes. In November 1988 Gorbachev visited New Delhi and had wide-ranging discussions on global as well as regional issues.

The end to the Soviet military involvements in Afghanistan had not meant an end to the crisis in the land, it only transposed it to a regional one, stripped of superpower rivalry.[74] The continuing crisis in Afghanistan had serious repercussions for India in the next decade. The end of the Cold War only vindicated India's persistent stance against superpower rivalry and against the consequent arms race since the end of the World War II and raised hopes in India that it would be, generally, conducive to India's interests. The 1971 Treaty was renewed in October 1991 for another 20 years during the Prime Minister P.V. Narasimha Rao regime. The Indian rationale for the extension of the Treaty was that despite the USSR's reduced stature and the horrendous problems it was facing at home, India had immense stakes in the USSR, particularly in trade and military fields. For the Soviets the extension had a greater symbolic significance as it represented Indian confidence in Soviet resilience. The Treaty extension reassured India that in a world of bewildering changes with political parameters dramatically altered, "the Moscow-New Delhi relationship is less ephemeral than the collapse of a hallowed ideology and a bipolar world."[75]

The August 1991 Coup

Incomplete understanding with little feedback and confusion over what was going on within the USSR and over what might be its implications for future Indo-Soviet relations, led Indian decision-makers of foreign policy to a faux pass – a slow, dilatory reaction to the Soviet coup of August 1991. However, the Indian government said nothing of approval either, as Prime Minister Narasimha Rao decided to ignore the letter by Yanayev, the leader of the coup, defending the actions taken.[76] In a letter, K. Natwar Singh, the former Minister of State for External Affairs, also accused the government of "incoherent management" of the country's foreign policy.

Subtle shifts in emphasis and their intonations were discernible in successive Soviet postures towards India during the perestroika period. The context changed with the end of the Cold War, with the two superpowers working together towards a better and cooperative relationship and with the definite improvement in Moscow's relations with Beijing. The subtle shifts in Soviet posture were evidenced in Gorbachev's 1986 visit when he advised New Delhi to work towards a negotiated settlement in Kashmir as the Soviets did in Angola and Afghanistan; in, when India was explicitly left out of the process of negotiations regarding the settlement of Afghanistan – an area vital to India's security; and in mid-1989, when the USSR denounced the US supply of F-16 planes to Pakistan for its security implications for Afghanistan, being evasive for the first time of its possible fall-outs for India. In November 1991, Moscow also signaled a deviation in its posture towards India in supporting a joint Pakistan-Bangladesh Resolution on Nuclear Weapons Free Zone in South Asia in the UN General Assembly.

The Disintegration of the USSR: The End of Indo-Soviet Relations

The Commonwealth of Independent States (CIS) – a new political entity in place of the USSR – was essentially born on 8 December 1991 when the Presidents of Russia, Belarus and Ukraine signed the Minsk Agreement. On 20-21 December at a summit meeting held in Alma Ata, the new body was formed that included eight more members, i.e. all the Central Asian Republics as well as Armenia, Azerbaijan and Georgia. The Upper Chamber of the USSR Supreme Soviet proclaimed on 26 December 1991 that "the Soviet Union no longer" existed.

Anatoly Dobrynin, "Moscow's Ambassador to Six Cold War Presidents," held Gorbachev responsible succinctly for the Soviet disintegration: "The Soviet Union that Gorbachev inherited in 1985 was a global power, perhaps somewhat tarnished, but still strong and united and one of the world's two superpowers. But in just three years, from 1989 to 1991, the political frontiers of the European continent were effectively rolled eastward to the Russian borders of 1653, which were those before Russia's union with the Ukraine."[77]

In his last Presidential Address to the nation on 25th December 1991, Gorbachev defended his ground as: "I have firmly stood for independence and self-determination – for the sovereignty of the republics – but at the same time for the preservation of the [Soviet] state and the unity of the country ..... The policy that has prevailed is one of dismembering this country and breaking up the state – and I cannot agree with it."[78] And he thereby discontinued his activities as President of the Union of Soviet Socialist Republics.

Gorbachev's mission and that of the *perestroishchiki* was to reorganize and revitalize the Soviet system as well as "to create the maximum favourable external conditions needed in order to conduct internal reform."[79] Another objective was to win the West's diplomatic and economic support for *perestroika*, while trying to maintain the USSR's superpower status. *Perestroika*, in Gorbachev's view, was the strategic mission of both foreign and domestic policy. "By remaining stuck in the old positions, we would not stop the arms race, which was bleeding our already anemic country, or reestablish cooperation with the West, or cease our involvement in regional conflicts, primarily in Afghanistan, or normalize relations with China."[80] We cite Anatoly Dobrynin's assessment of Gorbachev: "I believe that Gorbachev never foresaw that the whole of Eastern European (area) would fly out of the Soviet orbit within months or that the Warsaw Pact would crumble so soon. He became the helpless witness to the consequence of his own policy."[81] Dobrynin's assessment of Gorbachev as the helpless witness in this case equally holds good for his position vis a vis Soviet disintegration – which he endeavoured to avert/resist.

Now, two essential components of Indo-Soviet Relationship, the economic and military ones, will be discussed, alongwith the relevance of India's non-aligned stance for its relations with the USSR.

Indo-Soviet Economic Relationship

Undeniably, there existed active undercurrents that developed into an inter-relationship of the economic and the political elements of the Indo-Soviet relations. We have so far looked into the political aspect of the relationship, and this will lead to insights as well as perspectives from which to understand the urges and compulsions of both states to develop the economic relations to the level they reached.

The Soviet planning experience had become conventional wisdom for Indian political and economic leaders in pre-independence days, as evidenced in the Bombay Plan of 1944 that recognized the need for planning as a strategy as well as the need for a major role of the public sector in the development of heavy industry.

Within an overall import-substituting strategy – one of a number of options open to an industrializing economy – as enunciated by P.C. Mahalanobis (1953) – India adopted the option that is similar to the Soviet strategy: to import capital goods (machine tools) to make capital goods which in turn are used to make other capital goods, investment goods and so on.

Soviet and East European aid proved to be crucial to the implementation of the Indian development strategy as envisaged in the Second Plan's pattern of industrial investment. The first loan, for the Bhilai steel plant, was extended in early 1955 during the First Plan period. The planned nature of both economies induced the Soviets to commit project aid for the duration of a whole five-year plan period, and extend project aid for investments of an "interlocking character" – so that the Indian economy could achieve an independent technological capability in basic and capital goods. Almost every Five-year Plan coincided with the extension of a new Soviet loan as in the Second (1956-61), Third (1961-66), Fourth (1969-74) and the Seventh Plan (1985-90).

Soviet aid boosted growth of Indo-Soviet trade in the 1950's and 1960's and 1980's. Soviet aid utilised by India was 82.4 per cent of India's imports from the USSR between 1956-7 and 1960-1 and 66.1 per cent between 1961-2 and 1965-6.[82] That share fell dramatically from the late 1960's and rose again in the 1980's due to extension of several new credits since 1977. Utilization of these loans, in fact, was crucial for an increase in Soviet exports of machinery and equipments to India, an important policy goal of the USSR. Equally, credit utilized by India during the 1950's and 1960's helped expansion of Indian exports in the 1970's.

Sectoral composition of Soviet project aid differed from other donors in three respects:

(i) the Soviets gave a much larger share of its aid for steel;
(ii) Second, they were the first to come forward to help the oil sector,
(iii) Other donors, especially the International Bank for Reconstruction and Development (IBRD) gave a fifth of their aid to developing an infrastructure in transport,[83] unlike the Soviets.

Apart from Steel projects like Bhilai (1955), Bokaro (1965) and Vizag (1971), in the field of mechanical engineering, three Soviet-aided projects in late 1950's – Heavy Machinery Building at Ranchi, Mining and Allied Machinery Plant in Durgapur and Hardwar Heavy Electrical Plant – provided the basic foundation of Indian industry. In the power generation sector, Soviet assistance was enormous: "In most of the states of the Indian Union, one can see today Soviet-assisted power plants" – two in Tamil Nadu, one in M.P., two in U.P., one in Bihar, one in Punjab, two in Orissa, one in Andhra Pradesh and one in Karnataka, "amounting in all a power-generation capacity of 3.35 million Kilowatts"[84]

The Soviet involvement in Indian oil industry began in December 1955 when Prof. A.N. Kalinin, in his report, put on-shore "extractable oil reserves at four billion tonnes and gas reserves at about two trillion cu.m." Simultaneously, "Akademik Arkhangelsky" the Soviet research ship, surveyed the Indian Continental shelf and found the large oil deposit at Bombay High. Cooperation between ONGC and "corresponding Soviet organizations led to the identification of over 160 oil-bearing structures and 26 oil deposits in India."[85] In the sector of Drug and Pharmaceuticals, three Soviet aided plants were set up – Surgical Instruments Plant in Madras, Synthetic Drugs Plant in Hyderabad and the Antibiotics plant in Risikesh under the Indian Drugs and Pharmaceuticals Limited (IDPL) as per the 1959 agreement. Other areas of cooperation included the coal sector, agriculture sector (seeds, irrigation, dam and canal building, flood control, water management, weather forecasting, production of agriculture machinery etc.) and Soviet cooperation in science and technology including space.

Analysts on the subject have unequivocally emphasized and have agreed upon certain unique elements of Soviet economic assistance to India:

(i) The Soviet assistance preferred setting up of industrial complexes and not industrial plants, so much so that it helped "development of ancillary industries not only horizontally but also vertically," as pointed out by Muchkund Dubey.[86] Batuk Desai also showed, that the Bhilai steel project is supplied with iron ore by Rajar Pahar and Dal mines, limestone by Nandini querry, power by Korba plant and machinery by such plants at Ranchi, Durgapur and Hyderabad – "all Soviet aided endeavours."[87] Mehrotra also highlighted the creation of "vertically integrated industrial complexes" as part of a "whole strategy of import-substituting industrialization."[88]

(ii) The provision of making credit repayment through export of goods (even of goods manufactured in Soviet aided plants, in some cases) was another significant feature, also pointed out by both Dubey and Mehrotra.

(iii) Unlike the market economies, the USSR examined the techno-economic possibilities of only the "particular project, and not the entire gamut of India's economic policy", before providing any assistance (Dubey).

(iv) Mehrotra argued that Soviet help was crucial in stalling the monopoly of multinationals (MNCS) in certain sectors of the Indian economy, with the added benefits of a better bargaining position vis-à-vis MNCs and a resultant saving of scarce foreign exchange for India. Two such areas were exploration of oil and natural gas and manufacturing of drugs. India extracted valuable concessions from MNCs in their bids for oil refineries like the one in Madras, and the Soviet-aided public sector medicine plants in India attracted large scale investment from MNCs.

(v) Soviet equipments proved to be less sophisticated but more hardy than western equipments in the same category (Mehrotra).

Overall, Mehrotra discusses the costs of Soviet-technology-transfers to India as follows:

(i) First, inadequate planning and little understanding of the demand for specific products led the MAMC and the Surgical Instrument plants to disastrous failure.

(ii) Second, the practice of "one-off" sale of "design, documentation, and equipments" (with the design being at least ten years old) and with no further provision of supplying any improvement effected during the contract period was another problem with Soviet technology transfer.

Bernard D'Mello made a comparison between Soviet and Western collaboration in his doctoral thesis and his "hypothesis" is that although "the evidence is mixed and there are differences in detail, Soviet collaboration is essentially similar to Western Collaboration."[89] We may not always subscribe to his view but we can fruitfully use his arguments which are as follows:

(i) Very much like the Western collaboration, the motive of Soviet collaboration was also to find markets for its products, "though mainly in COMECON and developing countries," as the Soviet industry could not compete in the world market "because of its lower technological level."

(ii) Soviet long-term credits in the industrial sector are "double tied" – project- tied and source – tied (as in the Western case), but, significantly, with lower interest-rates and longer maturity period, in comparison with Western loans.

(iii) Both the Soviet and Western collaboration did not allow the Indian side to modify the "standard process design and sequence to suit Indian conditions."

(iv) In comparing respective pricing, he showed that "in BF (Blast Furnace) coke oven and sintering plant where the Soviet technical level is equivalent to the West, Soviet prices correspond more closely to western prices. In steel making furnaces and rolling mills where the Soviet technical level is lower than in the West, Soviet prices are lower."

(v) According to him, indigenisation of spare parts for plants was easier in Soviet collaboration.

(vi) In both Soviet and Western collaboration, there are several restrictions on horizontal transfer of technology.

Interdependence of the Economic Relationship

Though India's economic stake in the relationship might have been greater than the Soviet Union's, several economic factors that motivated the USSR to maintain, as also expand economic links, may be discerned. India provided significant quantities of certain raw and processed materials, some machinery and considerable quantity of consumer goods needed by the USSR. Soviet penetration in the Indian market with a wide range of goods might serve as a key to probable Soviet penetration into other Third World markets. Most significantly, India was a major purchaser of Soviet weapons. So the Soviet stake lay in promoting a stable Indian purchasing power through its economic initiatives to pay for the same. On the Indian side, the USSR had been for years India's first or second largest foreign customer, providing a major market for a significant range of commodities and consumer goods that helped Indian manufacturers gear up for world market.

India apprehended, in the 1980's, that if the value of Indian imports from the USSR fail to grow, both due to falling oil prices and a Soviet inability to meet India's requirements for more sophisticated military technology – it may, in the long term, be reflected in a declining growth in exports, even if such exports were secured in the short term by the large volume of the Indian debt to the USSR. In fact, total trade turnover between the two declined abruptly in 1983 in step with a decline in oil prices – Rs. 29.64 billion in 1983-84 from Rs. 30.82 billion in 1982-83.[90]

On both sides, however, the most important motive for bilateral relationship was political: India, like the USSR, wanted closer economic ties to safeguard the close affinity of political relations. Mehrotra has argued that in the 1970's the pursuit of economic advantages became a major goal of Soviet economic relations with LDCs (Less Developed Countries) as distinct from the period from 1954-64 when economic relations were used largely as a political weapon. In this, though, according to him, the relationship with India was distinctive and " conclusive" since Soviet arms export to and civilian trade with India were conducted in inconvertible rupees, it had no role in alleviating Soviet hard currency trade deficit with the West and thus Soviet economic interests in India were different in nature from its interests in LDCs, in general (as hard currency trade surplus from LDCs, mainly based on arms exports, relieved Soviet trade deficit with the West). Soviet preparedness to sell oil/oil products to India at the cost of its severe hard currency needs points to the fact that "it is for strategic political reason that India is important to the USSR rather than for economic ones"[91] So, a corroborative economic interest intertwined with reciprocal strategic political interests, that were not essentially identical, had built the range as well as the depth of the relationship.

Indo-Soviet Military Relationship

Till 1959, India's armed forces depended exclusively on Western equipment, especially British. The Soviet defence exports to India started only in the 1960's. Soviet use of the tool of military aid lagged behind the use of economic aid and foreign trade programmes. But in the short period between 1965-69, it gathered momentum to the tune of 80 per cent of all defence equipment imports of India, according to Stockholm International Peace Research Institute (SIPRI) yearbook 1971. The high Soviet share in India's defence imports, however, was in the context of the West's embargo on arms exports to India following the 1965 Indo-Pakistan war. In the early 1970's, the reasons for Soviet's high share were:

- (i) first, the USSR was replenishing Indian stocks during and after the 1971 War;
- (ii) second, the US stopped all sorts of assistance, military and economic.

So, by then it was an established fact that the USSR was India's singlemost important supplier. But there was a declining trend: in 1970-4 the Soviets share fell to 70 per cent of India's arms imports and in 1975-9 to 57 per cent.[92] But the fact remains that the Soviets were still India's most important supplier by far, in spite of India's fairly successful efforts in diversifying its sources of weapon systems. It suggested India's bargaining capacity in its dealings with the Soviets.

India opted for the MiG-21 in preference to Western alternatives since the Soviets offered its licensed manufacture in India and credits for the manufacturing programme. The US government, responsive to Pakistan's sensitivity, stalled the Lockheed move to transfer technology to India. The MiG deal was significant on account of Soviet refusal of Chinese approach for MiG-21 in the context of deteriorating Sino-Soviet relations.[93] After the 1962 Sino-Indian war, India responded positively to any offer of military aid from the Western Countries. The US promised $50 million of emergency assistance in 1962-3 and $60 million in 1963-4. In May 1964 as much as $500 million of military aid, half of it as a grant and rest as a loan, was promised for the period 1965-9. The 1965 Indo-Pakistan war led to a suspension of US military aid to both the countries, and India, as a result, could get only about $80 million. The USSR, on the other hand, came forward, as an addition to licensing production of defence equipments in India, to help set up repair and overhaul facilities in Chandigarh for the Soviet AN-32 medium transport aircraft. The biggest naval dockyard in the country, Vishakapatnam was constructed with Soviet assistance for servicing of naval vessels purchased from the USSR.

The inherent dissension between American and Indian perceptions of global issues was relatedly reflected in the unstable military relationship with the US. Several negative factors, however, contributed to the USSR's emergence as India's chief supplier: all military related sales over $25 million (lethal equipment ceilings were lower at $10 million) in the US were required to be presented to the US Congress for clearance that meant delay and, irritably, the exposure of the recipient's defence policy to scrutiny. Again, the US was generally eager to establish, on the ground of the sophistication of American equipments, an infrastructure, e.g., training and maintenance teams, in the recipient LDC. India was little interested in such broad-based military relationship. West Europe, as an alternative to Soviet supplies, though willing to transfer technology, proved expensive due to economies of scale, as they had rather limited productions in relation to the superpowers and were ill-prepared to extend long-term credits. In some cases, furthermore, European defence equipments included US technology and it might be a hindrance from American point of view.

In this context, the USSR was ready to extend long-term credit – initially for 10-12 years, later for as long as 17 years according to 1980 agreement – at lower rates of interest (2-2.5%) and under favourable repayment conditions – not in free foreign exchange but through export of goods in the way developmental loans were to be repaid. Additionally, the USSR offered licenses for the manufacture of weapon system: under the 1980 agreement, India purchased 70 T-72 tanks outright and 600 more were to be manufactured under license by the Avadi workshop in Madras and the deal was made on the basis of a loan of Rs. 13 billion at 2.5 per cent annual interest, to be repaid over 15 years after a 2-years grace period. MiG-21, the first Mach-2 aircraft, and MiG-23, the first variable geometry aircraft (as also the MiG-25 and MiG-29) were for licensed production in India – the first LDC outside the Warsaw Pact countries as the SIPRI 1983 yearbook wrote: "...the

Indian example remains one of a handful of exceptions..." K. Subrahmanyam, a leading defence analyst commented: "Only the USSR has adequate mutuality of interest in India's development of defence technology and necessary resources to support the effort with necessary credit."[94] The fact that the USSR emerged as India's preponderant defence supplier since the mid-1960's, more importantly with its readiness to transfer defence technology, was largely a reflection of the predominantly strong correspondence of geo-political interests between the two. The USSR resisted the trend in the arms market during the 1980's, that included the US, Britain, France, Italy and West Germany, to sell defence technology to the Third World. India was the exception.[95] And Soviet reluctance was due to its unwillingness to share the technology with countries whose future political leanings were unpredictable and to the fact that none of its biggest customers, other than India, could absorb the imported technology with the required development in infrastructure and technology.

Notably, periodic Indian efforts at diversification of its arms sources were met with simultaneous Soviet efforts to retain its position. In 1978, when India signed a $1 billion agreement with Britain for the purchase and subsequent licensed production of the Anglo-French Jaguar, the USSR offered the MIG-23 for licensed production at favourable prices.[96] The repetition of the pattern was perceived in 1982 with the Indo-French Mirage 2000 deal, when Defence Minister Marshall Ustinov, on his India visit, offered to sell more MiG-25s for rupees and hinted at allowing India to produce under license the MiG-27.[97] Marshall Ustinov's offer to sell India the MiG-29 (yet to be inducted in Soviet forces) and T-80 tank (recently tested) during his visit to New Delhi in October 1983, indicated the Soviet seriousness in retaining its hold on the Indian arms market.[98]

Soviet Compulsions for Building Defence Relations with India

Economic

During the 1960's the Soviet international supply of arms matched that of the US. During 1978-82, the USSR was the world's largest supplier of major weapons to developing countries, exceeding the US.[99] Apart from the quantitative rise, there was a qualitative transformation in the nature of Soviet arms trade with the developing countries during the period[100]: the arms tended to be sold rather than given as bilateral aid. In general, economic motivations came to the fore more prominently than the political or strategic considerations so common in the past. Balance of trade deficits with industrial countries, current account deficits in convertible currency and the cumulative debt burden were major problems for the Soviet economy which were to be resolved by earning hard currency and it was here that Soviet arms exports became relevant. Pierre put the point that "The Soviet defence industry routinely over-produces with potential exports in mind.[101]

As the Soviet defence industries had the privilege of excess supply within the framework of an economy, characterized by generalized excess demand, export of arms in preference to other goods was, therefore, more feasible. Data indicates that exports were well prioritized in total military output and not simply as an outlet for surplus: e.g., 58.2 per cent of the major naval combatants and 70 per cent of minor naval combatants were for export, while the corresponding figure for combat aircrafts was about 40 per cent during 1976-81.[102]

Deger analysed available data to show that on average for 1973-81, about 63 per cent of trade deficit in non-defence goods and services was financed by hard-currency earnings from international sale of armaments,[103] as the quantity of the export surplus available to earn hard currency from the energy sector was limited by the dependence of the Soviet allies on energy supplies from the USSR. In spite of the rise in direct sales of arms and convertible currency payments, relatively large amounts of arms were transferred on a commodity-exchange basis, to set right, primarily as a Soviet initiative, a sizeable trade deficit: large sales of arms to India in the early 1980's were, among others, partially prompted by large Soviet deficits in bilateral trade.

Political

Khrushchev's 1956 Report to the CPSU that announced the principle of peaceful coexistence, essentially de-emphasizing the potential for revolution in countries as a criteria for Soviet cooperation, was an ostensible signal to search out potential friends outside the Soviet bloc. The political initiative included promoting military relations for political ends to alternate Western military support to India in the 1960's, to skillfully out-manoeuvre Chinese influence in North Korea, to gain a political status in Ethiopia and so on.

Strategic

As the USSR grew to be a full-fledged superpower, its urgency for gaining overseas bases for its expanding "blue-water" navy was reflected, in separate cases, while making arms deals with countries. If the record of Soviet relations with Egypt, Somalia and Vietnam shows that arms transfers can be helpful in the quest for military bases in the Third World, Soviet experiences with Syria, Iraq, Algeria, Libya and India invalidates the premise. India, though a large recipient of Soviet arms, allowed only very limited *servicing facilities* for the Soviet navy, equally accessible for other countries.

The provisions in the 1971 Treaty were so adjusted to blend indigenous development of the defence potentials of India and committed the USSR, as a short term measure, to provide with a defensive shield to meet a threat affecting India's security. The Soviet arms supply to India was oriented to immediate defence needs, and the Treaty did not imply a permanent *locus standi* for the USSR in matters of military facilities and defence arrangements, adapted exclusively to Soviet interests.[104] India consistently refused to accept a military *quid pro quo*.

Influence: A Question

India, for over three decades, utilized arms imports from the USSR – as symbolized by the 1971 Treaty – to meet its security needs against Pakistan and China. Soviet arms had been also a counterweight to American and Chinese arms sales to Pakistan, there existed a compatibility between Indian security interests and Soviet policy.

The question of an influence-relationship through Soviet arms transfers to India must be viewed in relation to the totality of India's needs as well as its own investments: "a billion dollars in arms aid over a 10 year period must be related to an Indian defence budget of some $2 billion a year."[105] Equally important was the fact that Moscow had to compete with other countries, particularly the US, for India's approval, that automatically limited the scope of influence for the Soviets to alter India's preferred course of action. "A more dramatic sign" as Barnds pointed out "of Soviet influence would have been the establishment of Soviet naval bases in India – or guaranteed access to Indian bases."[106] Large Soviet arms transfers to India resulted in a large Soviet presence but not in proportionately large influence.[107] Whatever influence the Soviets could acquire was "*complementary*" in nature as against "*coercive*."

India's Non-Aligned Foreign Policy: Relevance

His own reading of the course of Indian history and of the world at large had convinced Nehru in pre-independence days that India is destined "to make a difference to the World." "A free, democratic and Socialist India" must take the lead in shaping out a new world order through its "continuous willingness to make friends of… opponents,"[108] that would deter any form of re-instatement of pre-war status quo that had sustained colonialism. Here we come across a seed[109] of the concept of non-alignment in Nehru's vision of the post-War India and the world, ready for transplantation subsequently. Nehru's ideas were rooted intimately in a sense of Indian civilization that had nurtured through ages the validity of the concepts of *diversity* and *pluralism* and had efficiently experimented them in interactions as with other civilizations, so with alien cultures and societies. He was confident of a capacity to steer independent India, alongwith like-minded nations of the Third World gaining or yet to gain independence, clear of the forming process of two opposite poles. Specifically here, India made "a difference to the World" through its continued efforts "to make friends of opponents."

By 1955, in the post-Stalin era, the Soviets discerned the anti-imperialist potential of the NAM. India's "progressive" stature, though neither "Socialist", nor of "Socialist orientation", was recognized in Soviet perceptions for its anti-monopoly, anti-feudal position in domestic fields and for its anti-imperialist stance in international arena. Notably, Soviet recognition of India's role in the NAM was best revealed in Gorbachev's 1986 Vladivostok speech: "The recognized leader of this movement is great India, with its moral authority and traditional wisdom, with its unique political experience and huge economic possibilities."[110]

Explicit assumption of the US was that India's non-aligned status demanded equidistance from both Washington and Moscow. Significantly, four carefully-organized dialogues between representative groups from India and America were held in Wisconsin and in New Delhi during 1982-84 that centred on what "non-alignment" means to both countries. An Indian participant observed in one of these exchanges that the metaphor of equidistance is misleading, since the superpowers are not "fixed polar stars" but are dynamic moving forces and "we must continually find ways consistent with our own interests to adjust and adapt to what you do." The phrase "genuine non-alignment" is redundant, like "honest truth." Similarly, non-alignment is the antithesis of "neutrality" because it calls for judging each issue on its merits, not abstention from taking a stand.[111] The general view of the American participants in the dialogues was that while virulently denouncing the US role in Vietnam, India did not condemn Soviet interventions in Hungary, Czechoslovakia and Afghanistan as strongly.

We may discuss India's stance in these three cases, cited often, and questioning India's non-aligned policy:

(i) On Hungary (1956), "Panditji's (Nehru's) clear instructions were that we have to oppose any fact-finding mission sent by the UN. The next day they would demand the same thing in Kashmir ... We totally resented the Soviet way of sending troops; but we didn't support the UN to go and meddle in the affairs of Hungary."[112] As India's interests were apparent in forestalling UN initiative, India abstained on November 4, 1956 and voted against, on November 8, the UN Resolution on Hungary.

(ii) On Czechoslovakia (1968), Mrs. Gandhi registered India's disapproval of the Soviet move in her statement in the Lok Sabha: "The right of nations to live peacefully and without outside interference should not be denied in the name of *religion* or *ideology* ... We have always stood for the right of every country to its own *traditions*, *aptitudes* and *genius*."[113] In the Security Council, India was willing to support all operative clauses of the Resolution except those condemning the USSR. Finally India abstained on the Resolution.

(iii) On Afghanistan (1979), the fact that India had reservations against the Soviet move, was evidenced in India's abstaining on the Resolution. Mrs. Gandhi reiterated, on every single available occasion, India's disapproval of interference by any country in the affairs of another, but was found quick to add that Moscow's "interference" in Afghanistan was not a "one-sided affair."[114]

What is notable of Indian stance on the three occasions is the consistency of approach over a long period of three decades. India denounced interventions, but stopped short of public condemnations, in cases of the USSR. A clue was provided by Mrs. Gandhi: "... we do not approve of foreign troops or any other type of interference in any country ... The other thing is how to deal with it: whether shouting about it is going to force the troops out or whether other initiatives could be taken?"[115]

Undoubtedly, she hinted at India's capacity to persuade as a consequence of the strength of its friendly relations with the USSR, which she was ostensibly not in a position to venture in case of American interventions in Vietnam and elsewhere. Indian persuasions were ineffective though, as she admitted in her interview with Nathalie Blime: "We have already asked for the withdrawal of Soviet troops. Without success. What is important is not what we ask but the situation in the country and what the Soviet(s) consider as their interest."[116] She pointedly referred to the "political realities" in Afghanistan as she did in 1968 regarding Czechoslovakia. The "political realities", in case of Afghanistan, included external supports for subversions there, President Amin's requests for assistance and the Soviet interests and commitments in that country. All these considerations of every aspect of a situation could only be made in case of a friendly country and as friendly gestures, though not deviating from India's principled and consistent stance against interventions.

The Relationship: A Review

Now, before proceeding towards the next chapters to examine closely and systematically the various aspects and dimensions of Indo-Russian relationship, it may be useful to pose a final question: what, in essence, was the nature of the Indo-Soviet relationship. "India has been described sometimes as a client state, a strategic partner or an ally of the Soviet Union" – thus Maya Chadda[117] introduced certain viewpoints of available literature on the subject. Some form of an unqualified answer to our key question is crucial, since it will determine significantly: first, the repercussions as well as reverberations of the disintegration of the Soviet Union on India; second, the nature of the growth of Indo-Russian relationship.

If. India played a subservient role in the relationship, India would have, in all probability, reacted to the consequences of the disintegration with utter dismay resulting in a sense of helplessness and a loss of direction. Nothing of the sort was perceptible in India's immediate reactions and the Indian point of view, as gathered from discussions[118] with key personalities in the Indian foreign policy community and analysts on the repercussions of the disintegration, was mature and matter-of-fact, far from being a perplexed one, and was most concerned with the resultant difficulties in bilateral trade and in getting military spare-parts.

That India did not play a subservient role has been corroborated by American analysts like Robert F. Goheen and personalities in the diplomatic field like Chester Bowles, who had the best advantage, as an US ambassador to New Delhi, to discern India's position as a partner to the relationship. "India's resultant friendship with the USSR" – Goheen commented "manifest in variety of ways, *but not, I would insist, as subservience* – has been galling to the sensitivity of the US policy makers.[119]

Subservience implies sycophantic compliance, suggesting a unilateral influence-relationship of the stronger partner. The influence-relationship between the two countries may be viewed against the candid admission in 1971 of Chester Bowles: that "by now", each superpower, the United States and the Soviet Union, "should have discovered that its own capacity to influence India . . . is strictly *limited*."[120] Chester Bowles, again, gave credence to India's hyper-sensitivity to being even distantly influenced. He commented that Indo-United States relations suffered setbacks "in part from India's own acute sensitivity, nurtured during the colonial period, to any act which can be interpreted as outside pressure."[121] So, India's position as a partner in the Indo-Soviet relationship is established by positive evidence – evidence stressed by a diplomat of the "other" superpower and a prominent analyst of the country.

Another point needs to be emphasized before going to elaborate on the nature of the relationship. There is no denying the fact that India could hardly sustain its non-aligned stature but for the material assistance, including economic and military, extended by the Soviet Union. If denied of assistance from both the camps in the context of the Cold War divide, India would have had no options but to compromise its posture to survive, having been a less developed country. The Soviet Union, however, had its own calculations: it had the *lead*, in the post-Stalin era, to discern the anti-imperialist potential of the non-aligned movement, initiated and activated by India, that could substantially serve its interests in *denying* the West a significant access to the Third World. The United States had a *lag* of some 25 years when President Reagan made conciliatory gestures to the 1983 NAM Summit in New Delhi.

Another pertinent point is the fact that India sufficiently strengthened its stature in the international arena through its leadership role in the NAM and its commitment to non-alignment and consequently got sufficient *leverage* in its relations with the Soviet Union to withstand any exertion of explicit influence. In building its relations with India, the Soviet Union treated India "as a great power, highly appreciating the role it plays in World affairs"[122] to a greater degree than did Washington.[123] The Soviet Union was much more ready to appreciate Indian interests as such rather than only viewing those interests in the context of broader strategic concerns as Washington often tended to.[124] The Indo-Soviet "Cooperation" had broader perspective, as Moscow proclaimed and persuaded, since it contributed to the "peace potential" of the world at large.[125]

The logic of geopolitics prompted the Soviet Union to discern its long-term interests in South Asia. Pakistan too was apprehensive of the logic as President Zia admitted early in 1980: ". . . you can't live in the sea and create enmity with whales . . . The Soviet Union is on our doorstep. The United States of America is 10,000 miles away."[126]

Among the factors that obstructed the exercise of influence by either State were the difference in foreign policy goals between the two: Moscow's policy of containment of China was in opposition to India's long-term interest in better relation with Beijing. Other Soviet interests, such as naval expansion in the Indian Ocean and intervention in Afghanistan, were in conflict with Soviet goals concerning India as well as with Indian interests. Indo-Soviet relations were guided by a reciprocal and co-responsive need of each other that belied the question: *who needed whom more*? The superpower, undoubtedly, had its own wider interests of global dimensions to project itself as one of the two contending poles, while India, though primarily a regional player, had earned for itself wider acceptability, transcending the limits of the region, i.e. South Asia, as the leader in its early years after independence and subsequently, as one of the leaders of the Third World, championing its cause for an equitable world order conducive to its development.

India needed Soviet support in times of crises vis-à-vis Pakistan over the persisting issue of Kashmir in the UN security council on various occasions or in times of uncertainty following the emerging Sino-United States rapprochement during the Bangladesh crisis and thereafter and the Soviet support was crucial for India for its impact as it fruitfully counterbalanced the "tilts" and interests of the other

Superpower in the region. India was also in dire need of the economic, technological and military assistance, that the Soviet Union was capable of providing, to come out of its colonial past and emerge as a powerful country.

The Soviet Union, on the other hand, needed India vis-à-vis the US interests and penetration in the region and against China to counterbalance its possible influence in Asia and in the Third World as well as to serve as a *conduit* for it for an access to the NAM to get sufficient exposure in the Third World. This was particularly evident when it wanted India to reciprocate past Soviet gestures, prior to the non-aligned Foreign Ministers' meeting in New Delhi in February 1981 and help it in its "time of trial" on the Afghan issue.[127] As the host country, India, entrusted with preparing the Draft Declaration, carefully avoided naming the Soviet Union in Afghanistan or Vietnam in Kampuchea and called for a settlement on the basis of withdrawal of troops and for strict observance of non-intervention and non-interference from third countries that was in tune with India's earlier stances as well as agreeable to Moscow's relief. Significantly, the West saw in the Declaration an end to "the pro-Soviet tilt" that had come to dominate the movement.[128] And China also saw it as a victory for the 'real nature" of the movement and a "heavy blow" to the Soviets.[129] India, thus, steered clear of any tilt toward one or the other country, while maintaining a *consistency* in its view of World affairs.

Mrs. Indira Gandhi, in the presence of Leonid Brezhnev at a civic reception in New Delhi in December 1980, brought out the essence of the bilateral relationship: "Indo-Soviet friendship . . . is of *equal* importance to both India and the Soviet Union",[130] stressing the fact that this relationship was important enough to pay dividends to both partners. Indo-Soviet relations reinforced mutual interests rather than *modified* each other's behaviour, looking forward to a stable relationship, where each exerted an implicit influence rather than a manifest one – a long-term rather than immediate one. And this was made possible between a weaker state like India and a superpower such as the USSR as a consequence of their mutual dependence. Moreover, this *implicit* and *long-term* mutual influence was made operational on the solid basis of convergence of interests of both, as well as of far greater *agreement* than difference of both in perceptions of issues of global dimensions.[131]

One US official in New Delhi in December 1980 interestingly provided a key to the Soviet success in building a lasting relationship with India.: the Soviet Union has "a good relationship with this country because the Soviets have never asked the Indians for anything the Indians couldn't *gracefully* give."[132] He pointed to Moscow's sensitivity while dealing with New Delhi and *by implication*, to its absence on the part of Washington.

This study so far has concentrated, generally, on reviewing India's place in Soviet foreign policy perceptions and has not taken into serious consideration the global implications of Soviet foreign policy goals and initiatives. The analysis on Gorbachev's "new political thinking" is attempted as it played a key role in effecting "tectonic" shifts in Soviet foreign policy goals and was alleged to have initiated/hastened Soviet disintegration, that has serious implications for subsequent Indo-Russian relations.

But the focal point lies elsewhere: the study is pursued to highlight the reverberations of Soviet strategic shifts on contemporary Indo-Soviet relations in general as well as on their prolonged and intensive impact on Indo-Russian relations that followed, in particular. The levels of cooperation reached at political, economic and defence sectors within the framework of Indo-Soviet relationship have come up as recurrent standards in subsequent writings and discussions on Indo-Russian relations to locate advancements/failures of the subsequent relationship. This study will be no exception, since earlier criteria are selectively helpful to assess the projections of Indo-Russian relations as well as to discern the twin factors of *continuity* and *change* in subsequent relations.

The global perspective on both sides has been altogether different and both countries are under compulsions to adjust and accommodate to other demands at various levels. Specifically, for instance, the short term foreign-policy goals of the Russian Federation have been inclined preponderantly to the West for potential help and cooperation in the post-Cold War context. So, while pursuing this study on Indo-Russian relations, it is necessary to be particularly mindful of the fact that the instruments of comparison between the Indo-Soviet and Indo-Russian relations are essentially dissimilar and not identical within a radically-altered global arena.

Notes and References

1. Dr. Arun Mohanty, Associate Professor, Moscow City Pedagogical University, had the privilege to have an access to these documents that help us study the above developments in a new perspective. I have

extensively used his materials from his article "55 years to Indo-Russian Diplomatic Relations", *Business Messenger*, June 2002.

2. K.P.S. Menon, *The Flying Troika*, London University Press, London, 1963.
3. Dennis Kux, *India and the United States: Estranged Democracies, 1941-1991*, National Defence University Press, 1993, Fn. 37, p. 92.
4. S. Gopal, *Jawaharlal Nehru: A Biography*, Vol. 2, Oxford University Press, New Delhi, 1979, pp. 60-61.
5. Richard J. Barnet, *The Alliance: America–Europe-Japan Makers of the Postwar World*, Simon and Schuster, New York, 1983, p. 153.
6. Sir Olaf Caroe, *The Wells of Power: The Oilfields of South West Asia*, Macmillan, London, 1951 p. 168–169, cited by Selig Harrison, *India and the United States: The First 50 Years*, India Abroad Center for Political Awareness, Occasional Paper, November 1997, p. 4.
7. Ralph De Toldano, *Nixon*, Dwell Sloan and Pearce, New York, 1958, p. 164 cited by Selig Harrison, *India and the United States: The First 50 years*, *Ibid.*
8. *Pravda*, 9 August 1953. Cited in R.C. Horn, *Soviet-Indian Relations: Issues and Influence*, Praeger Publications, USA, 1982, p. 3.
9. K.P.S. Menon, *op. cit.*, p. 58.
10. *Pravda*, 15 February, 1956 cited in R.C. Horn, *op. cit.* p. 5.
11. B.M. Jain, *India and the United States. 1961–63*, Radiant, New Delhi, 1987, p. 26–29.
12. John Kenneth Galbraith, *Ambassador's Journal*, Houghton Miffin, Boston, 1971, p. 445.
13. "Serious Hotbed of Tension in Asia", *Pravda* 19 September 1963 in *Current Digest of Soviet Press* (CDSP) 16 October 1963.
14. "What Russia Means to India" – Discussion between Nikhil Chakravarty, A.K. Damodaram and Madhavan K. Palat in Madhavan K. Palat – Geeti Sen (ed.) *Rethinking Russia*, UBS Publishers, New Delhi, 1994.
15. UN Security Council Official Records, 109th Meeting, 14th February 1964, as quoted in Hafeez Malik, *Soviet-Pakistan Relations and Post-Soviet Dynamics (1947–92)*, Macmillan Press, London, 1994, p. 180.
16. *Ibid.*
17. M.S. Rajan, "The Tashkent Declaration: Retrospect and Prospect", *International Studies*, Vol. 8, No. 1–2 July–October 1966.
18. Arkadii N. Shevchenko, *Breaking With Moscow*, Alfred A. Knopf, New York, 1985.
19. Hafiz Malik, *op. cit.*, p. 211.
20. Her interview in Tokyo and Jakarta, *Hindustan Times*, 19 June and 1 July, respectively.
21. G.W. Chowdhury, *India, Pakistan, Bangladesh and the Major Powers: Politics of a Divided Subcontinent*, Free Press, New York, 1975 pp. 141–142.

22. Pran Chopra, *India's Second Liberation*, MIT Press, Cambridge, 1974, p. 84.
23. *Ibid*, p. 84.
24. A.K. Damodaran, in his interview to Madhavan K. Palat in *Rethinking Russia*.
25. *Ibid.*
26. *Ibid.*
27. *Ibid.*
28. *Ibid.*
29. *Ibid.*
30. Hafeez Malik, *op. cit.*, p. 218.
31. Henry Kissinger, *White House Years*, Little, Brown, Boston, 1971, p. 878.
32. *The Statesman*, 12 December, 1971.
33. Vijay Sen Budhraj, "Moscow and the Birth of Bangladesh", *Asian Survey*, May 1972, p. 493
34. R.C. Horn, *op. cit.*, p. 72.
35. G. Yakarlev, "Conflict in Hindustan and Mao Group's Provocative Role", *Pravda*, 28th December 1971, p. 4 cited in Malik *op. cit.* p., 223.
36. T.N. Kaul, *Diplomacy in Peace and War*, Vikas Publishing House, New Delhi, 1979, p. 185.
37. Willam J. Barnds "Soviet Influence in India: A Search For The Spoils That Go With Victory" in A.Z. Rubenstein (ed) *Soviet and Chinese Influence in the Third World*, Praeger Publications, New York, 1975.
38. Christopher Van Hollen, "The Tilt Policy Revisited: Nixon-Kissinger Geopolitics and South Asia", *Asian Survey*, Vol. 20, April 1980, pp. 339-361
39. Thomas P. Thornton, in Harold Gould-Sumit Ganguly (ed.) *The Hope and the Reality: US-Indian Relations from Roosevelt to Reagan*, Westview Press, San Francisco, 1992, p. 98.
40. Baldev Raj Nayar, "Regional Power in a Multipolar World" in John W. Mellovl (ed.) *India: A Rising Middle Power*, Westview Press, Boulder, Colo, 1979, p. 147.
41. *Far Eastern Economic Review* (FEER), 24 June 1974, p. 5.
42. Cited by Baldev Raj Nayar, *American Geopolitics and India*, South Asia Books, Columbia, MO, 1976, p. 118
43. *Ibid*, p. 135
44. For the Text of the Agreement, See Surjit Mansingh, *India's search for power: Indira Gandhi's Foreign Policy 1966-1982*, Sage Publications, New Delhi, 1984, Annex B.
45. *Indian Express*, 11 September, 1976.
46. *The Statesman*, 9 June, 1976.
47. *Facts on File*, 27 April, 1979.
48. Her interview with the *Daily Express*, London, 22 January, 1980.

49. Her interview with *Stern*, Hamburg, 24 January, 1980.
    These excerpts of interviews are from *India's views on the Afghan Situation*, December 1980, Ministry of External Affairs, New Delhi.
50. *Los Angeles Times*, 12 January, 1980.
51. *Times of India*, 13 January, 1980 (emphasis added)
52. *The Statesman*, 12–15 February, 1980.
53. *Los Angeles Times*, 15 February, 1980.
54. Horn, *op. cit.*, p. 187.
55. For details, see Peter Schweiger, *Victory-The Reagan Administration's Secret Strategy that Hastened the Collapse of the Soviet Union*, The Atlantic Monthly Press, New York, 1994.
56. *Time*, 24 February, 1992, pp. 28-35.
57. R.C. Thornton, "Russo-Chinese Détente and the Emerging New World Order" in Hafiz Malik (ed.) *The Roles of the United States, Russia and China in the New World Order*, Macmillan Press, London, 1997, p. 224.
58. See "The Political Report of the Central Committee of the CPSU", Moscow, February 25, 1986, cited in Mikhail S. Gorbachev, *Toward a Better World*, Richarson & Steirman, New York, 1987, pp. 158-159.
59. *Foreign Boardcast Information Service (FBIS) Daily Report,*: Soviet Union, 17 February , 1987, p. AA17.
60. See "Gorbachev's Modernization Program: A Status Report", paper presented by CIA and DIA for submission to the subcommittee on National Security Economics of the Joint Economic Committee, 19 March, 1987, p. 1 cited in Robert S. McNamara, *Out of the Cold*, Simon and Schuster, New York, 1989, pp. 131-132.
61. "Gamble, Showman, Statesman", *New York Times*, 8 December, 1988, p. 34.
62. "NIE 11-4-89, Soviet Policy Toward the West: The Gorbachev challenge (Document 13)" under "Disagreements" section cited in Benjamin B. Fisher (ed.) *At Cold War's End US Intelligence on the Soviet Union and Eastern Europe 1989-1991*, Center for the Study of Intelligence, Central Intelligence Agency, Washington DC, 1999. (A compendium of newly declassified US intelligence documents).
63. *Ibid.*
64. See George Bush and Brent Scowcroft, *A World Transformed*, Knopf-Random House, New York, 1998, p. 282.
65. Cited in Michael Beschloss and Strobe Talbott, *At the Highest Levels: The Inside Story of the End of the Cold War*. Little Brown and Company, Boston, 1993, p. 240.
66. Eduard Shevardnadze, *The Future Belongs to Freedom*, Sinclair-Stevenson Ltd., UK, 1991, pp. 118-119.
67. *Ibid.*, p. 102.
68. Cited in Beschloss and Talbott, *At the Highest Levels*, p. 334.

69. Soviet Defence Minister D. Yazov. "Greatness of the People's Feat: Victory, Memory and Truth", *Pravda*, 9 May 1991. p. 3, cited in *At Cold War's End*, *op. cit.*
70. See "SNIE 11-182- 91. *The Republics of the Former USSR: The Outlook for the Next year*, September 1991 (Document 10)," cited in Benjamin B. Fisher, *op. cit.*
71. *Pravda*, 29 July 1986 (English edition).
72. Veshnik Ministersva Inostrannikh Del SSSR, No. 14, August 1988, cited in P.L. Dash, "Continuity and Change in Indo-Soviet Relations under Perestroika" in T.N. Kaul (ed.) *Indo-Soviet Relations: Prospects and Problems*, Patriot, New Delhi, 1991.
73. *Rethinking Russia*, *op. cit.*, p. 277-278, Emphasis added.
74. Z. Khalilzad – Barnett P. Rubin "The Fragmentation of Afghanistan", *Foreign Affairs*, Winter 1989–90, pp. 150–168.
75. S. Nihal Singh, "High Stakes in Trade, Military Fields", *The Hindustan Times*, 16 August, 1991.
76. See K.K. Katyal, "A Tardy, Diplomatic Reaction", *The Hindu*, 1 September 1991.
77. Anatoly Dobrynin, *In Confidence: Moscow's Ambassador to Six Cold War Presidents*, Times Books/Random House, New York, 1995, p. 615.
78. Cited in Michael R. Beschloss and Strobe Talbott, *op. cit.*, p. 463.
79. Eduard Shevardnadze, *op. cit.*, p. xi.
80. *Ibid.*
81. A. Dobrynin, *op. cit.*, p. 632.
82. Santosh Mehrotra, *India and the Soviet Union: Trade and Technology Transfer*, Oxford University Press, New Delhi, 1991 p. 209.
83. Pramit Chaudhuri "East European Aid to India" in D. Nayyar (ed.) *Economic Relations between Socialist Countries and the Third World*, Macmillan, London, 1977.
84. *Ibid.*
85. All quotations from Jyotirmoy Banerjee, *India in Soviet Global Strategy: A Conceptual Strategy*, Minerva Associates, Calcutta, 1977.
86. Muchkund Dubey "Indo-Soviet Economic Cooperation: Retrospect and Prospect" in V.V. Balababushevich – Bimla Prasad (ed.) *India and the Soviet Union: A Symposium*, People's Publishing House, New Delhi, 1969.
87. Batuk Desai "Contribution of Soviet Cooperation in India's Economic Development" in R.K. Sharma (ed.) *Indo-Soviet Cooperation to India's Economic Development*, Allied Publishers, New Delhi, 1982.
88. Mehrotra, *op. cit.*
89. Barnard C. D'Mello, *Foreign Collaboration In the Public Sector Steel Industry*, Ph.D. Research Thesis, 1986, submitted to the Indian Institute of Management, Calcutta.
90. Government of India, *Economic Survey*, 1985–86, New Delhi 1986.
91 Mehrotra, *op. cit.*, p. 208.

92. *World Armaments and Disarmament*, Yearbook, SIPRI, OUP, 1982.
93. K. Subrahmanyam, "Soviet Help for Self-Reliance in Defence" in S.D. Sharma (ed.) *Studies in Indo-Soviet Cooperation*, Lancer International, New Delhi, 1981.
94. *Ibid.*
95. See Rajan Menon, "The Military and Security Dimensions of Indo-Soviet Relations" in Robert H. Donaldson (ed.) *The Soviet Union in the Third World: Successes and Failures*, Westview Press, Boulder, 1981, p. 43.
96. *Ibid.*, p. 240.
97. *Strategic Survey*, IISS, 1982–83, p. 93.
98. Joseph G. Whelan, "The Soviets in Asia: An Expanding Presence", cited in Rajan Menon, *op. cit.*, p. 191.
99. World Armaments and Disarmament yearbooks, SIPRI, 1978–82.
100. *Ibid.*
101. A.J. Pierre, *The Global Politics of Arms Sales*, Princeton University Press, Princeton, 1982.
102. U. Albrecht, "Soviet Arms Exports" in SIPRI, *World Armament and Disarmament*, Yearbook, 1983, Chapter 12.
103. Saadet Deger "Soviet Arms Sales to Developing Countries: The Economic forces" in Robert Cassen (ed.) *Soviet Interests in The Third World*, Sage Publications, London, 1986, p. 167.
104. Zafar Imam, *Towards a Model Relationship: A study of Soviet Treaties with India and Other Third World Countries*, ABC Publishing House, New Delhi, 1983, pp. 94–95.
105. William J. Barnds. "Soviet Influence in India: A Search For The Spoils That Go With Victory" in Alvin Z. Rubenstein (ed.). *Soviet and Chinese Influence in the Third World*, *op. cit.*, p. 46.
106. *Ibid.*
107. See Rajan Menon, *Soviet Power and The Third World*, Yale University Press, New Haven and London, 1986, pp. 214–237.
108. Jawaharlal Nehru, *India and the World*, Allen and Unwin, London, 1937, p. 223.
109. See Gould, *op. cit.*, p. 30.
110. *Pravda*, 29 July 1986 (English edition).
111. *India and the United States* (A Review of Dialogues of June 1982, at Wisconsin and of March 1984 at New Delhi). p. 28 cited in Selig Harrison, *op. cit.*, p. 26.
112. Nikhil Chakravartty's interview, in *Rethinking Russia*, *op. cit.*, pp. 80-81.
113. *Indian and Foreign Review*, 1 September, 1968, p. 5 (Emphasis added).
114. *Overseas Hindustan Times*, 24 January, 1980.
115. Extracts from the transcript of Press Conference in New Delhi on 21 October 1980, "*India's views on Afghanistan*", December 1980, Ministry of External Affairs, New Delhi.

116. In *Le Figaro*, December 8, 1980, *ibid.*
117. Maya Chadda, "Indo-Russian Relations in the Post-Cold War Era", in Hafeez Malik (ed.) '*The Roles of the United states, Russia and China in the New World Order*', Macmillan Press Ltd., London, 1997, p. 105
118. I interviewed in late December 2002 in New Delhi ex-Foreign Secretary J.N. Dixit, K. Subrahmanyam, ex-Director of Institute for Defence Studies and Analysis and Brahma Chellany, Defence analyst on the subject.
119. Robert F. Goheen, "US Policy Toward India During the Carter Presidency" in H.A. Gould, *op. cit.*, p. 122.
120. Chester Bowles, "America and Russia in India", *Foreign Affairs*, July 1971, pp. 637–638. Emphasis added.
121. Chester Bowles, "*Promises to Keep*", Harper and Row, New York, 1971, p. 471.
122. *Backgrounder*, Information Department, USSR Embassy in India, New Delhi, November 1986, p. 7
123. Chester Bowles, "America and Russia in India", *Op. cit*, pp. 637–638.
124. Leo E Rose, "The Superpowers in South Asia: A Geostrategic Analysis", *Orbis*, Summer 1978, pp. 395–413.
125. *Backgrounder*, *op. cit.*, p. 9.
126. *Los Angeles Times*, 16 January, 1980; cited in R.C. Horn, *op. cit.*, p. 217.
127. Andrei Fialkovsky, "We Rejoice at Your Achievements", *New Times*, No. 4, January 1981, pp. 8–9.
128. *Los Angeles Times*, 14 February, 1981, cited in R.C. Horn, *op. cit.*, p. 207.
129. *Beijing Review*, no. 8, 23 February, 1981, pp. 11–12, cited in R.C. Horn, *ibid.* p. 207.
130. *Soviet Review*, No. 58, 15 December, 1980.
131. See R.C. Horn, *op. cit.*, pp. 219–220. Emphasis added.
132. Christian Science Monitor, December 8, 1980, cited in *ibid.*, p. 221, Emphasis added.

Chapter 2

Economic Dimensions of Indo-Russian Relations

Bilateral economic relations between India and the Russian Federation, the successor the former Soviet Union, nose-dived substantially in the initial years following the Soviet disintegration when compared to the levels achieved by Indo-Soviet economic cooperation. Such bilateral economic relations then came to reach at a relatively stable stage subsequently. Against this background, as this was a transitional period for the Russian economy in particular, in view of its restructuring process from a command-economy to a market-economy, the wild commotions it faced in adjusting itself to the new realities, need to be discussed as a backdrop to account for the vicissitudes in the relationship. Similarly, the Indian economy from 1991 was in a transitional phase from a "controlled" economy toward "greater market coordination of economic decision-making"[1] and this equally serves as a backdrop.

The Indo-Russian economic relationship, in the initial years post 1991, witnessed a period of uncertainty and crisis, partly due to chaos uncertainty after the Soviet disintegration in 1991 and partly due to reciprocal policies of both countries that had a discouraging effect on mutual trade. Moreover, while rupee-trade was officially discontinued by the May 1992 agreement, switching over to hard currency-trade was not operationally easy for Indian exporters. Delay on the part of both governments in fixing exchange rate of rouble to rupees for calculating debt-repayment, further affected Indo-Russian trade. We may use as a reference point the statistics of Indo-Soviet trade from 1960–61 to 1990–91 for a comparative study of Indo-Russian trade in the initial period:

Table 1: Indo-Soviet trade 1960–61 to 1990–91[2]

(Rs. Crores)

	Indian Exports	*% share in Indian total exports*	*Indian Imports*	*% share in India's total imports*
1960 – 61	29	4.5	16	·1.4
1970 – 71	210	13.7	106	6.5
1980 – 81	1226	18.3	1014	8.1
1990 – 91	5255	16.1	2528	5.9

The following Table depicts India's tumultuous trade relations with the USSR, during the last year of the existence of the Soviet Union, then trade with the CIS and, in the next year, with Russia.[3]

Table 2: Indias' Trade: 1991–92 to 1993–94

	India's Exports (Rs. Crores)	*India's Imports (Rs. Crores)*	
1991–1992	4040	1795	USSR
1992–1993	1756	737	CIS
1993–1994	2036	806	Russia

The immediate causes for the sudden decline in bilateral trade were external factors that, like tips of an iceberg, had surfaced from the internal and domestic systemic turmoil that Russia, in particular, had to undergo.

The Backdrop

The 1991 "Revolution" made a radical change in the development model of Russia from one of excessive bureaucratic centralism to one of market-oriented capitalism.

The Joint Report in February 1991 by the "Houston-4", viz., the International Monetary Fund (IMF), the World Bank, the European Bank for Reconstruction and Development (EBRD), and Organisation for Economic Cooperation and Development (OECD) made some policy prescriptions for the Russian economy for conversion to a market economy. A "conservative" approach, it was argued, would gradually adjust prices till their total decontrol over two to three years, while the "radical" approach presented a "macro-economic stabilisation programme to reduce budget deficit to 2-3 per cent of the GDP", and "immediate decontrol of most prices." The Report rejected the "conservative" approach, and, while anticipating that the "radical" approach might result in sharp "fall" of output and rise of unemployment, hoped that after a few years, a "period of catching up with western standards of efficiency could begin, during which growth in productivity and output would likely (to) exceed that of most mature market economics .... Further strong growth of output and rising living standards could be expected for the remainder of the decade and beyond." Another study of the Russian economy by the Russian government (RET 1992)[4] expected that during 1992–93 production would stop declining, the rate of inflation would drop to less than 3 per cent per month, that there would be "social stability, law and order" and that during 1993–95 there would be "a return to the pre-crisis level [1990] of the GDP."

But the policy of economic "shock therapy", implemented by Prime Minister Yegor Gaidar and President Boris Yeltsin from 1992, following the line of IMF-WB prescription at a rapid pace without taking into account the prevalent ground realities of the Russian economy, failed to reverse the economic decline, despite the expectations. The policy of price liberalization before effecting privatization was criticized even by Vice-President Alexander Rutskoi and Ruslan Khasbulatov, the Speaker of the Russian Supreme Soviet. The process of privatization, termed "illegitimate privatisation"[5] by the Russian analyst Sergei Lounev, benefited only two strata of the population, the nomenklatura and the criminal world. Viktor Chernomyrdin replaced Gaidar in 1993 and sought to pursue the basic policies of the IMF-WB prescription at a slower pace-opting for a middle-path to the transition to market. But the high expectations of both the studies to achieve economic stability by 1995 was found illusory, as by early 1997 Yevgeny Yasin, the Russian Economics Minister, conceded Russia's failure to rejuvenate the economy. Former Soviet President Mikhail Gorbachev writes, in his Foreword to a book,[6] of the "irreparable harm" to the Russian economy, which in his view was caused by shock therapy. Joseph Stieglitz, former Chief Economist at the World Bank and Nobel laureate in economics in 2001, in his Preface, criticizes the "excessive reliance on textbook modes of economics" and reasons that the success of a market economy "cannot be understood in terms of narrow economic incentives", because "norms, social institutions, social capital and trust play critical roles." He continues that "shock therapy may be occasionally effective (e.g. in an anti-inflation move) but is not appropriate for "installing" in (previously non-existent) institutions."[7]

The hindrances to the growth of the Russian economy included: Russia's limited exposure to the workings of market economy systems, lack of good infrastructure, under-developed and under-regulated security markets, fragile small and medium – sized companies, segmented markets, very low amount of foreign direct investment (US$ 4.4 billion at the end of 1995)[8] due to unfavourable investment climate, poor level of adaptability of the banking sector to the rules of the new economic system, the failure of the policy of privatization of the Russian military-industrial complex, coupled with the huge fiscal burden inherited by Russia from high military expenditure[9] by the USSR. All these factors gave rise to a chaotic economic atmosphere. The breaking-up of economic ties within countries of the former Council for Mutual Economic Assistance (CMEA) and within the former USSR, high rise in prices, due to abolition of state monopolies in foreign trade, the lack of customs norms and, most importantly, the sudden exposure of the economy to foreign competition, exacerbated the crisis.

In place of a western-style market economy, a "pseudomarket-economy" gained ground in Russia as it was characterized by "the operation of market forces in a criminal environment with weak legal and contractual parameters and dominated by a government favoured elite".[10] What emerged was classified as a "robber-baron form of capitalism" by Peter Truscott, "wild capitalism" by J. Soros or "pirate capitalism" by Alexander Solzhenitsyn.[11] Sir Karl Popper in an interview to Radio Liberty had a word of warning and his predictions, made in 1991, about post-Cold War Russia are worth-noting: "The will to build a market economy... must come from the people ..... If and when the Russians get their capitalism they will be in for a profound disappointment for it will not be rich capitalism ... and it will lead to sharp popular reactions when the dream is shattered."[12]

The Russian economy went through bad to worse phases during the period following 1992. In 1995, Russian GDP growth rate was (–4%), rate of industrial output (–3%), rate of agricultural output (–8%), rate of gross fixed investment (–13.4%), rate of unemployment (8.2%), real disposable income rate (–13.4%) and rate of growth in consumer prices (196%).[13] The gap between rich and poor sections of the Russian population had a rapid increase, as an estimated 45 million people suffered impoverishment after the economic reform process began.[14] By October 1994 wage arrears totaled 22.5 trillion roubles but came down to 6.4 trillion roubles in June 1995. Also, poor collection of tax revenues meant that the department of public health got 60 per cent of their estimated budget, while the education department got 65 per cent.[15]

The fall in investment was also very sharp – in 1995 it was 27 per cent lower than in 1994 and in first three months of 1996, it was 8–10 per cent below the level in 1995. Expectedly, the fall was much sharper in productive sectors like industry (about 60% lower in 1995 than the 1990 level) and agriculture (output in 1994 was 21% lower than in 1990 and in 1995, –10 to -12% under the level of 1994) than in non-productive sectors like housing, education etc.[16]

Interestingly, industrial structure also underwent a change: in 1990 natural resources based industries accounted for 15.5 per cent of GNP while processing industries 84.5 per cent, but in 1995, the rate was 25 per cent and 75 per cent respectively. Decline in agricultural output led to rise in import of food – in 1995, overall food imports comprised 40 per cent of total food consumption in Russia, according to Institute of Research on Market Situation.[17]

Another notable development was the increase in income-disparities in Russia. For example, Ingush and Dagestan regions, Altai region in West Siberia, Buryat in East Siberia with very low resource – potentialities became the poorest regions with the lowest per capita income in Russia. Likewise, Central, Volga region, Central Black soil region, North-Western region also were most affected as their production of engineering goods and consumer goods, failing to compete with imported goods because of their outdated manufacturing technology. On the other hand, oil and natural gas-rich Yamalo-Nenets region in West Siberia registered almost 10-fold increase in per capita income, whereas oil-rich Mansiiskiy and West Siberia and diamond-rich Yakutia registered 6–8 fold increase by exporting their products to world market.[18]

Capital outflows became the order of the day: in early 1996, in a conference organized by the Russian Industrial Development Bank, it was discussed that the amount of capital flight from Russia was around $20 billion per annum. The Russian Federal Currency Control Service also estimated the total capital flight during 1990–96 was $120–$150 billion. Interestingly, independent experts opined that the governmental estimate of capital flight at $1.5–2 billion per month was rather understated.[19] N.K. Chandra suggested that capital outflows of such a magnitude "are intimately related to the fast expansion in the shadow economy, the power of the mafia, drug trafficking etc..."[20] Regarding this shadow economy, Melnikov, a high-level Russian official, stated in a confidential cable to the US State Department, "Much of the money was used for illegal purposes, including narcotics ... Russian organised crime now controls between 50 and 80 per cent of the country's banks, and has turned Russia into one of the world's major money laundering centers...."[21]

A grave financial crisis faced by Russia in August 1998 made the matters worse for the Russian economy: fiscal mismanagement by the Russian government leading to huge fiscal deficits, its attempt to solve the problem through borrowing, overdue short-term foreign exchange liabilities and the sharp decline in tax collection were the domestic factors, while the fall in world oil prices and the impact of the Asian financial crisis aggravated the crisis. Russia clinched the $22.6 billion IMF-led rescue package in July 1998 as a final effort to halt the devaluation of the rouble and to keep struggling Russian businesses and banks afloat. But despite this help, Russia was forced to devalue its currency by at least 30 per cent and default on some foreign debt.[22]

After the August 1998 financial crisis in Russia, the mainstream media in the West seriously asked whether bad foreign advice might be partly responsible. A British political scientist[23] put the matter succinctly: Russia's mischance was that the collapse of communism coincided with market triumphalism in the West. The crackpot policies that were foisted on it had little to do with Russia's needs and everything to do with the neo-liberal hubris that had gripped Western governments. It was clear from the beginning that the country's uniquely daunting problems required pragmatic solutions, not ideologically driven programmes. This crisis became complicated by the domestic political crisis – Prime Minister Victor Chernomyrdin was replaced by Sergei Kiriyenko in March 1998, was re-appointed a few months later by President Yeltsin, and was finally replaced by Foreign Minister Yevgeny Primakov, as the Russian State Duma declined to endorse Chernomyrdin's re-appointment.

And all this had a negative impact on the Russian economy – real wages reduced by 2.5 times, compared between 1990 and 1999 level; unemployment reached more than 11 per cent by the end of 1999;[24] GDP fell by 83 per cent between 1991 and 1997; unemployment rate rose to 9.2 per cent in 1997[25] and according to the Human Development Index (by the UN Development Programme), Russia went down from the 33rd place in 1990 to the 44th place in the world in 1992, to the 57th place in 1996, 67th in 1997 and 71st place in 1998.[26]

But the pro-reform economists viewed Russian economic transition from a different viewpoint:

Anders Aslund[27] supported speedy and radical reforms in all the economies of the former Soviet bloc and suggested "severe" shocks for achieving "macroeconomic stabilization." To him two so-called "shocks", proved effective in Russian transition – while the currency collapse of October 1994 taught the Russian policymakers "their need for stabilization", the financial crisis of August 1998 speeded up "its transformation" to a market-economy.

Andrei Shleifer and Daniel Treisman[28] took pains to show that reforms in Russia "were a remarkable success" in many regards – e.g., by August 1996 monthly inflation came to naught from a peak of 245 per cent in January 1992, exports rose from about $54 billion in 1992 to about $87 billion in 1997, real per capita income rose by 3.4 per cent in 1997 and proportion of the population below poverty level came down to 20.9 per cent in 1997 from 26.2 per cent in 1995. And they concluded that the reforms could not become totally successful in Russia because the reformers there faced an unenviable complex task unlike in the countries of the former Soviet bloc – centre-region conflict over reforms of the tax systems and macro-economic stabilization programmes; concentration of profitable enterprise in a few resource-rich regions that generated economic inequalities; compromises made with barons, bankers and regional leaders; and the constitutional struggle between the Parliament and Presidency because of the semipresidential nature of the Russian political system. The authors have analogized the conducting of reforms in Russia with "embarking on a journey through mountains without a map.... To understand their (the mountaineers') chances of success, it is not enough to consider their will power, their integrity, and the climbing kits or cash international friends have supplied. One also has to consider the shape of the mountains."[29]

All considered, the fact remains that the reforms process in Russia was not as successful as it was intended to be for various reasons as argued both by analysts who have questioned the wisdom of radical reforms and who have welcomed them.

During this period of transition, the various sectors of the Russian economy experienced a tumultuous process of restructuring that had a devastating impact on the socio-economic environment. It is essential to keep in mind this persistently irritating *domestic factor,* while assessing the Indo-Russian economic relationship, that had been, by implication, conspicuously a non-factor in the Indo-Soviet economic relations of the previous four decades.

The Indian Perspective

As a matter of coincidence, India too experienced an unprecedented balance of payments crisis in mid–1991 that prompted it to initiate a process of restructuring of its economic policies and priorities, oriented towards a market-economy. The process had a prelude in the policy changes of 1980–81, linked to a $5 billion IMF credit to withstand the second oil shock and had a continuation in mid-1980's with the deregulation of the industry and trade, diversification of financial sector and promotion of stock market.

Jayati Ghosh[30] has linked the balance of payments crisis of 1991 involving an erosion of Indian foreign exchange reserves and difficulties in repayment of short-term external commercial debt to "the unsustainable domestic fiscal position resulting from the government's use of large deficits to fuel the economic growth of the late 1980s." Other events contributing to take up the reform package were the sudden fall in inward remittances from the West Asian States due to the 1991 Gulf War, the growing instability in India's domestic politics and, most significant, the collapse of the Soviet economy.

India asked for an immediate stand by loan from the IMF to tide over the crisis in mid–1991, made a two-stage devaluation of the rupee by about 20 per cent and went on to take up a structural adjustment programme, defined as "a process of market-oriented reforms in policies and institutions with the goals of restoring a sustainable balance of payments, reducing inflation and creating conditions for sustainable growth in per capita income."[31] The programme, undertaken by India, covered delicensing of industrial investment and production, financial liberalization measures for both resident and external investors, decanalisation of a number of imported items, along with the shift from import quotas to tariffs and reduction of average tariff rates, substantial easing of the rules governing foreign capital inflow and removal of export subsidies. Also, foreign institutional investors were allowed to operate in Indian stockmarkets with full repatriability, permitted after a relatively low lock – in period.

The performance of Indian economy, after the reforms were initiated, can be judged from these economic indicators[32] in Table 3:

Table 3: Indian Economy after Economic Reforms

Economic Indicators	*1985–90 average*	*1990–91*	*1991–92*	*1992–93*	*1993–94*	*1994–95*	*1995–96*
Rate of growth of real GNP	5.8	5.2	0.5	5	4.5	6.7	7
Rate of growth per capita NNP	3.6	3	–2.1	2.9	2.3	4.8	5.1
Rate of growth agriculture	3.4	4.2	– 2	6.1	3.6	4.6	–0.1
Rate of growth industry	7.5	7	–1.7	4.2	6.8	9.4	11.6
Gross domestic investment (% of GDP)	23.1	27.7	23.4	24	23.6	26	27.4
Fiscal deficit (% of GDP)	10.1	8.3	5.9	5.7	7.5	6.5	5.8
Foreign exchange reserve ($ billion)		3.2	5.8	6.4	15.1	20.8	16.3
% of population in absolute poverty		36.4	37.4	43.5	38.7		

As the Table shows, the economic indicators used here, nosedived during 1991–92 as compared to 1990–91, as well as to the average of 1985–90; only the foreign exchange reserves increased from 1990–91 level – a factor that might be attributed to the IMF loan extended to India in mid–1991. During 1995–96 all the economic indicators showed stable growth except the rate of growth in agriculture that showed a volatile trend.

A comparative study of the Russian and Indian economies shows that Indian economy was in a much stabler position than the Russian during the period.

A clue to the strength of the Indian economy in relation to the Russian economic performance has been provided by P.V. Narasimha Rao, the Hon'ble Ex-Prime Minister of India, who initiated the liberalization process in 1991, in his written answer early in 2003 to my pertinent question: "On our side the change-over was in bringing a liberalized orientation in our mixed economy. On the Russian side it was a straight jump from an established command economy to an unfamiliar system, which obviously entailed a much greater effort at change. Once in a lighter vein, President Yeltsin told me, 'We don't know how to run a shop!' I replied that we had no such difficulty because our instincts and initiatives on trade and economy were part of our ancient heritage."[33]

At the backdrop of an emerging new economic world order and the adopted policy of economic liberalization by the two countries to integrate their respective economies with the world economy, it is needed to keep in view the intrinsic change factor in their economic relationship:

A. Both the countries had to confront new global competitors in each other's domestic markets. Barring Russia's trade with CIS countries (accounting for 28–30% of Russia's total trade), main trading partners of Russia now are the US and the European Union (EU). Germany is the largest partner accounting for 9 per cent and the US for 6 per cent of Russia's total trade. Region-wise, Western Russia's main trading partners are Germany, Finland and Turkey, whereas Japan, South Korea and China are favourable partners in Eastern Russia. In case of India too, the US, Japan, Germany and the UK are significant trading partners.

B. Soviet aid played a significant role in Indo-Soviet economic relations, now the aid factor comes to be non-present in view of Russia's deteriorated economic capabilities.

Growth and evolution of the Indo-Russian economic relations from 1992 till 2002.

Bilateral economic relations between Russia and India evolved in a fluid situation, susceptible to changes that the new post-disintegration realities demanded. The developments, during the period under study, came to be distinguished by certain basic trends towards stabilization of the relations – prompting the study to classify the entire period in three definite phases: from 1992–1995; from 1996–1998; and from 1999 till 2002. To start with, the study of bilateral economic interactions in 1991, the last year of Indo-Soviet relationship, will be helpful in evaluating the developments in successive years.

1991

In 1991, before Soviet disintegration, Izvestia, representing the views of the Kremlin leadership, commented that the result of following the Soviet model, began to tell on Indian economy's performance: its foreign trade deficit reached the record level of Rs. 106 billion and foreign debt to $70 billions. It continued, "Financial confusion(s) in India have acquired a permanent character, and reflects the difficulty its economic system has been facing."[34] It felt that the model adopted by India, taking the USSR as an example, led to a situation where the call for self-reliant national industry put the economy into protectionism, leading to tight bureaucratic control.

The trends in the transitional Soviet economy of this time and their impact on Indo-Soviet trade was presented briefly by Alop Mittal:[35]

(i) As most of the Soviet organisations which imported from India were in transition from central authority to self-control, there had been a lag in their dealings with India due to lack of organisational infrastructure, inexperience and very little knowledge of the Indian market in the newly-created "operation level of bureaucrats and technocrats."

(ii) The Soviet companies now wanted to concentrate only in hard-currency areas.

(iii) The Soviet companies had very few saleable products, due to obsolete technology, uncertain deliveries due to non-availability of spares and machineries (as resulted from growing closures and strikes in state-aided industries), and their "non-commercial approach" restricted Indian imports from the USSR.

(iv) The stringent new controls on value addition norms, put by the Indian government, on goods (to be exported to the USSR) having "high import content financed in hard currency," restricted Indian exports to the USSR.

(v) As there was a big global market in hard currency sector for crude oil and petrol products, the USSR was "reluctant to supply the committed quantities" of these products to India.

(vi) There was a gross fall in demand for Indian goods in view of the near cessation in the earlier practice of "diverting Indian goods by the USSR to its East European allies and other countries."

(vii) The problem of rupee-rouble adjustments was also present.

In late 1991, India had an estimated Rs. 1500 crores of technical credit (i.e. the difference between commodity exports of one trading partner with the other) outstanding against the USSR. As per the 1991 Indo-Soviet Trade Protocol, Indian government had to pay the Indian exporters in rupees for exports to the USSR. But the problem arose as imports from the USSR stopped since October 1991 and with this loss of matching imports from the USSR, the payment the Indian government had to make to Indian exporters, got reflected in the annual budgetary deficit of India. The problem became more serious as one of the conditionalities of the loan provided by the World Bank and the IMF to India, following the fiscal crisis of June–July 1991, was to control the budgetary deficit and so the maintenance of technical credit became a major fiscal irritant for India. With many Indian exporters opening Letters of Credit in advance for deliveries to be made to the USSR in mid-1992, the Reserve Bank of India suspended payments to Indian exporters to the USSR since 27 December 1991 and on 31 December 1991, the total amount of technical credit (alongwith the LCs) stood at Rs. 3200 crores. But in view of the long-standing friendship with the USSR and the politico-economic crisis it was facing, India agreed to honour the LCs already opened and to liquidate the pending technical credit in two instalments.[36]

The Incipient Phase (1992–95)

The economic relations were built up from scratch in this phase and this was marked by a number of threatening problems faced by the incipient relations – necessitating the signing of two notable agreements, first, on trade in convertible currency and second, on rupee-rouble exchange rate. The latter subsequently called for a proper mechanism to utilize the clearing of the accumulated rupee-fund at the disposal of Russia and that again called for rupee auction as a corrective measure from Russia's end, virtually representing a cycle: problems begetting corrective measures-measures taken begetting further problems and so on to be dragged on to the next phase, i.e., 1996–98.

1992

In January 1992 a high-level Indian team, led by Foreign Secretary J.N. Dixit visited Moscow and signed Memorandum of Understanding on trade and defence supply.

The first trade Protocol with the new Russian government was signed on 22nd February 1992 by Indian Commerce Secretary A.V. Ganesan and Deputy Chairman of Russian State Committee of Foreign Economic Relations, V.A. Shibaev. It was agreed that trade would be denominated in rupees as a transitional arrangement and India offered a technical credit of Rs. 850 crores for the calendar year. It was decided the Russia would export crude oil, diesel, kerosene, non-ferrous metals, polyethelene, synthetic rubber and newsprint, and India would export tea, coffee, textile products, black pepper, soyabean extractions, castor oil, medicines, shoe uppers, paints, cosmetics, detergents, and plastic products.[37] The Protocol envisaged a two-way trade of $1100 millions on each side and on Russian side, it was decided, that $750 millions would be on the central account and Russian firms would buy goods worth the remaining amount. A major part of the Protocol was on delinking of the debt aspect from trade[38] and Russia agreed to grant limited credit in sectors like defence, power generation, steel and coal.

During the visit of Russian Secretary of State Gennady Burbulis to New Delhi, both sides signed a five-year agreement on trade and economic cooperation and another agreement on setting up of an Inter-Government Commission (IGC) on Trade, Economic, Scientific and Technological Cooperation. These two agreements were signed by

Burbulis for Russia, whereas P. Chidambaram, the Minister of State of Commerce, signed the trade agreement and Eduardo Faleiro, Minister of State for External Affairs, signed the other agreement.[39] They decided to accord Most Favoured Nation (MFN) treatment to each other. Russia decided to renew export of oil, newsprint and military equipment and India opened a $ 285 million technical credit to Russia for 1992. Of this, $85 million would be disbursed immediately for Russia to buy tea, coffee, tobacco and spices and the balance $200 million would be used "commensurate with the flow of goods from Russia.[40] In a significant departure from the past, it noted that all payments and settlements under this agreement would be designated in dollars, unless otherwise specified by Inter-Governmental Agreement. During 1992 the trade would continue in rupee-terms based on a dollar-clearing mechanism and from next year, in free currency.[41] It was also stipulated that all Indian exports to Russia would be made on the basis of confirmed letters of credit issued in dollars by the Russian Vneshtorg Bank, subject to confirmation by three Indian banks – State bank of India, Punjab National Bank and Union Bank of India. Payments would be debited and credited to the central account, operated by the aforesaid Russian Bank and the Reserve Bank of India and that the Russian Bank would issue letters of credit considering the balance available in the central account.[42] It was decided that the technical credit of Rs. 3500 crores India extended to the former USSR in 1991, would be adjusted against India's debt to the successor state, Russia. But the Russian side opined, despite all these agreements, that bilateral trade relations would continue to go through an ad hoc phase[43] in view of Russia's sudden and unprecedented economic decline.

India and Russia signed an agreement on September 17, 1992 in which Russia agreed to "provide State Credit in Special Drawing Rights (SDR) units to India….. for financing long term projects in the field of technical co-operation and for purchasing special equipment."[44] 10 per cent of the repayment would be made in US dollars, credited directly to the existing dollar Escrow Accounts of the Russian banks and organisations. "The balance 90 per cent and the interest would be paid in equal annual instalments in US dollars within 7 years beginning from the year, following the year in which the relevant credit amount was utilised, into Bank for Foreign Economic Affairs' (BFEA) non-repatriable US dollar based on central account with the Reserve Bank of India." The funds (upto 90%), credited to the BFEA's account with the Reserve, Bank would be utilised by the Russian side for purchase of goods and services from India as permissible under the extant EXIM policy of the India Government.[45]

In the first meeting of the Indo-Russian Joint Commission held in New Delhi during 22-24th October, 1992, both sides finalized some compromises on matters of trade and credit.

The study of Indo-Russian Trade, published by the Russian Embassy,[46] New Delhi, attempted to show how effective Indo-Russian trade was for Russian economy, as "Without wasting any hard currency, this country uses rupees to buy tea, coffee, rice, medicines, knitted wear and leather." It noted that "The search for new outlets would take a lot of time, to say nothing of the need to spend hard currency." Also, the importance of trade with India was proved by the fact that in the field of medicine and medical raw materials, India remained their "one and only supplier." India, according to this study, paid in full and as per schedule for the credit granted for construction and military hardware devices and "the acquired resources are used by Russia to buy consumer goods in short supply. Long-term payments account for over half of Russian's Indian imports." Interestingly, it referred to the ongoing bilateral talks on the problems of trade and rupee-rouble exchange rate as: "This is a hard business not only due to the woes of the crisis-stricken national economy during its transition to market relations; the inertia of certain Russian departments and the Western market priorities of many enterprises are quite tangible."

But Izvestia[47] referred to a paradoxical situation arising out of the 1992 Protocol: though the Russian state committed to supply 4 million tonnes of crude oil and 600,000 tonnes of diesel fuel to India, but it was left to commercial organizations to fulfil the promise. Naturally, Russia could not deliver the promised amount and India got only 1 million tonnes of crude oil in the end.

1993

Before President Yeltsin's visit to New Delhi in late-January 1993, Finance Minister Manmohan Singh and V.P. Shumeiko, the First Deputy Chairman of the Russian Council of Ministers, discussed issues of India's debt to the former USSR, and new arrangements to govern bilateral trade in terms of credits and cash and rupee-rouble exchange rate.[48]

Indo-Soviet bilateral trade was to be conducted through the Rupee Trade System based on annual plans, it was agreed, and the exchange value of rouble in relation to rupee was kept very high. The 1978 Indo-Soviet Protocol tied rupee to a basket of currencies while the value of rouble was retained constant. And if the value of rupee were lowered in relation to these currencies, rupee's value in relation to rouble also got affected and this became a major irritant in bilateral economic relations. During talks between India and Russia on this particular matter, Russia insisted "on India agreeing to pre-1989 arrangements while we stuck to our point that monetary arrangements, governing economic relations, should be related to existing realities regarding the rouble's standing in the international currency markets."[49]

However, during President Yeltsin's visit in New Delhi, an agreement was signed by Manmohan Singh and Shumeiko on the repayment of outstanding state credit extended by the former USSR for defence and civilian projects in India. The agreement[50] worked out India's total debt at Rs. 31,377 crores. The debt was divided in two parts: the "non-rescheduled portion" of the debt was the rupee-equivalent of the rouble debt using the exchange rate of Rs. 19.9169 per rouble (as on January 1, 1990) amounting to about Rs. 19,643 crores. This part was to be paid over a period of 12 years with the rupee-value indexed to a basket of six SDR currencies. The average interest rate was to be around 2.4 per cent per annum.

The rest of the amount (i.e., the balance between Rs. 31,377 crores and Rs. 19,643 crores) was to be repaid in equal annual instalments over a period of 45 years at zero interest rates. There will be no indexing to any depreciation of the rupee for the first five years, after which a review would be undertaken, only if the rupee then would be found to have depreciated on an average by more than 3 per cent annually against the SDR currencies and then the future payments would be indexed to the depreciation. For both parts of the debt, repayment would begin on April 1, 1992 and in rupees, to be used by Russia to buy goods and services from India. Secretary for Economic Affairs, Montek Singh Ahluwalia made it clear that this agreement was valid only in the case of repayment of old debts and for any future trade transaction, both sides might negotiate new arrangements.

Many economists argued that India conceded too much to Russia regarding the exchange-rate in the Agreement. Some noted that during negotiations India suggested to make January 1, 1987 as the cut-off date, with the exchange-rate then being Rs. 14.3 per rouble. But the Agreement finally decided to January 1, 1990 as the cut-off date with the exchange-rate being Rs. 19.92 a rouble, which was closer to what Russia suggested (Rs. 22.7 as on November 1, 1990).[51] Some also agreed to what The Economic Times[52] suggested – that India made a "$10 billion gift to Yeltsin", as with January 1993 auction rate of 488 rouble = 1$, India's total debt of $9,871 million would amount to a meager $20.2 million. But Nirmal Kumar Chandra[53] put up the rationale from an economist's point of view behind India's consent to this agreement:

(i) First, it required nothing more than common sense to understand that a huge gap existed between the value of rouble in 1993 and that of rouble in 1989 and earlier when the USSR supplied India military and civilian goods on credit.
(ii) Second, as Russia's was a highly volatile economy, so to specify what should be the "correct" exchange rate, would be a very difficult task.
(iii) Third, as no other trading partners of the former USSR asked for a scaling down of their debt, India had "no logic" to do so.
(iv) Fourth, by reneging on rouble debt, India might lose a "valuable outlet" and a steady supplier of "hard goods" like oil, fertilisers and metals, but most significantly, India's defence capacity would get a major shock as the USSR provided India with military supplies at rates far below the world market price level (as compared by the SIPRI).

In his interview granted to me J.N. Dixit, the then Foreign Secretary pointed to the political dimension of the deal. In response to my question whether we gave away too much to Russia in this deal, he commented:

> "That's true. Technically true. We gave away too much to Russia in purely economic and technical (terms). Then, had we not done that, Russians would not give us... certain very important supplies – oil, certain defence equipments. We carefully balanced all the difficulties which might have arisen if we had taken a totally tough negative stand. There were lots of differences of opinion between the Finance and External Affairs Ministry. The Finance Ministry wanted to

> be absolutely strict. Defence and External Affairs (Ministries) felt that it is unimaginative given our larger interest. We advised Prime Minister Mr. Rao to give some concessions which he gave."[54]

Mr. Pranab Mukherjee, the ex-Finance Minister in Indira Cabinet and the ex-Commerce Minister and the ex-External Affairs Minister in Narasimha Rao cabinet during 1994–96, in his interview granted to me commented:

> "I don't subscribe to the theory (that India conceded too much in the deal). It (pressing on the market-rate) would be like *taking advantage of Russia's helplessness*. I think, it would be unbecoming (of India)."

To my question whether it was a gesture towards building the Indo-Russian friendship, he answered:

> "Exactly. (The gesture indicated) that India did not want to take advantage of Russia's wretched state of affairs."[55]

The comments cited clearly indicate that India did not compromise its interests but "accommodated" Russian viewpoints, as a friendly gesture, for a larger interest to engage Russia in a comprehensive and long-term relationship.

It is significant that few economists like Pronab Sen argue that this rate is a "unit of account" with "no operational significance", and that the rate "is notional in the sense that it is an artificial rate of exchange between two inconvertible currencies."[56] To them, the non-significance of the exchange-rate in matters of trade gains ground as there exist three exchange-rates for rupee and rouble: the "commercial" rate for tourists, the "protocol" rate for trade transactions and the "basket" rate for credit transactions. And the chain of arguments are as follows: the price of "hard" goods (constituting 90% of Indian imports from the USSR) is measured in "world market price, i.e. dollar price and the quantity is fixed ex-ante by bilateral trade protocols and then the "dollar" price is converted to their equivalent price in rupee terms according to the rupee-rouble rate and is credited to the Soviet account in rupee terms. For "soft" goods the prices are directly quoted in rupee-terms, so in this respect rouble seems irrelevant. And as Soviet imports from India are covered by rupees available partly from Soviet exports and partly from debt servicing, protocol-rate of rupee-rouble "can have no operational role to play in trade transactions." Sen stated that though having some superficial logic, these arguments rest on two implicit and unstated assumptions: that "the desired supply of all Soviet exports to India are completely independent of the rouble equivalent of the rupee prices paid" and "Soviet imports from India are completely and effectively limited by the availability of rupee resources from current sources."

The points raised by Sen indicate that rupee-rouble exchange rate mechanism had limited viability in the growth of Indo-Russian trade, that has ostensibly led to the reversal of the mechanism to convertible currency in 1992. But there is no denying the fact that the old mechanism played a crucial role in moderating the vulnerabilities of the two economies to pay in hard currencies in the context of their limited expendable foreign-exchange reserves. On 11th June 1993, India and Russia signed an accord to convert the denomination of most of India's debt from roubles to rupees – justifiably since the variations in the prevailing value of the rouble caused great confusion.[57]

1994

The declining trend of bilateral trade continued even after the 1993 Protocol on rupee-rouble exchange rate because of lack of a proper mechanism to utilise clearing of rupees. This task of working out a proper mechanism became toilsome because of lack of experience of Russian leadership in this matter (India being the first such case) and the existence of multiple lobbies for dealing with this problem, e.g., Central Bank of Russia, Ministry of Finance, Ministry of Foreign Economic Relations and the industrial trading lobby.[58]

Various options were considered by Russia to clear the annual debt: auction of rupees, granting of deferred payment facility, reinvestment of a part of the debt in industrial projects like in energy or electronics sector and contract tenders.

In May 1994 the first Indo-Russian Business Seminar was organized in Moscow jointly by the Indian Embassy in Moscow, Indian Business Association in Moscow and the Russian Foreign Policy Foundation. And in this Seminar, Margarity Gretskaya, a senior official in the Russian Foreign Ministry, announced her government's plan to auction Rs. 400–700 crores which would be available from India's debt repayment scheme so that Russian private companies could use it for imports from India.[59]

During Prime Minister Rao's visit to Moscow in June-July 1994, both sides stressed on the issue of auctioning rupee funds to solve this problem of debt clearing. During his visit to India in June 1994, Russian Commerce Minister Yuri Yarov declared that.[60]

(a) Russia would not auction more that 30 per cent of the clearing rupees received from India's debt repayment scheme and rupee auction would be open for Russian buyers only;
(b) there would be the stipulation for buyers that the purchased rupees from this auction could be used only for import of goods from India and re-export of goods to third countries would be strictly prohibited; and
(c) the larger part of India's annual debt repayment amount would be used to settle outstanding debts of Russian state enterprises (estimated at Rs. 7–8 billions) to their Indian partners.

But a confusion remained over the exact amount of rupee to be auctioned: while Yarov said it to be Rs. 13 billion, Deputy Foreign Minister Albert Chernyshev said the amount would not exceed Rs. 2–3 billion.[61] Also, there were apprehensions that rupee auction at a discount might lead to switch trade, detrimental for India's economic interests. Naresh Minocha commented that rupee auction was one of the two Russian initiatives to improve the debt repayment mechanism: while the auction would "improve cash flow" of the Russian government and "reduce budget deficit", granting of a 180 – days deferred payment scheme to Russian importers would enable them to buy Indian goods.[62]

However, in July 1994 at the first-ever tender of government contracts worth Rs. 386 crores for rupee-imports from India, the demand for rupee was as high as 70–90 per cent of rupee-rouble crossrate through dollar. This success was due mainly to the giant state monopolies (now most of them were being privatised) which raised their offer for rupee biddings, so as not to lose the lucrative Indian market. The success led the Russian government to prefer the contract-tender formula to the auction formula as this would enable the Russian government to encourage purchase of those Indian commodities badly needed by Russia and second, it would help the Russian government to avoid the threat of re-export of Indian goods to the third countries.[63] But later the auction was made the decisive means of disposing of the debt, as we shall see, in 1997.

During Prime Minister Rao's visit to Moscow, it was decided to engage in joint ventures to make use of the rupee fund available from the debt repayment, and to set up a joint bank in Russia with the participation of the State Bank of India and Rosexim Bank of Russia. India also agreed to modernize the Novorossisk port and build warehouses in return of getting priority in berth-facilities there.

During his visit in June 1994, Yarov discussed a proposal to bring up bilateral trade to Rs. 5000 crores in the next two years at a meeting with Indian Commerce Minister Pranab Mukherjee.[64] Both sides also discussed the setting up of the Indo-Russian Inter-Governmental Commission (IGC) which would have five working groups on: Trade and Economic Cooperation, Power and Non-conventional energy sources, Oil and Coal industries, Ferrous and non-ferrous metallurgy and Science and Technology. The Commission's main task was to create favourable political, trade, economic, financial and regulatory conditions for the subsequent development of multifaceted Indo-Russian relations on both state and individual entrepreneurs level.[65] It is important to note that the Inter-Governmental Commission now covers some more working-groups, on viz., Pharmaceuticals, Cultural Cooperation, Information Technology, Environment and natural resources, and Cooperation with the Regions.

The Joint Statement, issued after the first meeting of the Indo-Russian Joint Commission in September 1994 in Moscow, stated that the ground reality was that "the present level of trade and economic cooperation does not correspond with the potential of both countries" and resolved to double the bilateral trade in the next year or two.[66] An agreement was also signed on opening of offices of the State Bank and Canara Bank in Moscow and St. Petersburg.

During Prime Minister Chernomyrdin's visit to New Delhi in December 1994, both sides signed 8 agreements covering among other sectors, trade, investment promotion, merchant shipping, etc. on 23rd December.[67] The "Agreement for the Promotion and Mutual Protection of Investment" covered protection of investment (even intellectual property rights) from either country made on or after January 1, 1987 as foreign investment was not allowed in the former USSR before that date. It asserted the MFN status for both the states and agreed that this status could become null and void only if both the states participate in a common market/free trade area/customs union/ economic union. It provided that nationalisation or expropriation could be undertaken only in extreme circumstances and under judicial review.

The Agreement would remain in force for 10 years, but for the investments made during this period, its provisions would continue for 15 years after its termination. An elaborate mechanism for dispute settlement was also made, though taxation matters were excluded from its purview. Both sides also agreed to settle the problem of non-payment by some Russian organisations to Indian exporters, for goods supplied before 1993, within three months.[68] The agreement on shipping replaced the 1976 Merchant Shipping Agreement and provided the legal framework for bilateral shipping operations. Russia also agreed to buy 20,000 tonnes of tobacco, 30,000 tonnes of tea, 100,000 tonnes of soyabeans and $100 million worth of medicines from India against the rupee debt, annually through 1997.[69]

1995

In July 1995, the visiting Russian Deputy Prime Minister Yuri Yarov and External Affairs Minister Pranab Mukherjee agreed,[70] in a meeting in New Delhi, to use debt repayment funds for investment in joint-venture projects in both states. Initially, about Rs. 400 crores was allocated for five projects: two in Russia (a grain terminal in the Port of Novorossisk and the second phase of a tourist hotel in Novgorod) and three in India.

The proposal for the development of oilfields in Siberia by India marked a new era of collaboration, as earlier the USSR invested in offshore and onshore oil-projects in India. Also, Indian petroleum industry agreed to implement projects for production of titanium dioxide and a polypropylene plant.[71] They also signed a Protocol of Co-Chairmen Meeting of the Indo-Russian Intergovernmental Commission.

But, still a number of issues remained unresolved. The Joint Business Council Meet on September 21 and the Meet of the Joint Working Group on Trade and Investment (October 3–6) discussed these issues. For the Indian side, these were the failure of Russian authorities to provide a single-window system for exporters, the inability to raise number and value of commodities earmarked for export, and most important, lack of transparency in the system of rupee-auctions; while for the Russian side, it was the lowering of 100 per cent VAT on export items, as levied by India.

In the New Delhi Meet of the Indo-Russian Joint Commission on Trade, Economic, Scientific, Technical and Cultural Cooperation (9–13 October, 1995), Deputy PM Yarov led a high-level delegation of a number of First Deputy Ministers. Pranab Mukherjee, in lead of the Indian delegation, expressed satisfaction after the Meet, that debt repayment was on the right track to cross the target of Rs. 5000 crores by next year.[72]

In this session, the much-disputed issue of non-acceptance (by Indian organisations) of guarantees from Russian Banks for Russian agencies was positively resolved and both sides mapped out possibilities for cooperation in power, engineering, coal and oil production, metallurgy, science and technology, information science, environmental protection and culture. Both sides also discussed problems like long time taken by the Reserve Bank to process letters of credit, application of a 100 per cent surcharge on import-components on items exported to Russia, demands for the presentation of certificates regarding arrival of goods in Russia, and holding up the shipping of commodities to Russia until registered letters of credit were produced, among others.

In October 1995, all of a sudden the repayment issue became the eye of a storm. Russian Finance Minister wrote a letter to the Indian Finance Minister, Manmohan Singh, to pay a part of India's debt in hard currency – Pranab Mukherjee announced this during the Joint Commission Meet in New Delhi. In mid-October, Manmohan Singh categorically rejected the proposal, put forward again by his Russian counterpart when they met in Washington. But two high ranking Russian officials reiterated the demand under the logic that since India made its currency fully convertible on current account and accepted the obligations under Article VIII of the IMF, India should denominate its debt to Russia in hard currency. India rejected the demand on grounds that:

(i) First, it was totally against the letter and spirit of the 1993 agreement which particularly provided for rupee repayment; and

(ii) Second, if Russia wanted reneging on the 1993 agreement, then the relevant currency parity to be considered would be the rouble-dollar parity at that time and at the rate India's rouble debt would come down to a paltry $2.5 million a year.[73]

Later the issue was dropped altogether.

To dispel any confusion regarding debt repayment, it is needed to note what the Reserve Bank has to comment on the repayment issue:

> "As per this (1993) agreement, which is effective from January 1, 1993, credits by Indian organisations including payments against overdue liabilities, if any, are to be repaid in Indian rupees direct into the special accounts of the Russian organisations which are maintained, with commercial banks in India .... The export of goods and services done under this arrangement (special Rupee Account Mechanism) is to be invoiced in Indian rupees only .... Export to any country other than Russia is not permissible under this mechanism."[74]

The Intermediate Phase (1996–98)

In this phase, new areas of cooperation were identified—as in Information Technology Sector and in oil and gas sector, where joint ventures were contemplated in both the countries and in third countries as well. This was an intermediate phase – from a fluid situation towards solidity.

1996

During the first meeting of the Indo-Russian Working Group on Pharmaceuticlas, in New Delhi in early April 1996, Commerce Secretary Tejendra Khanna (the head of the Indian delegation) pointed out that though Russia agreed in December 1995 to purchase pharmaceuticals worth $100 million annually over the next three years under the debt repayment scheme, yet the actual purchase was only $59 million in the first 9 months of the last financial year. On the other, AE Vilken, the Deputy Minister for Medical Industry and Drugs, noted that some problems like registration and quality control of drugs should be taken note of to further bilateral cooperation in this sector.[75] Russian ambassador to India, Albert S. Chernyshev declared, on 9th August 1996, the formation of a special Russian-Indian Business Council in Moscow.[76]

And there were no dearth of suggestions on what India should do to promote exports to Russia. E.A. Isayev, the Russian Trade Commissioner, suggested at a meeting organized by the Federation of Indian Export Organisation on 16th September 1996, that Indian companies should aggressively market their products in Russia, just like their American, German, French and Israeli counterparts. On 29th October 1996, at the Plenary Session on "A New Era of Business and Economic Partnership between India and Russia" at the India

Economic Summit organized by the CII, the Russian delegation analyzed that Indian share in Russia's total trade was only 9.3 per cent and suggested that India should export hi-tech products instead of agricultural and raw materials and that value-addition norms on such products should be done away with to promote these products in the Russian market.[77]

1997

On 1st January 1997, India relaxed the value-addition norms (from 100% to 75%) on certain hi-tech items, like electronic goods, computer hardware and software, pharmaceuticals etc., for export to Russia – a move expected to boost Indian exports to Russia.

After the Moscow Meeting of the Indo-Russian Joint Commission, several documents[78] were signed on February 11. The Memorandum of Understanding (MoU) on the Protocol on Trade, Economic, Scientific and Cultural Cooperation was signed by Co-Chairman I.K. Gujral and Russian First Deputy P.M....Ilyushin. The MoU on Information Technology decided to establish a permanent group (Rus Indtech) to certify both software and hardware products for export. Both sides also decided to further cooperate in areas like science, commerce, metallurgy etc and to set up a sub-group on finance and banking under the existing Joint Working Group (JWG) on Trade and Economic Cooperation. They also agreed on rough guidelines to use 10 per cent of the Debt Repayment Fund (DRF) for Russian investments in projects in India and also Ministry of Power identified four projects of a total outlay of Rs. 8000 crores for such ventures. MoUs were signed as oil and gas sector joint ventures were decided to be set up – between the ONGC – Videsh Limited (OVL) and Zarubezhneft for third country projects; between OVL and Machinoexport for projects in India; and between OVL-and Rosneft for projects in Russia and Kazakhstan.

For the coal sector, it was decided to prepare a masterplan for the development of Talcher–15 valley coalfield, to exchange data on hydraulic mining technology for Namdung coalfield, to use Russian technology for evaluation of mining deposits technology and that Russia would participate in the global tender for Jhanjhra – II project.

To control the large-scale misuse of the Escrow Account and export schemes, both sides considered an Agreement for mutual assistance in the investigation of frauds in exports and imports, with the exchange of information on the misuse of the value-based Advanced License

Scheme and Duty Drawback Scheme, as unscrupulous exporters to Russia cause loss of Rs. 600 crores annually through over valuation of goods, diversion of goods (bound for Russia) to other countries and export of junk materials. The Agreement, based on the Draft World Customs Organisation Agreement, was signed during Prime Minister Deve Gowda's visit to Moscow.[79]

After completion of the fourth meet of JWG on Trade and Economic Cooperation in New Delhi, a Protocol on Trade was signed, on 12th December by Commerce Secretary P.P. Prabhu and V.G. Karastin, Deputy Minister of Foreign Economic Relations and Trade, to take concrete steps to establish long-term trading arrangements for export of tea, tobacco, pharmaceuticals etc. from India and for import of fertilisers and newsprint from Russia. Trade Basket would be made broad based to include engineering goods and hi-tech items like electronics and products for information technology.[80]

On 18th December, Finance Minister P. Chidambaram and Deputy P.M. Anatoli Chubais signed a very important Protocol that proposed to set up a bilateral free trade zone[81] including the CIS. An expert group was proposed to be set up to explore which of the CIS countries should be included for this "preferential trade area."

1998

After the end of the fifth meeting of JWG[82] on information technology in late-October 1998, a Protocol was signed on widening of cooperation in trade, commerce, and electronic governance, to utilise DRF for financing joint projects in this sector and certification of products including software, strategic electronics, micro-electronics, electronic and digital components.

The fifth session of the Indo-Russian Inter-Governmental Commission, under the co-chairmanship of Finance Minister Yashwant Sinha and First Deputy PM Yuri Maslyukov, was held in Moscow during 26-28 November1998. Transport, power, coal and oil and natural gas were earmarked for further cooperation. Also, Russia agreed to double its import of pharmaceuticals from $100 millions to $200 millions a year. Sources at the Russian Trade Ministry said that Indian offer, at the Meet, to increase debt repayment amount was conditional on setting up of an effective and transparent mechanism to use rupee funds by Russia, in view of the various corrupt practices attached to the system of rupee-auctions in Russia.[83]

During Russian PM Yevgeny Primakov's visit to India in December 1998, a Joint Document on the Development of Trade, Economic, Industrial Financial, and Science and Technology was signed; agreements on cooperation in telecommunications and air transport were also signed.[84]

The Third Phase (1999–2002): Towards Stability

Alexander M. Kadakin, the Russian ambassador in New Delhi, admits there was a period of "long stagnation" in Russian economy with the bilateral trade "fluctuating in the range of $1.1–1.9 billion."[85] This "stagnation" was only a reflection of the sorry state of affairs in Russian economy. But President Vladimir Putin (since 2000) seemed to have turned the wheel, so far as Russian economy is concerned. A package of laws was introduced to cut all major taxes and abolish most of the minor taxes, to reduce business profit from 35 per cent to 24 per cent and VAT from 20 per cent to 15 per cent, and to fix a unified rate of tax on personal income at 15 per cent,[86] among other reform-measures. As a result, Russia's tax collection increased by 75 per cent in 2000 over the level of 1999, inflation came down to below 40 per cent, exchange rate of rouble also came down at 26-27 roubles per dollar and Russia achieved a trade surplus of $ 38 billion with countries outside the CIS, as against $ 20 billion in the previous year.[87] All these positive signs have prompted Michael Mussa, the IMF Research Director, to observe that "after years of dithering and delay, important areas of structural reforms are beginning to move forward in Russia."[88] Martin Gilman, the Moscow representative of the IMF, also opined that Russian government's budget-policy played a positive role in laying the foundation for macro-economic stability.[89] And as a recognition of the improvement in Russian economy. Thomson Bank Watch, the international bank rating agency, upgraded Russia's debt rating from CCC to B.[90]

The Russian economy grew during the (1999-2002) period at an average annual rate of more than 5 per cent that well exceeded the OECD average of around 3 per cent a year. The economic recovery initially was stimulated by the massive devaluation, before the August 1998 crisis, of the rouble (R6 = $1), resulting in an average 1999 exchange rate at (R 24.6 = $1). Import substitute production was revitalized with the recovery of food processing, textiles, clothing and engineering sectors, that had been struggling for survival from competition of the imported items. The devaluation stimulus was further activated by a rise in oil prices in the international market in early 1999 that prevailed more or less till late 2002. Inflation rate declined to about 15 per cent a year (consumer prices) in 2002 and the rouble recovered in real terms against the dollar– all this restricted the scope for financing capital flight. Domestic fixed investments grew by 17 per cent and the Moscow Development Centre estimated that accumulated corporate funds, held both in Russia and abroad, could keep in investment growing at 5-6 per cent a year in the near future. The sustainability of this upward inclination of investment and consumption evidently is an indicator as well as a catalyst of business confidence in the economy.

Table 4: An Estimate of Capital Flight From Russia[91], 1998-2001

($ mn)

1998	23,971
1999	22,535
2000	29,625
2001	17,653
2002	10,400

1999

During the early phase of this "recovery", both Indian and Russian sides agreed to utilize the debt fund for investments in steel (for the modernization of IISCO plant in Burnpur) and in power (the Koodankulam project), during the visit of Viktor Kristenko, the First Deputy PM for the Inter-Governmental Commission meet in New Delhi in July 1999. Kristenko and Finance Minister Yashwant Sinha also signed a Protocol to set up a JWG on civil aviation. After reviewing the reasons for the 23 per cent fall in bilateral trade during 1998-89, Kristenko expressed hopes that India's decision to relax value-added norms for exports to Russia further (from 75% to 33%) and diversification of the trade basket would definitely push up bilateral trade volume.[92]

2000

At the end of the 6th meet of the JWG on Trade and Economic Cooperation, a Protocol on trade was signed by Commerce Secretary PP Prabhu and Russian Deputy Minister of Trade Igor Mitrofanov. Both sides also decided to encourage bilateral trade through a focus on high value-added items like diamonds and hi-tech goods, trade facilitation measures and launch of a joint liner service. Russia agreed to help Indian consignment exports, especially tea and tobacco, to be stored in customs bonded warehouses in Russian ports. Indian demands for VAT exemption on consignment exports and reduction in customs duty for tea was also discussed.[93]

During President Vladimir Putin's visit to India in early October 2000, a number of agreements were signed, viz., on the extension of the Integrated Long-Term Programme (ILTP) of cooperation in science and technology till 2010, on Mutual Legal Assistance in Civil and Commercial matters, on Cooperation in Agriculture, on Establishment of another Inter-Governmental Commission on Technical Cooperation, a MoU on peaceful uses of nuclear energy and a Production-Sharing Contract between GAS Authority of India and Gazprom for exploration and development of an oilfield in the eastern coast of India under the New Exploration Licensing Policy (NELP).[94] Also, sectors like metallurgy, fuel and energy, information technology, banking and finance and communications were identified for further development.

2001–2002

During Prime Minister Vajpayee's November 2001 Moscow visit, both sides agreed that some steps needed to be taken to set up a monitoring mechanism to check on the implementation of the decisions taken on trade and economic matters. They also stressed on the need to ensure that the Russian imports of tea and tobacco did not suffer when rupee-funds would run out in another 3 years (bilateral trade stood at a miniscule $ 1.4 billion in 2000–01).[95]

In the eighth session of IGC in New Delhi for trade, economic, scientific, technological and cultural cooperation between the two countries in February 2002, Russian Dy. Prime Minister Klebanov and Indian Finance Minister Yashwant Sinha signed an economic protocol, envisaging joint development of a 100 – seater multi purpose transport aircraft, more investments in the energy sector and the opening up of the North-South corridor and to set up a JWG to examine restructuring of Burnpur IISCO.[96]

In the "Joint Declaration on Strengthening and Enhancing Economic, Scientific and Technological Cooperation," signed between the two countries in New Delhi on 4 December 2002, both noted that in the last decade, "with the stimulus of reforms and liberalization, the economies of two countries have acquired a new dynamism and significant new capabilities and requirements have emerged." The Joint

Declaration identified the following areas, among others, to "provide for a positive environment for the conduct of business interaction and investment": strengthening transportation links and infrastructure in different modes, with special importance on bilateral and trilateral consultations to operationalize the North-South Transport Corridor; streamlining customs administration; recognizing the importance for a sustained business sector dialogue between Russian Union of Industrialists and Entrepreneurs and Confederation of Indian Industry; developing trade in and joint ventures for the production of Knowledge-based high technology goods and services; exploring jointly possibilities of regional trade and economic cooperation with other countries in harmony with their respective national interests; emphasizing on possibilities of working together in key areas, such as telecommunication, computerization, information technology and space research; maximizing the opportunities, provided by the presence of large reservoirs of skilled manpower in their respective countries for the creation of knowledge-based industries, while ensuring the protection of intellectual property rights in each other's markets; and indicating their common desire to intensify long-term cooperation in energy security, which could be extended to other areas including the Caspian Sea as well as to other aspects of the energy sector.[97]

Consequences for Bilateral Economic Relations

So far, this discussion has followed and closely studied the important policy-decisions of the two governments on the bilateral economic relations and the important agreements signed. But these are projected as high expectations and, at best, good intentions in the context of achievements in real terms. The focus will now be on what are reflected in related data. It is already shown, in the beginning, India's exports to Russia and imports from Russia from 1991–92 to 1993–94. Here are data for successive years till 2002.[98]

The figures in Table 5 show that Russia's share in India's total exports was just 2.4 per cent, and 1.6 per cent in India's total imports in 1996–97 and 2.6 per cent of India's total exports and 1.7 per cent of India's total imports in 1997–98.[99] In 1998–99 Russia's share in India's total exports was 2.14 per cent and in India's total imports, 1.29 per cent. In 1999–2000, the figures were 2.53 per cent in India's exports and 1.3 per cent in imports.[100]

After a total downswing in bilateral trade following the Soviet-disintegration, the total trade turnover showed an upward trend during

Table 5: India-Russia Trade: 1994–95 to 2001–02

(Rs. Crores)

Year	*India's Exports to Russia*	*India's Imports from Russia*
1994–95	2534.36	1583.76
1995–96	3495.49	2864.16
1996–97	2879.60	2230.93
1997–98	3541.67	2520.53
1998–99	2984.57	2295.13
1999–2000	4122.85	2675.68
2000–2001	4054	2344
2001–2002	3787	2558

1999-2000, when it grew by 28.75 per cent. It once again declined by 6 per cent during 2000-01, compared with 1999-2000. During 2001-02 trade turnover showed a decline of 4.31 per cent compared with the previous year.[101] Since approximately 80 per cent of the bilateral trade is through the debt repayment track, an end to annual debt repayment of Rs. 3000 crores from 2005 onwards might eventually affect the fledgling trade turnover, negatively or positively, through Indian entrepreneurs' ventures, in the competitive milieu, into Russia's virgin markets in the distant regions and through investments of private firms without much of government protection.

We shall now look into commodity-composition of India's exports to Russia and India's imports from Russia.

The data in Tables 6 and 7 reveal a perceptible trend in Indian exports and imports that an upswing is followed by a downswing in the successive year. India's imports nearly doubled in 1995–96 from the earlier year and after that, successive fluctuations were restricted within a very short range. India's exports in 1999–2000 show a virtual jump from the earlier year, and it is important to note that the "total value of export has been higher than the total debt repayment amount."[104]

Road Blocks

Despite persistent efforts by the two governments, the Indo-Russian trade level could not be raised to the Indo-Soviet level. It indicates that there must have been some persistent reasons that deterred the growth of trade:

A. *Debt-Repayment route:* Though around 80–85 per cent of India's annual export to Russia is carried through Debt

Table 6: Composition of Imports from Russia 1993–94 – 1999–2000[102] (*US $ million*)

	1993-94	*1994-95*	*1995-96*	*1996-97*	*1997-98*	*1998-1999*	*1999-2000*
All Commodities	256.89	504.54	857.53	628.98	679.02	545.42	618.23
Fertiliser manufactured	78.34	82.69	168.33	29.52	77.17	149.44	191.16
Iron & Steel	3.65	40.50	130.66	77.17	157.42	65.16	63.27
Non-Ferrous metals	72.07	135.25	179.10	164.33	136.17	55.57	59.52
Newsprint	35.54	41.34	85.38	74.13	82.26	60.93	50.26
Coal, coke & briquettes	–	–	–	–	–	5.71	40.96
Non-electrical machinery	13.18	36.86	47.57	27.83	39.09	21.88	30.13
Primary steel pig iron based item	1.35	15.79	28.68	8.51	10.46	4.15	23.72
Metalliferous ores & metal scrap	2.82	7.88	9.97	10.89	17.21	13.40	20.04
Synthetic & reclaimed rubber	0.83	4.01	4.42	4.83	8.10	12.41	16.18
Cotton raw & waste	0.42	3.95	5.36	1.51	15.64		
Organic chemicals	5.36	22.08	45.72	29.19	34.73	19.19	15.24
Project goods	11.76	57.01	16.30	9.27	1.18	18.32	14.95
Gold and silver	0.91	16.61	3.06	1.22	35.28	9.56	
Transport equipment	6.80	18.26	12.90	37.58	16.82	5.90	7.80
Electronic goods	0.70	1.55	2.00	1.52	1.51	1.34	7.09
Printed books, newspapers etc.	0.15	–	1.98	0.84	0.05	0.08	5.44
Medicinal & pharm. products	1.96	1.74	2.57	5.22	5.78	5.56	4.98
Sulphur & unroasted iron pyrites	–	–	0.78	1.70	–	–	3.74
Inorganic chemicals	1.48	5.49	1.88	14.43	17.89	13.11	3.17
Manufactures of metals	0.79	1.19	2.49	1.40	1.56	2.36	2.97
Electrical machinery	0.11	0.44	0.86	0.47	1.36	1.27	2.66
Professional inst, optical goods etc.	0.06	0.29	1.29	1.64	1.09	0.94	2.10
Non metallic mineral mnfs.	0.15	0.77	0.71	0.32	1.47	1.70	1.87
Raw hides and skins	0.88	0.42	0.86	1.11	0.79	1.02	1.33
Artificial, resins plastic matrl. etc.	2.83	2.81	4.65	1.98	1.73	0.29	1.13
Puip & waste paper	5.47	9.59	23.23	6.44	10.73	0.70	0.85
Machine tools	0.39	0.27	9.31	4.61	2.24	2.58	0.66
Pearls precious & semiprecious stones	0.15	0.35	2.20	1.35	0.99	0.01	0.50
Leather	0.57	0.08	0.07	0.05	0.34	0.71	0.30

Table 7: Composition of Exports To Russia 1993–94 – 1999–2000[103] (*US $ million*)

	1993-94	*1994- 95*	*1995-96*	*1996-97*	*1997-98*	*1998-99*	*1999-2000*
All Commodities	648.60	807.38	1046.56	811.84	954.12	709.26	952.60
Tea	99.82	86.36	142.69	75.04	198.49	197.89	160.23
RM Garments of cotton incl accessories	28.29	27.03	39.66	30.47	52.92	93.13	157.86
Drugs, pharm, & fine chemicals	89.82	89.84	90.92	108.99	106.07	47.65	113.94
Cotton yarn fab. madeups etc.	14.56	31.67	35.52	61.78	76.61	51.23	68.27
Coffee	26.10	44.96	102.10	85.78	93.97	59.17	51.91
Tobacco un-manufactured	48.07	4.77	21.63	30.35	59.27	25.12	44.63
RM Garments of wool	21.39	21.95	33.23	33.52	25.76	15.74	39.12
Non-basmati rice	–	0.46	31.61	89.51	41.37	33.51	36.08
RM Garments of manmade fibers	13.07	8.30	12.26	12.22	16.06	26.01	34.21
Plastic & linoleum products	59.88	25.01	27.94	32.82	30.80	12.64	24.24
Machinery & instruments	16.97	26.54	20.39	20.92	14.15	18.84	20.95
Electronic goods	21.29	37.58	18.20	4.75	20.10	5.84	18.98
Spices	7.44	15.07	8.96	9.09	14.70	8.29	11.86
Castor oil	8.07	15.18	13.54	2.20	1.83	1.06	11.67
Leather goods	13.68	9.64	5.61	6.41	8.28	5.37	9.84
Footwear of leather	20.44	31.97	18.89	12.34	27.94	11.84	9.72
Manmade yarn fab. madeups	9.55	21.53	6.77	6.72	5.02	2.65	8.53
Cosmetics/toiletries	25.47	51.24	34.88	19.09	20.26	7.86	7.84
Manufactures of metals	2.09	3.74	2.37	2.16	2.26	2.91	6.14
Processed minerals	15.62	50.37	60.38	31.62	0.75	15.53	6.12
Oil meals	21.95	22.02	9.58	3.47	10.94	2.80	5.39
Rubber manufactured products	2.89	1.74	4.78	2.34	3.77	3.81	5.37
Handicrafts excl. handmade carpets	0.77	0.86	1.41	0.90	0.98	0.53	4.57
Leather garments	–	–	6.43	7.41	8.66	3.96	3.48
Groundnut	1.70	2.95	1.55	0.67	7.42	1.39	2.59
Non-Ferrous metals	0.01	0.21	–	2.96	2.97	0.10	2.47
Woolen yarn fab. madeups etc.	2.53	2.48	0.46	1.56	0.80	1.50	2.33
Paper/wood products	1.81	1.88	2.17	2.42	0.55	1.64	2.31
Basmati rice	0.31	1.01	2.83	1.17	0.28	0.03	2.01

Repayment Fund (DRF) route, the export basket mainly consists of some traditional items like tea, coffee, tobacco, rice, spices, sugar, chemicals, jute products, pharmaceuticals etc. and exports of non-traditional items and items with hard currency content are not encouraged.

During the visit of an Indian delegation led by Finance Minister Yashwant Sinha to Moscow in October 1998, the Indian side accepted the Russian proposal for repayment of half of its rupee-debt in the form of goods and the remaining half of the non-convertible rupees would continue to be auctioned off[105] by the Russian government to private Russian firms wanting to make purchases in India. But the auctioning of rupee funds in the Russian markets led to malpractices and to the encouragement of switch trade in third world countries to the detriment of Indian exports there.[106]

Three problems, noted by CII, are—trade in free foreign currency, counter trade and barter.

B. *Trade in Free Foreign Currency:* Problems here include:
   - (i) buying of hard currency by Russians which is costly and time-consuming as value of rouble is constantly volatile;
   - (ii) the lack of nationwide network of banking,
   - (iii) stipulation of depositing full money in advance for opening of Letters of Credit (LC),
   - (iv) the time gap between opening LC and actual delivery of goods,
   - (v) difficulty in obtaining loans and high interest rates in Russia (over 200%).
   - (vi) On the Indian side, the absence of ECG cover for exports to Russia acts as an impediment.

C. *Counter Trade:* This mechanism is supposed to overcome the problem of constraints in trading in hard currency. However, "stipulation of Russian exports prior to Indian exports, sharp fall in Russia's oil production, desire of many organisations to export independent of former state enterprises, preference of Russians for hard currency exports are some of the major irritants."

D. *Barter (Commodity Exchange):* Though most practical and potentially useful, this method has not been fully exploited. "Lack of networking among exporters and importers, lack of institutional arrangements for counselling – facilitating interface between exporters and importers are the main constraints."[107]

E. Other problems include poor storage facilities in customs bonded warehouses for Indian tea and tobacco.

F. Bilateral credit and insurance arrangements need to be improved to provide proper shipment credits, export credits and contract insurance.

G. Relaxation of value-added norms on Indian goods, especially on Indian hi-tech items, has been a long-standing demand by Russian importers.

H. Exports from India take a relatively longer time to reach Russia (45 to 60 days as compared to 5–6 days for exports from Europe to Russia), and this involves extra cost, making Indian goods less competitive in Russian markets.

I. Another problem faced by Indian exporters in new Russia has been highly organised "mafia" networks. Since 1992, the crime wave is estimated to have cost the Russian economy over 60 trillion roubles (over £ 9 billion), causing severe damage to the economic reform process as a whole.[108] Faced with threats from mafias, Indian exporters have to go by their dictates, to conclude deals only with them and to accept lower margins of profit. The exporters with greater resources have to take a costly and circuitous route to arrive at Russian market – selling through front companies in Singapore and other places on a consignment basis to the established importers.[109]

J. The SGS inspection agency of Russia has the sole authority to certify the quality, quantity and safety of India's export-items to Russia. Variation in fees (from 1% to 1.3%) during the immediate post disintegration years affected the competitiveness of Indian goods in Russian market.[110]

The Indian Trade Promotion Organisation (ITPO) a Government of India enterprise, has identified three general problems.[111]

K. (i) As pointed out earlier, ITPO also noted that trade between Russia and India within the framework of debt repayment scheme has generally been detrimental to market mechanisms. The system of rebates granted to some Russian traders has been more corruptive than helpful and often led to illegal re-export of Indian goods to third countries.

(ii) Second, perception of India as a low tech, agrarian country, makes Russian consumers suspicious of such Indian products as software, machinery and auto spare parts.

(iii) Third, most Indian goods lack active branding and advertising support in Russia.

As the former USSR was the largest importer of Indian Tea and Jute, so there is the need to look into the pattern of trade of these two items in post-disintegration Russia.

Table 8: Trends in Indian Tea Export

(Million Kgs)

Year	*Total Indian Export to World*	*Indian Export to USSR/CIS*	*Indian Export to Russia*
1990	209	120	117
1991	202	104	Not earmarked
1992	172	46	-do-
1993	174	72	-do-
1994	149	47	-do-
1995	164	81	-do-
1996	160	51	-do-
1997	201	95	-do-
1998	210	95	82[112]
1999	190	98	88[113]

The figures in 1990 and in 1991 were relatively the highest, whereas the lowest point was in 1992, i.e., just after the break up of the USSR. Problems of Indian tea-exports to Russia, as noted by the Indian Tea Association are as follows.[114]

1. Indonesia, Kenya, Sri Lanka, Turkey etc. are the new entrants in Russian tea market. And Sri Lanka has become the toughest challenger to India. First, Sri Lankan government subsidises their tea export (nearly 95% of their tea-production is exported), but no such measure is undertaken by the Indian government, though the cost of production is much higher in India. Second, Sri Lanka sometimes blends Indian tea with other brands of inferior quality and market these products as Indian tea. So the marketing of genuine Indian tea faces stiff challenge. Kenya, with high production

and high export level, is another major competitor of India in Russian market.

2. Tea export (or for that matter, any export to Russia) has to go through a long arduous process when hard currency business is undertaken. First, Indian exporters have to fix tea-importers in Russia (who, then, are required to open LCs in Russian banks) and to secure permission from the Reserve Bank of India; and after the export, the exporters' money remains blocked till the export – amount is sold, as offloading from Russian warehouses is allowed only when there is a particular buyer.
3. Though earlier import-duty on bulk tea and packet tea in Russia was approximately 5 per cent, in 1998–99 import-duty has been increased to approximately 20 per cent on packet tea, subject to 0.4 per cent ECU. Though later 25 per cent concession was provided for tea exporters from developing countries, still the existing duty is very high. So, export of packet tea has been badly hit as well as packaging industry in India has become the sufferer.
4. As it was stipulated that 85 per cent of Indian tea-export to Russia must be done through the debt repayment fund route, the tea export business suffers as a consequence. It does not have the advantage of hard currency operations there, that other markets provide.

Jute is another product that has suffered a steady downfall in India's trade with Russia. Like tea, jute had a large market in the former USSR: for example, in 1986–87 the USSR imported 112,000 tonnes of hessian from India, out of total Indian export of (approximately) 178,000 tonnes in that year. Even in 1989–90, the USSR imported (approximately) of 163,000 tonnes in that year. Now, the graph of India's export to Russia shows a completely different picture.[115]

The course of this discussion so far, corroborates the prevalent Indian view that the state of bilateral economic relations presents an over-all grim picture. N.K. Chandra[116] also has subscribed to this view.

The enthusiasm of the 400-odd Indian companies, that started various enterprises with representative offices in Russia in early 1990's has been eroded by persistent problems and recession in Russian economy – Tata's tea processing and packaging unit failed to make a dent in the Russian market; Balmer Lawrie, Larsen and Toubro and Bharat Forge are also reportedly reluctant to continue their Russian operations. But against the recessional trends, some big Indian

Table 9: Trends in India's Jute Export

('000 tonnes)

Year	*Hessian*	*Sacking*	*Carpet Backing*	*Other goods*	*Total goods exported to Russia*
1990–91	81.7	4.2	–	0.3	86.1
1991–92	57.9	0.1	–	–	58.0
1992–93	15.7	1.0	–	–	16.7
1993–94	–	–	–	–	5.0
1994–95	–	–	–	–	2.3
1995–96	–	–	–	–	1.2
1996–97	–	–	–	–	1.2

companies like the Sun group, SIA International, Unique Pharmaceuticals, Dr. Reddy's Laboratories, Ranbaxy and Videocon successfully competed with western competitors with brand-images of their own and were able to survive the 1998 financial crisis in Russia.

The image of India and Indian goods have been shaped mostly in the Soviet period, when bilateral trade contacts were quite intensive. This plays only a role of a "positive background" against which a new image of modern India can be built. The following countries are referred to, by ITPO, as key competitors to India in the Russian market: Turkey, China, Poland, Indonesia, Malaysia, Thailand, Singapore and South Korea. The images of China, Turkey, Poland have become somewhat "infamous" in the last ten years due to a "conglomerate" of low key products. The example of a number of Indian companies' performance-report in the Russian market reveals that to succeed in the Russian market, a company should have long-term objectives and use western methods of business, the Russian consumers need to be well-informed about modern India and India needs measure to re-position itself as a country with advanced science and high technology. Indian goods, generally, lack branding and advertising support in the Russian market. Failings in these areas cost Indian trade dear. India lost its Russian cigarette market to major international manufacturers, who stressed on the importance of advertising and marketing.

A ground-level sector-wise SWOT analysis of Indian products in Russian market, showing Strengths, Weaknesses, Opportunities and Threats, will be useful in the assessment of the sectors' potentials and prospects, simultaneous with the weaknesses and hindrances. Six singularly important sectors for SWOT analysis have been chosen based on the Final Report of market study for Indian products in Russian market by India Trade Promotion Organisation (ITPO).[117]

1. Indian Drugs and Pharmaceuticals.

Strengths: State support. Good reputation of drugs prepared from herbs. The biggest market share. Good value for money. Ramified network of representative offices and distributors in Russia.

Weaknesses: Low share of high-end market.

Opportunities: Growth in Russian market. High dependence of the Russian market on import.

Threats: End of state support. Active black "PR" (against Indian products). Local production. Detrimental effect of low-quality medicines produced by small Indian companies.

2. Leather

Strengths: Good-quality sheepskin leather (e.g. for gloves). Buff of competitive quality (e.g. for military shoes). Consumer awareness and favourable images of Indian leather goods (except footwear).

Weaknesses: Unsuitable boot-tree for Russian consumers. Leather soles are not good for Russian climate. Old-fashioned design.

Opportunities: Steady demand for leather products. Low local production. Growth of leather haberdashery market (especially gloves).

Threats: Protectionist policy of the Russian Government. Strong competition from China and Turkey. Leather substitutes from Japan.

3. Indian Ready-made Garments

Strengths: Favourable image/memories about the quality of Indian ready-made garments.

Weaknesses: Indian products are perceived as not fashionable and not European. Unstable textile colouring. Logistic difficulties.

Opportunities: Limited colour-range of domestic ready-made garments of Russia. Indo-Russian joint ventures. Production of more fashionable, European garments.

Threats: Increasing local production. Competition with European exporters.

4. Gems and Jewellery

Strengths: The leader in ruby and sapphire mining.

Weaknesses: Old-fashioned design. Low quality. Unusual colour of gold (Russian Consumers are used to "reddish" gold).

Opportunities: Broader range of jewellery products. Modern design. Switch to modern technologies (of production).

Threats: High/complicated customs duties. Obligatory marking of all parts of imported jewellery-items. Loyalty to local products. Special design-license for import of gems.

5. Indian Machinery and Equipment

Strengths: Value for money in three categories of equipment – packaging, pharmaceuticals and food processing.

Weaknesses: Indian equipment is manufactured under licenses from Western Europe, but Russian companies prefer original equipment. 100 per cent pre-payment (for Indian products). Long delivery time.

Opportunities: Focus on strong categories. Credit agreement (for six-months) signed in October 2000 and for five years, signed in December 2000 by the EXIM Bank of India and the Vnesheconombank. Work on individual basis.

Threats: Strong competitors. Image of India as a primarily agricultural country.

6. Indian Software

Strengths: Broad experience in off-shore programming. High professional level of Indian programmers. Low manpower costs.

Weaknesses: Insufficient number of unique, know-how software. Low awareness of Indian software potential. Lack of Indian presence in Russian market. Perception of India as a traditional, primarily agricultural country.

Opportunities: Free training of Russian bank managers in India using Indian software. Student exchange programmes in accordance with the agreement signed during President Putin's visit to India in October 2000. Setting up of joint ventures for software development. Cooperation with world known system integrators.

Threats: Strong competition of domestic companies and Western brands. (Russian distrust to Indian high-tech branches. Software piracy.)

The uniqueness of this study lies in the fact that it has evaluated the prospects of Indian goods in Russia's domestic market in terms of exclusively ground-level business perspective, and the positive points in favour of Indian exports to Russia, made in this study, give substance to the visage of sound bilateral economic relations.

Soviet aid, technology transfer and technical expertise in joint venture projects in key industrial sectors of India played a crucial role in building a strong modern industrial base for Indian economy. Russian help is continued in joint ventures in certain areas like the energy sector, mining and science and technology. Unlike during the Soviet period when India was the "recipient" country, now Indian companies, in the changed scenario, make capital investments and offer their expertise and experience for joint ventures in Russia. For example, the Videocon group signed a MoU with the Voronezh company (VELZ) in 2000 for production of colour TV picture-tubes in Russia with an investment upto $ 100 million, the "Sun Group" of companies are engaged in a number of joint projects in beverage and food-processing sector with a total investment of $ 500 million since 1991, Dr. Reddy's Laboratories and Ajanta Pharma are also engaged in a number of small-scale joint venture projects in the pharmaceuticals sector.

CII has identified a number of areas where "tremendous synergies can be identified for working together"[118]: financial services, information technology, biotechnology and telecommunication among others. The joint venture projects in these sectors not only target the large domestic markets in these two countries but aim at the more lucrative markets in America, Europe and Asia.

A. Financial Sector

The decade of the 1990's was a period of reforms in the Indian financial sector covering banking, capital markets and the insurance sector.

In Russia, foreign banks were permitted entry in 1996 but the total share of the foreign banks in this sector's total capital is only 12 per cent, according to a study by Economic Intelligence Unit (EIU).[119] The EIU study also said that inadequacy in custody arrangements has hindered the development of stock markets in Russia, which started in 1991. More than 2000 insurance companies started operations in Russia during 1992-98 but most of them targeted short-term tasks or a narrow clientele. And only 1400 of them could survive the 1998 financial crisis. The EIU study commented that insurance companies in Russia are generally under-capitalized with limited skills and financial resources.

And in all these areas, Indian experience can help Russian entities face competition from foreign companies and build a sound financial sector.

B. Information Technology

The Indian Information Technology (IT) industry had a size of $8 billion in the 1999-2000 financial year. India's strengths in this sector include a huge pool of skilled and English-speaking manpower, cost-effectiveness, world-class quality, high reliability, rapid delivery and the use of state-of-the-art technologies. And the software industry has been the engine of growth of this booming industry with a steady growth of 61 per cent during 1995-2000 and accounted for 10 per cent of total Indian exports in 1998-99.

On the other hand, Russia has a lot of experience in hardware designs and advanced computing but lacks English-speaking IT professionals as also the expertise to market its products in the Western markets and India can help in both areas through joint ventures. Significantly, when asked by the interviewer what can be done to change the stalemate in bilateral trade, President Putin has remarked: "... (to improve the relations) we are drawing up a whole programme of joint activity in development and cooperation in modern computer technologies. This is of great importance to Russia with its underdeveloped communications and transport infrastructure, coupled with a vast territory."[120]

C. Biotechnology

India has a large pool of highly trained scientists in this field and a wealth of biotech resources, whereas Russia has a long and rich tradition of research and development in this field, apart from a wide range of biotech resources. While Indian companies can utilize the huge research facilities available with the Russian companies, the Russian companies can utilize the financial liquidity and marketing skills (which they lack) available in India. And joint ventures in this field will help companies of both the countries commercialise the available resources for third country markets.

D. Telecommunications

India has one of the fastest growing telecommunications systems in the world with total connections growing at an average of more than

20 per cent during 1996-2000. On the other hand, according to the EIU Report, the Russian telecommunications system is undersized and outdated and will require $40 billions of investment for the next ten years to remedy past deficiencies and meet demands of the subscribers. And this sector has great scope for Indian private companies as well as for the VSNL (Videsh Sanchar Nigam Limited) and MTNL (Mahanagar Telephone Nigam Limited) for providing technical support and for investments as well.

Promises

The course of this discussion so far, may be compelling to conclude that there was a stalemate in the economic relationship during the decade, though certain significant projects were initiated during the period that promise new vistas for the future economic relationship. It is, now, essential to concentrate on these projects in terms of their long-term potentials:

A. Integrated Long-Term Programme (ILTP) of Cooperation in Science and Technology:

Knowledge in science and technology is a powerful tool to create economic wealth and to drive societal transformation. The acquisition of knowledge has, therefore, become the thrust area throughout the world. Cooperation in science and technology is closely interlinked with economic cooperation. The agreement on ILTP was signed on 3 July 1987 by President Gorbachev and Prime Minister Rajiv Gandhi, and has been renewed for another 10 years on 30 October 2000. Under this programme, a total of 146 projects are being implemented. The programme covers nine thrust areas of applied science and technology, like, Biotechnology and Immunology, Engineering and Electronic Materials, Laser Science and Technology, Catalysis, Space Science and Technology, Physics and Technology of Accelerators, Water Technology and Computers and Electronics. Furthermore, joint research projects are pursued in seven selected areas of *basic research in science*, namely, Mathematics and Applied Mechanics, Earth Sciences, Radiophysics, Astrophysics, Ecology and Environment, Chemical Sciences and Biology. Some major achievements of this programme include[121] establishment of a Unit to produce oral polio-vaccines, using the technology supplied by IPVE of Moscow, at Bharat Immunological and Biologicals Corporation Limited (BIBCOL); installation of the

Param 10000 supercomputer system (designed and developed by the Centre for Development of Advanced Computing, Pune) in the Russian-Indian Centre for Advanced Computing in Moscow to conduct joint research – projects; development of medical and industrial lasers at the Centre for Advanced Technology, Indore; development of payload jointly by the Tata Institute of Fundamental Research and PN Lebedev Physical Institute for launching, aboard a Russian rocket; joint development by Bhabha Atomic Research Centre and the Lebedev Physical Institute, Moscow of an imaging unit for the gamma-ray telescope TACTIC, installed at Gurushikhar near Mount Abu and the development of the multi-purpose light transport aircraft Saras-Duet by Indian National Aerospace Laboratory and Myashisheav Design Bureau, Zhukovskii; the establishment of Advanced Research Centre for Powder Metallurgy and New Materials (ARC-1) at Hyderabad and of Indo-Russian Centre for Biotechnology at Allahabad; and the commissioning of synchroton radiation source INDUS-1 at the Centre for Advance Technology, Indore.

S.K. Lamba, the ex-Indian ambassador to Moscow, has added to the relevant point when I interviewed him:

> "The old commitments (of the Soviet era) continue on both sides. Science and technology is one such area in which the ILTP Agreement of the 1980's continues right to this day and the joint cooperation between India and Russia in that sector is the *largest for each country with any other country*".[122]

Simultaneously, under the JWG on Science and Technology, eight Sub-Working Groups (SWG) have been formed that emphasize on collaboration of basic research in various identified areas of mutual interest which would catalyze marketing of technologies in the third world market through the proposed Science and Technology Centre (Technology Clearing House). The SWGs include, among others,: on Agricultural Research, on Biotechnology, on Medical Sciences, on Meteorology; on Oceanology and on Industrial Realisation of High Technology.

The ILTP programme, also encourages close cooperation between Indian industry and Russian industry as the latter lack money and expertise to commercialize many technologies under its command to meet market- demands. And Ambassador A.M. Kadakin has expressed hope that practical implementation of projects under the ILTP "will undoubtedly and inevitably improve the living standards of common people both in Russia and India."[123]

B. Sakhalin-1 Project

India's interest in investment in prospecting and extraction of oil in Russia was first discussed in the fifth meeting of the JWG on energy in Moscow in October 1998. In that session ONGC and the Russian companies like Gazprom, Zarubezhneft, Rosneft, Luk Oil, Tatneft, Mashino export and others discussed ventures in Russian oil fields like Sakhalin, Astrakhan and operations in third countries like in gas fields in Iran and in oil fields in Iraq. After two sessions that followed the [the sixth in (1999) and the seventh in (2000)] – in February 2001, OVL signed an agreement with Rosneft. Under this agreement, OVL acquired the 20 per cent stake in the Sakhalin-1 project from Rosneft-S and SMNG-S, two subsidiaries of Rosneft, and besides an upfront cash payment for its share, OVL will invest in further development of the project, and finance Rosneft in its remaining participation in this project until the project becomes cash flow positive.[124] OVL's total investment in the project will be $1.7 billion and India will get 5 million metric tonne per annum (mmtpa) for the first five years from 2005–2006, and after that, 2.5 mmtpa. S.K. Lamba, in his interview to me, has pointed out that the OVL's investment "is the *largest Indian investment abroad* and also one of the largest investments in Russia in recent years".[125]

The importance of Sakhalin-1 project (with estimated reserves of 1.15 billion tonnes of oil and 20 trillion cubic feet of gas) lies in the fact that it heralds cooperation of a new type in the new world economic environment which, in turn, lends viability to this relationship. The project also is a major part of India's energy security. "This project is a clear manifestation", as A.M. Kadakin has remarked,[126] "of how mature the Russian – Indian strategic partnership in the economic and investment fields is all set to be in the 21st century." The oil from this project will feed such highly solvent and remunerative but at the same time energy deficient markets as Japan, South Korea, China and APR (Asia-Pacific Rim) countries. In an interview to the "Business world", Subir Raha – the Chairman of Oil and Natural Gas Corporation (ONGC) – has identified the significance of India's Sakhalin venture: "First, the fact that an Indian company could invest billions of dollars was established. Effectively, we were financing 40 per cent upfront. Second, Sakhalin is a major area now: there are the Sakhalin 1, 2, 3, 4, 5 fields. We are in Sakhalin 1. The fact that we got into one of the emerging areas was another first."[127] Here we refer to two related projects in the energy field: A.M. Kadakin has referred to the project between OVL and LUKOil for joint offshore exploration of oil in the Arabian Sea, which is on the anvil and the project at Block # 26 in Bay of Bengal where Gazprom has started operations.[128]

C. North-South Corridor

A significant Inter-Governmental Agreement on the creation of International North-South Corridor for Mumbai-Moscow transport route via Iranian ports of Bandar Abbas and Anjeli was signed by Russian Prime Minister Mikhail Kasyanov, Indian Minister for Surface Transport, Rajnath Singh and Iranian Minister for Roads and Transport, Mahmoud Hojati in St. Petersburg on 12 September 2000.[129] The route details of the Corridor are proposed to be: 40-feet containers from Mumbai would reach Bandar Abbas by shipments, from there to the port of Anjeli on the Caspian Sea through trucks, then to Russian port of Astrakhan by ship and then, by trucks and trains to customers in Russia, and the CIS and later, to the countries of North-Western Europe. Under the Agreement, duties and taxes, except payment for transit services, would not be levied on transit carriage.[130]

This 6,245 kilometers (km) long corridor from Mumbai via Bandar Abbas-Astrakhan-Moscow-St. Petersburg-Helsinki (proposed) has been termed by the India-CIS Chamber of Commerce and Industries (ICCCI) "as innovative as the Suez Canal",[131] it being a strategic transport link between Indian production centres and the extensive international market. The importance and immense possibilities of this project are:

(a) It will help reduce delivery time (from India to Russia) by 10-12 days, compared to the traditional route through Suez Canal and the Mediterranean, and cut operational costs by around $2000 per container.

(b) A conservative estimate puts that this corridor is expected to handle 15-20 million tonnes annually with the trade turnover reaching annual $10 billion mark. And it will help India increase its share in the global trade from the present 1 per cent.

(c) India's trade with Russia will increase manifold and, more important, India will get more connectivity with Central Asia – a potential huge market for Indian products. Kazakhstan has already evinced its keen interest in the project. Future rail and road links will help India reach not only the other CIS states like Georgia, Armenia and Azerbaijan but also the East European, Scandinavian and Baltic countries. The corridor will allow Central Asian states (alongwith countries like Finland, Estonia, Bulgaria, Romania etc.) relatively easier access to the markets of South and South-East Asia.

(d) The route is relatively free from flare-ups in the Middle-East, Pakistan and Afghanistan.

Some analysts hold the view that the corridor has the potential to become the silk route of the 21st century.

For an overall evaluation of the bilateral economic relations, it must be noted that the trade and economic interactions are not on par with other aspects of the relationship, namely, the political and the defence. The economic aspect continues to be the weakest link in the relationship that purports to bind them together. A.M. Kadakin, too, has noted the fact: "Unfortunately, our trade and economic interaction has fallen far behind the scope of cooperation in all other fields."[132] S.K. Lamba, the former Indian ambassador to Russia,[133] has also subscribed to this view. He has identified certain key areas to concentrate India's efforts on for the overall improvement of the economic relations:

- "Firstly, we need to establish contacts between the top corporates in India and the new business class in Russia, the two have not shaken hands properly.
- Secondly, new fields like energy and diamonds should be exploited.
- Thirdly, the banking channels must be revitalised.
- Fourthly, organizations like the CII, the FICCI, and others must take more interest and penetrate, set up offices in Russia, and revive interest in the business sector.
- Fifthly, direct contacts between regions (as they are becoming more important in Russia) and the Indian states should be further encouraged."

To substantiate his last point, here are some of the efforts hitherto initiated: consequent on Russia's free-market policies, regions like

Voronezh, Ryazan, Omsk, Yaroslav and Bashkartstan have participated in annual trade fairs in India. The following members of the Russian Parliamentary delegation, headed by Yegor Stroyev (Chairman of the Federation Council, the Upper House of the Russian Parliament), came to India in February 1999[134] to interact with their counterparts in Indian states and to recover their lost ground in India: G. Aliev, (Chairman – People's Assembly of Daghestan); B.A. Govorin, (Governor-Irkutsk region); V.N. Tikhomirov, (Governor – Ivanovo region); V.V. Sudarenkov, (Governor – Kaluga region); V.N.P. Pivnenko, (Chairman, Chamber of Representatives – Karel region); O.A. Bogomolov, (Governor – Kurgan region); L.K. Polezhaev, (Governor – Omsk region); L. Yu. Roketsky, (Governor – Tyumen region) and I.M. Shabanov, (Governor – Voronezh region).

As a consequence of such connections, a Memorandum of Understanding with Republic of Bashkartostan on cooperation in Science and Technology for a period of three years was signed on 18 May 2001 in Ufa (Russia); and another MoU for Cooperation with the Novosibirsk region was signed on 14 May 2001 for four years. A Protocol on trade, economic, scientific, technological and cultural cooperation was signed between the Samara region of Russia and the state of Karnataka during President Putin's visit to India in December 2002.

There is no denying the fact that the bilateral trade and economic interactions have been prevailingly sluggish during the decade. Pranab Mukherjee,[135] while admitting the fact, has pointed to other repercussions of Soviet disintegration:

> "It was a major earthquake-like event. A strong monolithic character disintegrated into separate units. That must have an impact (on bilateral trade). A new system has arrived in, naturally it gets reflected in the relationship." At the same time, he stressed that: "We mustn't forget that during the period of 52 years from 1947 to 1999, India has suffered from B-O-P (Balance of Payment) crisis. We were offered the advantage to make defence purchases through the rupee-rouble agreement (during the Soviet period). If one wants to forget the past completely, he can ignore history, but the fact remains."

A sympathy with this Indian viewpoint has been echoed by President Putin,[136]: "We have a Russian saying, one old friend is better than two new ones" while responding to the pertinent question, put to him by the interviewer, that for much of the 1990's Russia ignored India and he pointedly suggested a come-back.

Russia's rationale for engaging India in "strategic partnership" has been thus suggested by Ambassador Kadakin[137] "In the envisioned multipolar structure of the 21st century, Russia views India as an economic and strategic power centre not only in Asia but in the whole world." He has elaborated, "Its (India's) growing weight as one of the important poles of world politics owes much to the progress achieved in economic development..... With the growth rate exceeding 6 per cent, the GDP amounted approximately to 400 billion US dollars in 1999, it makes India the fifth largest economy after the USA, China, Japan and Germany."

The Declaration of Strategic Partnership, signed in New Delhi in October 2000 by Prime Minister AB Vajpayee and President Putin, professed to include enhanced cooperation in the field of "Trade and Economy," among others. In this field, both countries identified certain areas for bilateral cooperation. These are the areas that envisage a mature economic relationship in the 21st century beyond bilateralism: "...... further enhancing the quality and international competitiveness of their goods, by, inter alia, promoting the joint development and sharing of the latest technologies; exploiting to mutual benefit the new opportunities arising out of the integration processes under way in the world economy; enhancing cooperation and coordination at international trade, economic and financial bodies; jointly exploring the possibilities of regional trading arrangements with third countries."[138]

This study attempts on objective assessment of the development of the bilateral economic relations during the decade, as it locates the new areas of promises while analyzing the downturn of the relations, as compared to the earlier Indo-Soviet economic interactions.

Notes and References

1. R. Nagaraj "What Has Happened Since 1991?" *Economic and Political Weekly*, 8 November, 1997, p. 2869.
2. Economic Survey, Government of India, cited in Gulshan Sachdeva "Indo-Russian Trade and Economic Relations: Present Realities and Future Possibilities" in Sham Uddin-Bhaswati Sarkar (ed.) *India and Russia: Towards Strategic Partnership*, Lancer's Books, New Delhi, 2001.

3. *Statistics of the Foreign Trade of India by Countries* (Volume 1 for Exports, Volume 2 for Imports). Various Issues of Directorate General of Commercial Intelligence and Statistics (DGCIS), Kolkata.
4. Both Reports are cited in Nirmal Kumar Chandra, "Dimensions of Social and Economic Crisis in Russia Today" in *Economic and Political Weekly*, 11 May, 1996, pp. 1139-1150.
5. Sergei Lounev, "India and Russia on the Threshold of XXI Century" in Shams–ud–din (ed.) *India and Russia Towards Strategic Partnership, Op. cit.*, p. 59.
6. Lawrence R. Klein-Marshall Pomer (eds.), *The New Russia: Transition Gone Awry*, Stanford University Press, Stanford, 2000, p. i
7. *Ibid*, pp. xxi-xxii.
8. Report of the UN Economic Commission for Europe, cited in Peter Truscott, *Russia First: Breaking With the West*, IB Tauris Publishers, London, 1997. p. 123.
9. Economic Intelligence Unit, EIU Country Profile 1995–96: The Russian Federation, cited in Truscott, p. 109.
10. Truscott, *ibid*, p. 105.
11. Cited in Lounev, *op. cit*, p. 60.
12. Sir Karl Popper, interviewed by George Urban, *Report on the USSR*, RFE/RL Institute, Munich, 3, 22, 31 May 1991, pp. 20-22.
13. F. Clairmont, "Yeltsin: The Death Rattle" *Economic and Political Weekly*, 18 May, 1996.
14. Russian Centre for Economic Policy, "Russian Economic Trends, Monthly Update," 13 June 1996, cited in Truscott, *op. cit.*, p. 130.
15. Truscott, p. 131.
16. N.K. Chandra, *Economic and Political Weekly*, 11 May, 1996.
17. *Ibid.*
18. R.G. Gidadhubli, "Growing Regional Economic Disparities in Russia", *Economic and Political Weekly*, 17 August, 1996, (pp. 2226–2227).
19. Lounev, *op. cit.*, p. 59.
20. N.K. Chandra, *Economic and Political Weekly*, 11 May, 1996.
21. *The Economic Times*, 1 January, 1996.
22. Reuter, *Asian Age*, 8 September, 1998.
23. John Gray, "Russia's Fall", *The Guardian*, 22 August 2000.
24. "Report by the International Labour Organisation," cited in Lounev, *op. cit.*, p. 60.
25. Tahir Asghar "Indo Russian Trade: An Overview" in Shams–ud–din, (ed.), *op. cit*, p. 210.
26. Related Issues, for respective years published by the UNDP, www.undp.org
27. Anders Aslund, *Building Capitalism: The Transformation of the Former Soviet Bloc*, Cambridge University Press, 2002, p. 451-453.
28. Andrei Shleifer-Daniel Treisman, *Without A Map: Political Tactics and Economic Reform in Russia*, MIT Press, Cambridge, 2000.

29. *Ibid.*, p. 184.
30. Jayati Ghosh "India's Structural Adjustment As Assessment in Comparative Asian Context," *Economic and Political Weekly*, May 17–24, 1997, pp. 1113–1131.
31. By Corbo and Fisher, 1995 – cited in R. Nagaraj. *op. cit.*
32. *Issues of Economic Survey*, Government of India and *Reserve Bank Reports on Currency and Finance*, cited in Jayati Ghosh, *Economic and Political Weekly*, 17-24 May, 1997, *op. cit.*
33. I met Hon'ble Ex-Prime Minister P.V. Narsimha Rao at his New Delhi residence on 7.12.2002. He sent me his written response to my questionnaire in January 2003.
34. Quoted in *Patriot*, 7th July, 1991.
35. Alop Mittal, "Indo-Soviet Trade: Death and Rebirth", *Times of India*, 25 June, 1991.
36. *The Hindu*, 22 March 1992.
37. *The Hindu*, 23 February, 1992.
38. *The Hindu*, 22 March, 1992.
39. *The Hindu*, 5 May 1992.
40. "Trade With Russia New Beginning", Editorial, *Economic and Political Weekly*, 30 May 1992, p. 1105.
41. *The Hindu*, 5 May 1992.
42. *Economic and Political Weekly*, 30 May, 1992.
43. *The Hindu*, 21 January 1992.
44. *Payment Procedures: Exports to Russian Federation*, Reserve Bank of India, December 1995.
45. *Ibid.*
46. Cited in *Hindu*, 3 May 1992.
47. Nikolai Palkin, Izvestia, 25 January 1993 in *Current Digest of Post-Soviet Press (CDPSP)*, Vol. XIV, No. 4, 1993.
48. *The Statesman*, 23 January, 1993.
49. J.N. Dixit, *My South Block Years: Memoirs of a Foreign Secretary*, UBS Publishers, New Delhi, 1996, p. 221.
50. *The Hindu*, 30th January 1993. Also see Sunil Kanwar "Rupee-Rouble Agreement: Was It a Sell-out ?" *Economic and Political Weekly*, 13 March, 1993, pp. 431-432.
51. Sunil Kanwar, *Economic and Political Weekly*, 13 March, 1993.
52. Editorial, *The Economic Times*, 1 February, 1993.
53. N.K. Chandra, "India's Rouble Debt and Depreciating Rouble", *Economic and Political Weekly*, 3–10 July, 1993, pp. 1443–1552.
54. I interviewed Mr. J.N. Dixit at India International Centre, New Delhi on 17.12.2002
55. Taken on 14.11.02 at his Calcutta residence and has been translated from Bengali.

56. Pronab Sen, "Rupee–Rouble Exchange Rate", *Economic and Political Weekly* , 24 March 1993, pp. 613–618.
57. Itar–Tass, quoted in *The Times of India*, 12 June 1993.
58. R.G. Gidadhubli, "Russia's Economic Relations with Asia", *Economic and Political Weekly*, 17 June, 1995, pp. 1424–1427.
59. *Indian Express*, 2 May 1994.
60. *Indian Express*, 29 June 1994.
61. *Ibid.*
62. Naresh Minocha, "Rupee Auction by Russia a Mutually Beneficial Exercise", *Indian Express*, 5 July, 1994.
63. *The Hindu*, 15 July 1994.
64. *The Statesman*, 4 June 1994.
65. *The Statesman*, 8 June 1994.
66. *The Hindu*, 16 September 1994.
67. *The Hindu*, 24 December, 1994.
68. *Hindustan Times*, 24 December 1994.
69. Editorial, *The Hindu*, 21 July 1995.
70. *The Hindu* 19 August, 1995.
71. Editorial, *The Hindu*, 21 July 1995.
72. *The Hindu*, 10 October 1995 and *The Statesman*, 13 October 1995.
73. *Times of India*, 13 October 1995.
74. *Payment Procedures*, Reserve Bank of India, December 1995.
75. The Hindu, 4th April, 1996.
76. Jyotsna Bakshi, "India–Russia Cooperation in Economy, Science and Technology" in Shams–ud–din, (ed). *op. cit.*, p. 250.
77. *Hindustan Times*, 30 October 1996.
78. *Hindustan Times*, 12 February 1997, *The Statesman* 12 February 1997 and *The Hindu* 12 February 1997.
79. *Indian Express*, 10 February 1997.
80. *The Hindu*, 13 December 1997.
81. *Times of India*, 19 December 1997.
82. *The Hindu*, 31 October 1998.
83. *The Hindu*, 26 November 1998.
84. *www.meadev.nic.in/news.*
85. A. Kadakin. "Indo-Russian Relations", *Journal of Indian Ocean Studies*, Vol. 9, No. 3, December 2001, p. 378.
86. *Ibid.*, p. 379.
87. R.G. Gidadhubli "India-Russia Economic Relations: Challenges and Opportunities", in *India and Russia Towards Strategic Partnership, op. cit.* p. 205
88. Radio Free Europe/Radio Liberty (RFE/RL) Report 28.9.2000. *www.rferl.org*
89. *Ibid.*, 20.9.2000.
90. R.G. Gidadhubli, *op. cit.* p. 207.

91. Source: RECEP, "Russian Economic Trends Monthly Update," October 2002, Table 10, cited in Philip Hanson "The Russian Economic Recovery," *Europe-Asia Studies*, vol. 55, No. 3, 2003, pp. 365-382.
92. *The Hindu*, 30 July 1999.
93. *The Hindu*, 14 January 2000 and India-CIS Chamber of Commerce and Industry (ICCCI) *Newsletter*, February 2000, p. 3–4.
93. *ICCCI Newsletter*, November 2000.
95. *Hindu*, 8 November 2001
96. *Hindu*, 8 February 2002
97. *http://meaindia.nic.in/event/2002/12/03events01.htm*
98. *Statistics of the Foreign Trade of India*, DGCIS.
99. *Economic Survey 1997–98*, Government of India, Ministry of Finance, Economic Division.
100. "*India–Russia The Road Ahead*", CII, 2000, p. 16, 18.
101. DGCI&S trade figures *http://meadev.nic.in/foreign/newrussia.htm*
102. Source: Centre for Monitoring Indian Economy, cited in Gulshan Sachdeva in Shams-Ud-Din- B. Sarkar. (ed), *op. cit.*
103. Source: Centre for Monitoring Indian Economy, *ibid.*
104. "*India–Russia The Road Ahead*", CII, 2000, p. 2.
105. *Ibid*, p. 2.
106. Jyotsna Bakshi, "India–Russia Cooperation in Economy, Science and Technology", in Shams–ud–din, (ed.). *op. cit.*, p. 247.
107. Seminar on "India–Russia Economic Partnership" 11 October 1995, *Background Paper*, CII.
108. Truscott, *op. cit.*, p. 135.
109. See N.K. Chandra "Russia's Sinking Economy: External Dimensions", *Economic and Political Weekly*, 15 May, 1993 (pp. 995–1003) and Satish M.–S. Dinaker, *Economic Times*, 9 April, 1993.
110. R.L. Varshney "Trade Relations between India and Russia" in V.D. Chopra (ed.) *Indo-Russian Relations Prospects, Problems and Russia Today* Kalpaz Publications, New Delhi, 2001, on behalf of International Institute for Asia–Pacific Studies. p. 98
111. *Final Report of the market study for Indian products in Russian market*, commissioned by ITPO, 2000.
112. Source: The figures from 1990 to 1998 were provided to me by Mr. Sarit Patra of Indian Tea Association, Calcutta. He could not provide me figures of Indian exports of tea exclusively to Russia (save in 1998), the rest were included in CIS figures.
113. *Issues of Tea Production and Export Scenario*, 2000, Publication of Indian Tea Association (ITA).
114. Based on my discussions with Mr. Manojit Dasgupta, Additional Secretary, ITA and Mr. Sarit Patra of ITA, in July 2000.
115. Data source: various *issues of Annual Summary of Jute and Gunny Statistics*, issued by Statistics Department, Indian Jute Manufacturers'

Association, Calcutta. Sarit Roy of the Association was kind enough to provide me with these issues but he declined to comment on the pressing problems the jute industry faces in trade with Russia.

116. In my interview of N.K. Chandra, at the Indian Institute of Management, Kolkata on 8.5.2003.
117. *Final Report of the market study for Indian products in the Russian market*, ITPO, 2000.
118. "*India-Russia: The Road Ahead*", CII, 2000, pp. 1-14.
119. *Ibid.*
120. In his interview with Raj Chengappa in October 2000 in *www.india-today.com*
121. Dr. Hari Mohan Saxena, Counsellor (Science and Technology), Embassy of India, Moscow; "Scientific and Technological Cooperation between India and Russia: Existing Programmes, Achievements and Future Possibilities", *Business Messenger*, December 2002, Special Issue dedicated to President Putin's visit to India, Moscow, pp. 22-31.
122. Interview in New Delhi on 25.12.02. Emphasis added.
123. A.M. Kadakin, *op. cit.* p. 378.
124. Sanjib Kohli, "Indo-Russian Economic and Commercial Engagement," Counsellor (Commerce), Embassy of India, Moscow. *Business Messenger*, December 2002, p. 27.
125. In my interview of S.K. Lamba, *op. cit.* Emphasis added.
126. Kadakin, *op. cit.*, p. 378.
127. *Business world*, 14 July, 2003, p. 31.
128. Simultaneously, in the Indian power sector, Russia assists in the construction of Vindhyachal thermal power project in Uttar Pradesh, the hydel power project in Tehri and the renovation of Bhakra project. Russian participation in some other projects like Patratu in Bihar, Tuvey Hydel power plant in Mizoram and Kameng hydel power plant in Arunachal are under discussion. Russia's assistance in the nuclear power sector will be discussed in the next chapter.
129. *http://meadev.nic.in/foreign/newrussia/htm.*
130. *ICCCI Newsletter*, October 2000, p. 14.
131. *Ibid.*
132. Kadakin, *op. cit.*, p. 377.
133. My Interview of Lamba, *op. cit.*
134. *Russian-Indian Relations, Annexure-IV*, 2000, CII, *op. cit.*
135. His discussions with me in Kolkata on 14.11.02.
136. Putin's interview with Raj Chengappa; Deputy Editor, India Today in Moscow in October 2000. The text is from *www.india-today.com*
137. A.M. Kadakin, "Russian-Indian Relations: A View into the Third Milennium" in V.D. Chopra (ed.), *Indo-Russian Relations Prospects Problems and Russia Today*", Kalpaz Publications, New Delhi, 2001. See pp. 44-45.
138. Text is from *http://www.meadev.nic.in.*

Chapter 3

Towards A Strategic Partnership

This chapter concentrates penetratingly on the political as well as the defence-related aspects of the relationship: from the initial uncertainties that persisted till 1995 to a stable relationship in 2002.

The Main Features of Russian Foreign Policy (1992-95)

The cross-currents in locating and fixing foreign-policy goals and priorities for the USSR during the Gorbachev-era (1985–1991) lend us the needed vital perspective for an exact and factual view of the evolving Indo-Russian relations. The policy of westernization and the concept of a "Common European Home" formed the central theme of Soviet President Mikhail Gorbachev's foreign policy, as was evidenced in significant shifts in various policy-decisions concerning the on-site inspection of military facilities [at the 1986 Conference on Security and Cooperation in Europe (CSCE) conference], the scrapping of intermediate-range ballistic missiles under the 1987 Intermediate-range Nuclear Forces (INF) Treaty, reducing conventional forces under the 1990 Conventional Forces of Europe (CFE) Treaty, the Soviet withdrawal from Afghanistan in 1989, its assent to the reunification of Germany in 1990 and its support to UN sanctions on its old ally, Iraq during 1990–91.

After the Soviet disintegration in December 1991, this policy got enhanced strength and fuller support during 1992–95 under Russian President Boris Yeltsin and his Foreign Minister Andrei Kozyrev. This period was termed as "the honeymoon period" with the West by foreign observers as well as by Russian analysts, while Kozyrev coined the term "Romantic period" in reference.

But it must be noted that Gorbachev held the view that the US and the USSR were essentially rivals: "Economic, political and ideological competition between capitalist and socialist countries is inevitable."[1] Yeltsin, on the other hand, sought to build a genuine partnership with the US: he asserted in the US Congress on June 17, 1992. "In joining the world community, we wish to preserve our identity and history ... at the same time Russia does not aspire *to remake the world in its own image*."[2] Yeltsin favoured this policy, first, to outbid Gorbachev's reputation as a westernized reformer in the West and second, to create a benign, non-threatening international environment to resist potential foreign adversaries from taking advantage and to carry on the transformation of Russia's economy unhindered.[3] Kozyrev bade goodbye, as a deliberate attempt to break away from the past, to the ex-Foreign Minister of Gorbachev, Eduard Shevarduadze's concept of "the unique opportunities the Soviet Union had for the formation of a *Eurasian* zone of security and stability, bringing together West and East, Europe and Asia"[4] and concentrated on strengthening relations with the US and the NATO to pursue the goal of developing democracy and free economy in, and security for, Russia.

In return, the US pledged support to Russia in the Camp David Declaration of 1st February 1992 and in the Freedom Support Act of 1992. The Washington Charter on American-Russian Partnership and Friendship (of June 17, 1992) went a step further and delineated the roles of both the US and Russia in politico-economic and security matters of the Euro-Altantic area and decided to settle disputes peacefully.

In February, 1994, Kozyrev identified the benefits of his policy for Russia: Russia avoided the international isolation as the USSR experienced after 1917; it avoided also the fragmentation as engulfed Yugoslavia; a peaceful international environment was created which lessened Russia's burden of military expenditure; Russia joined the IMF and the World Bank and got economic assistance from the West; NATO (North Atlantic Treaty Organization) adopted the Partnership For Peace Programme with Russia rather than a policy of rapid expansion to its borders and the tripartite agreement among the US, Russia and Ukraine was reached to eliminate Ukraine's nuclear weapons.[5] Simultaneously, with Russia's overtures towards a closer relationship with the West, a particularly vigorous debate developed between two schools of thought – the "Atlanticist" and the "Eurasianist", as coined by Sergei Stankevich, Russian State Counsellor.[6] The Atlanticists' foreign-policy orientations was established on the premise that Russia's identity should be defined as a civic state within the boundaries of the Russian Federation, which was in tune with the goals of liberal democracy, market reforms and the preferred inclination towards the West. Their *weltanschaung* was one of a peaceful, benign and non-antagonistic world. They repudiated the Eurasianist idea that Russia could become a bridge between Europe and Asia. Contrarily, they would like to view Russia as a "normal" power, with no overarching mission beyond. They deemed the return of Communism or its growth elsewhere as the only threat to Russia and their policy proposals towards the states of the former Soviet Union (FSU) were based upon the principles of equality of states and non-interference in other states' domestic affairs.[7]

Eurasianism is based on the premise that Eurasia- the territory of the erstwhile Soviet Union and Russian empire – is unique in itself as a civilization and therefore it will be a blunder for the present day Russia to replicate the development of Europe or to mould its cultural consciousness into an European character. The Russian ethos or culture is only the leading element of the "symphonic personality of Eurasia," which has evolved over the past 700 years since the Mongol conquest of Russia. The doctrine was pronounced after the Russian revolution of 1917 by a group of eminent émigré scholars. Eurasianism has been ideologically diversified, yet there is an idea which was common to all representatives of the movement: "All Eurasianists insisted that Russia is a unique cultural and quasiethnic entity which consists of both Slavic and non-slavic people. Eurasianists also stressed the Asiatic ingredient of Russian culture and ethnicity."[8] The present day Russia is in need of an ideology to determine what is to be held together and to provide it a direction of course to aim at. An eminent scholar has pointed out: "Modern 'democracy' however dogmatic, does not possess the ideological certainties, the theoretical comprehension, or organisational capacity to do the job. Russian multi-culturalism which the Eurasianists have pondered so deeply is a datum to work with."[9]

The principal characteristics of the Eurasian school of thought are: recognition of Russia's status as a "great power", a policy of re-integrating the former Soviet republics, instead of efforts to build new integrative links; the quest for new allies and cooperation partners outside the West; a search for independent Russian positions on almost all subjects of global affairs, even at the risk of alienating Moscow's relations with the West; and an assertive stance against the issue of NATO expansion. The Eurasianists, moreover, argued that China, India, the Middle East and the Pacific rim countries were more connected to Russia's political and economic interests, among whom Russia could be an ally, even a leader, while with the West, Russia would never become more than a second-class citizen.[10] In March 1992 Stankevich wrote, 'It is obvious that we will have to look for a new balance of Western and Eastern orientations that is distinctive to today's Russia and our times. Initially, however, we will most likely have to devote special attention to the strengthening of our positions in the East, rectifying the obvious distortion caused by the creators of the conceptions of the "Common European Home".[11] The Eurasian idea received a strong support from N. Nazarbayev, the President of Kazakhstan, who in 1994 mooted the concept of transforming the CIS into an "Eurasian" union.

The frustration with "Atlanticism" and the apparent deadlock to which "Eurasianism" led, prompted some influential members of the Russian elite-like academicians Andrannik Migranyan, Georgii Arbatov, First Deputy Defence Minister Andrei Kokoshin, and leaders of Yabloka bloc like Vladimir Lukin and Alexei Arbatov – to search for a way out: their concept paper entitled "Strategy for Russia" ("Realism") was published by the non-governmental organization "Council for Foreign and Defence Policy" in May 1994 and advanced the following assumptions: Russia's endeavour to adopt Western standards ("Atlanticism") used up itself, the differences, however, between Russia and the West were not so unsurmountable (as suggested by "Eurasianism") that confrontation could not be averted; a singular fixation on either Europe or Asia should be avoided; the opposition to NATO's enlargement was not relevant (as this was a lost case), while the strengthening of Russia's position in the sphere of the former USSR, was.[12]

The main refrain of all these debates were reflected in the stance of various parties critical of Yeltsin (the so-called "Opposition") against the official foreign policy orientations of Russia during the Kozyrev era. Kozyrev's support for sanctions against Serbia, voted through the UN Security Council in May 1992, was vehemently attacked by the Opposition in the Duma for abandoning Russia's traditional ally – the Serbs. In an article in the Journal of the IMEMO, officials of the Russian Ministry of Foreign Economic Affairs harped on the need to give closer attention to India and other old friends of Russia – a view reiterated by Alexander Lukin, the-then Ambassador to Washington, in an article in Moscow News.[13]

Relatedly, there was a frontal clash between the Atlanticists and the Eurasianists in mid-1992 on the Kurile islands issue that had deadlocked Russian relations with Japan. The Russian Foreign Ministry prepared President Yeltsin's visit to Japan with a remarkably commercialized "islands-for-cash-and-credits" agenda, while the military supplied the opposition with ammunition regarding the strategic importance of the Kurile passages for the Russian Pacific Fleet. The abrupt cancellation of President Yeltsin's Japan visit at the very last moment was taken by some analysts as the turning point in Russian diplomacy.[14]

In October 1992, Yeltsin told the Foreign Ministry officials that he was disappointed with the West's attitude of treating Russia as a country saying "Yes" always and that the only ideology the Foreign Ministry should follow was to defend Russia's interests and security. Yeltsin's statement may be taken as a prelude to Kozyrev's famous speech to the CSCE in December, 1992, that shocked the West as it subscribed wholly to the views of opponents of Russia's pro-West lobby: Kozyrev told the Western powers to keep out of the states of the former Soviet Union, demanded an end on Serbian sanctions, and promised full military support to Bosnia[15] – all in an effort to forewarn the West, what could happen were Yeltsin to be defeated by his domestic opposition.

In that speech, Kozyrev also stressed that the entire territory of the former USSR was an area where Russia had to protect its own interests even by military and economic means. This point was suggested by Yevgeny Ambartsumov, Chairman of the Supreme Soviet's Joint Committee on International Affairs and Foreign Economic Relations, while expressing the nationalists' view in a report to the Russian Parliament "As the internationally recognized legal successor to the USSR, the Russian Federation should base its foreign policy on a doctrine declaring the entire geopolitical space of the former union to be the sphere of its vital interests (like the US's Monroe Doctrine in Latin America)…."[16]

An overall perceptible shift to substantive assertiveness and a partial cooling of relations with the West in Russian foreign policy came to the fore at the beginning of 1993: In February 1993 Yeltsin himself proposed the adoption of a Russian Monroe Doctrine in the space of the former USSR.[17]

A nationalist orientation in Russian foreign policy manifested itself in asserting Russia's role in influencing political developments in its "near abroad" through a variety of means ranging from economic pressure to military support: the establishment of an Eurasian security system through the Tashkent Collective Security Pact of 1992; Russia's military support to the pro-Russian Rakhmanov government in Tajikistan against the armed opposition in the Tajik civil war during 1992–94; the finalization of basic documents for the CIS Economic Union in September 1993, and the adoption of the first Military Doctrine in November 1993 that emphasized Russia's "special interests" and peacekeeping role in the "near abroad." This process got a boost after the December 1993 elections, in which the ultra-nationalist Liberal Democrats came in the forefront with 64 seats out of 225 seats in the Duma and the communists got 48 seats with the third place. This led to the weakening of Parliamentary support to Kozyrev's obsession with pro-Western foreign policy.

In April 1995 after a meeting with his American counterpart Warren Christopher in Geneva, Kozyrev came out to declare: "The honeymoon has come to an end."[18] Discussions in the meeting centred on Chechnya, NATO enlargement, the peace process in former Yugoslavia and the planned sale of Russia's nuclear rectors to Iran.

The fall in living standards, rising unemployment, soaring inflation, rampant corruption and growth of mafia – all this, to Russian people, was a direct fall-out of the economic reform programme undertaken by the Russian government under the direction of the IMF and the World Bank and this helped the growth of anti-Westernism in Russian public opinion.

The trend of self-assertion in its foreign policy was reinforced when Russia had to confront the Chechen crisis and the NATO's eastward expansion programme. This precisely precipitated the emergence of what Truscott termed as the "Russia First" policy-meaning "a Russian attempt to find uniquely Russian solutions to the country's domestic and foreign policy conundrums", as commensurate with its "unique Eurasian identity."[19] So, though the West condemned the large-scale human rights abuses and massacre of innocent lives by Russia during the Chechen War of 1994–96, but to Russia "its territorial integrity and national security were not a matter for international negotiation."[20] Apart from the security perspective of NATO's expansion (as it would bring the alliance within 150 Kilometres of St. Petersburg on Russia's north-west boundary), Kozyrev complained that Russia fell into a trap set by the West through the NATO'S PfP (Partnership for Peace) offer. In May 1994, Kozyrev signed a framework document with NATO in Brussels, the details of which were left for future negotiations. Russian Foreign Ministry assumed wrongly that the final decision on NATO enlargement was indefinitely postponed, to be caught by surprise by the Western change in attitude. In December 1994, Kozyrev refused to sign the individual NATO Partnership programme and Yeltsin was prompted to speak about an emerging "Cold Peace" in Russia's relations with the West in the CSCE Summit in Budapest a few days later.

The spectacular success of the Left in the 1995 Duma elections (221 seats in the 450 – Seat Duma) and the subsequent sacking of both Foreign Minister Kozyrev and reformist Finance Minister Anatoli Chubais by Yeltsin were indicators to this change in Russia's foreign policy making. The appointment of Yevgeny Primakov, a quiet protagonist of resuming good relations with the USSR's old allies, as Foreign Minister in early 1996 marked a determined break from Kozyrev's pro-West policies of the preceding three years and "an assertion of a 'Russia First' syndrome at the Ministry of External Affairs."[21]

Truscott discerned a trend of periodic shifts to Westernization and the subsequent shift away from it since the days of Peter the Great (1682–1725). So, after the initial euphoria over Westernization during the last years of Gorbachev and the first two years of Yeltsin-Kozyrev, Russia – as an heir to that legacy – turned to reprioritize its foreign policy goals to project a more assertive image in areas of its interest, like in the Balkans, the Near Abroad, China and India.

Indo-Russian Relations

The wild commotion in prioritizing and re-prioritizing Russian foreign policy goals during these years was reflected with discernible transparency in Indo-Russian relations. The most important consequence of the on-going orientations in Russia's foreign policy regarding Indo-Russian relations was that India's strategic importance steadily dwindled in the Russian scheme of things and India had to adjust to this short– and medium term reality.

Indo-Russian relations evolved essentially in three distinct phases: from 1992–95, when the relationship grew through uncertainties and confusions, from 1996 -1999, when India's place in Russian foreign policy perceptions was re-prioritized, and from 2000-2002 when the compulsions from both ends to come closer crystallized the relationship towards a stable form.

First Phase (1992–95):

This period has been distinguished by Russia's foreign policy orientation towards the West. India had to make relations with a new country, a new entity, with altogether new orientations, necessitating its accommodation with this emergent fact.

1992

In January 1992, at the behest of Prime Minister Rao, Foreign Secretary, J.N. Dixit led a delegation – comprising of Defence Secretary N.N. Vohra, Commerce Secretary AV Ganesan and others – to Moscow to resolve immediate and specific problems. Notably, Kozyrev was not available for a meeting ostensibly for his view that there was no need to preserve the "special relations" with India that had existed in the Soviet era and he never paid a special visit to India throughout his tenure. At their very first meeting, Vice Foreign Minister Kunadze told Dixit: "India should recognize that 'the Russian Federation is not the Soviet Union.' He went on to state that '... (Russia) had a new identity; it had a new status and new interests; and its foreign policy had new orientations."[22] This was reflected in the Concept Paper of the Russian Federation's Foreign Policy of January 1993 that put India in the seventh place out of Ten in the list of Russia's priorities:[23] 1. The CIS; 2. Arms control and international security; 3. Economic reforms; 4. The US; 5. Europe; 6. Asia-Pacific; 7. West and South Asia; 8. Near East; 9. Africa and 10. Latin America.

Hindustan Times cited two contradictory views of Kozyrev on India within a span of two weeks in late-1992 that brought to the fore the prevailing confusions of the Russian foreign policy – making an about face over India's place in the Russian scheme of things: in November 1992 Kozyrev told Hindustan Times that a fundamental principle of Russian foreign policy is "strategic partnership with democracies around the world" and that India remains a key partner for Russia because it is "the largest democracy in Asia." Barely two weeks later, he told a largely western audience in Moscow's International Press Club that Russia sought strategic partnership only with First World industrial democracies – in Asia he named Japan and South Korea – and warned that critics, who urged other priorities, "seek to drag Russia down into Third World backwardness."[24]

Andrei Kozyrev, however, was unambiguous on Russian foreign

policy orientations towards India in his Memoirs: "This (Russia's national interest) affects first and foremost our traditional cooperation with a great Asiatic country – India. As distinct from the Soviet period, cooperation now is shorn of elements of counterbalance and counterweight vis-a-vis China, Pakistan and the USA in South Asia. Such attempts at counterbalance in the past led to a one-sided aspect to Soviet foreign policy, and limited the opportunities for development of relations with other important countries of the region, turning them into possible opponents of our country."[25]

But at the same time dissenting views were also forthcoming. Important members like Ambartsumov and Pudovkin argued: "India was, is and should remain Russia's first priority."[26] Also according to the Moscow correspondent of the "Washington Post", Sergei Stankevich, Russia's State Councillor on Political Affairs, would like Russia to develop relations with the "second echelon" countries like India and Brazil, which share the Russian goal of integration with the world economy, since "for many years the best we would be able to count on would be the role of a junior partner (in the Western alliance)."[27] In September 1992, Ruslan Khasbulatov, the Chairman of the Russian Supreme Soviet, emphasized that it would be "a mistake for Russian diplomacy to regard India as an unpromising partner" during his visit to New Delhi. He also ruled out the possibility of any re-orientation of Russian foreign policy away from India.[28] Significantly, the Russian Minister – Counsellor to India, Alexander Kadakin, at a press meet in New Delhi in January 1992, asserted: "Russia is still a superpower in a world which is multipolar", while he listed the other poles as being the US, Japan, China, Germany and India.[29] A publication of the Russian Embassy in New Delhi also suggested that "we should gain (from Indian experience) a deeper insight into its ways of balancing different interests and retaining unity in versatility" and that both states "are conscious of strengthening stability in South Asia and the Asia Pacific region..."[30]

The list of other Russian views suffices to corroborate the Russian urge for a closer tie with India, as against the "embryonic under currents of distance"[31] between the new Russia and India.

But there were factors of uncertainty and confusion during early years (1992-93) in Indo-Russian defence relationship. These posed a grave problem as India desperately needed uninterrupted and steady supply of spare parts for MiGs, that accounted for nearly three-quarters of the Indian Air Force (IAF) and the IAF had only one year's spares left with them. An uncertainty factor was there, as domestic political upheaval and economic transition in Russia led to bottlenecks in production, supply and marketing of defence products, and as manufacturing units of armaments were not centrally located in Russia but were scattered in other newly independent states of the former USSR. For example, some parts of AN-32 transport aircrafts (made only for export to India) are manufactured in Russia and Belarus but are finally assembled in Ukraine, and IL-76 transport jets are produced in Uzbekistan.

There was also a confusion, as an article in Izvestia, while analyzing the financial bottlenecks with India, questioned the mode of debt-repayment by India and brushed aside barter-trade or rupee payment as unacceptable to Russian arms producers.[32] But another article in Izvestia in June 1992 reported that Russia's failure to supply military hardware and spares to India would result into non-availability of imported food, medicine and consumer durables from India.[33] It was clear that arms trade would now be more on a commercial basis, as in May 1992, Russian Economy Minister Andrei Nechayev stated that new trade credits for defence supplies to India would be double the existing interest rate, with one-tenth of the payment being made in advance.[34]

Indian Defence Minister Sharad Pawar visited Moscow in September 1992 and met his counterpart Pavel Grachev to chalk out the plan for restoring the bilateral defence links.[35] Gennady Burbulis, the Secretary of State, acknowledged Russia's "considerable obligations" towards India for delivery of arms and spares, during his meeting with Pawar.[36] During Pawar's visit to Ukraine in October 1992, it was decided that Ukraine would supply weapons and spares for AN-32 aircrafts, in return for medicine, clothings and partial payment in hard currency.[37]

A realistic account of Indo-Russian arms relationship was presented in an article in the VEK Journal: that despite earlier contracts, "arms and spares are not reaching India in practice", and that visiting Defence Minister Pawar inquired about "guided missilecrafts from the Black Sea Fleet of Ukraine."[38] Significantly, Indian Defence Ministry officials stated that as against the Ukrainian offer to sell India an aircraft-carrier from its Black Sea Fleet, Russia offered an aircraft-carrier for US $ 458 million-half under barter and half on easy cash payment.[39] It is notable that the Russian offer suggested that Russia could hardly afford to allow other republics of the CIS to steal a march over Russia in defence supplies. And both sides finalized a deal worth $466 million for India's purchase of 20 MiG-29M and 6 MiG-29UM Fulcrum multi-role fighters with related spares and support package,[40] and $830 million of defence credit to India during Pawar's December visit to Moscow. To solve the perennial spares problem for India, President Yeltsin suggested three proposals: improving the workings of specific Russian enterprises, which manufacture spares for India; setting up of joint ventures to produce those spares; and transfer of technology to India to produce those spares.

1993

Russian Defence Minister Grachev and Sharad Pawar signed an agreement on bilateral military cooperation on January 28, 1993, during President Yeltsin's visit to India. It was decided that deliveries would be resumed at previous level with guaranteed product-support and comprehensive services for maintenance, repairing and modernization. The agreement envisages cooperation in defence, science and technology and joint research and development projects.[41] Pawar expressed satisfaction that the agreement would "greatly relieve pressure on our armed forces."[42] And the Report of the Ministry of Defence commented that the agreement "provides a framework for a continuing defence supply relationship with Russia and paves the way for implementation of mutually beneficial programmes of cooperation in the defence sector."[43]

1994

On 30 June 1994, a bilateral agreement was signed to form the Indo-Russian Aviation Private Limited as a joint venture – between Hindustan Aeronautics Limited (HAL) and the Industrial Credit and Investment Company of India (ICICI) from India and MAPO, Rosvoorouzhenie and the Raizam State Instrumenting Plants from Russia – to manufacture spares for the MiG series of combat aircrafts.[44] Also, a comprehensive upgradation programme for MiG-21 aircrafts was undertaken by HAL, in association with the Mikoyan Design Bureau of Russia. The upgradation would be completed in three phases and would install new avionics and weapon systems in MiG-21s to meet the requirements of the IAF.[45]

In the first meeting of the Russian-Indian Commission on Military and Technical Cooperation, a bilateral Military and Technical Programme till 2000 (worth over $7 million) was endorsed. In

December 1994, the Military Cooperation Agreement was signed during Russian Prime Minister Viktor Chernomyrdin's visit to India and the comprehensive agreement covered bilateral defence cooperation till 2000.[46] The Defence Ministry Report commented that "Russia continues to be a dependable source for India's military modernisation at affordable costs."[47]

Besides these various commitments and plans, the highlights of this first phase were the 1993 Indo-Russian Treaty, the 1994 Moscow Declaration and the cancellation of the Cryogenic rocket deal.

A. The 1993 Treaty

The 14-clause Treaty of Friendship and Cooperation, signed by Prime Minister Rao and President Yeltsin (during his one and only visit to India in January 1993), was the first political document to guide Indo-Russian future relations.

Notably, Russian Vice Foreign Minister Kunadze pointed out to visiting Foreign Secretary Dixit in January 1992 in Moscow (regarding the drafting of a new treaty) that: "New Russian policies would not have any linkage with the Soviet Union's ideology or its world view."[48] He wanted the word "Peace" to be dropped from the title of the new treaty, since "'Peace' was a communist word and smacked of Soviet ideology."[49] According to J.N. Dixit, (regarding his response to Kunadze's disapproval of the word "Peace"), "(I said to him) We have no desire to insist on an old relationship which you don't want. You have a new relationship, we have a new relationship."[50]

Consequently, the word "Peace" was dropped from the new document. The kernel of the old arrangement – Article IX of the former Treaty – was expunged. This Article had provided that: "Each High Contracting Party undertakes to abstain from providing any assistance to any third party that engages in armed conflict with the other Party. In the event of either Party being subjected to an attack or a threat thereof, the High Contracting Parties shall immediately enter into mutual consultations in order to remove such threat and to take appropriate measures to ensure peace and security of their countries." It was now intended to downplay the old strategic relationship card. Dixit commented in his interview that the "1971 Treaty was against all sorts of security challenges to both the countries. As the world changed, so the Article became irrelevant. We (felt) that Russia will not be as intensely interested in an operational defence cooperation, so we agreed (to downplay the strategic relationship)."[51]

The connotation of the new Treaty was not to form "blocs, axis, triangles or quadrangles"[52] as President Yeltsin emphasized during his visit. He further elaborated that during the 1970's, Moscow used to play the India card "against world imperialism and Chinese hegemonism" but now "We do not want to build our relations with India on that special basis" but rather "on a solid basis of mutually advantageous partnership, not directed against any third country ..."[53] The Cold War context of the Article IX lost its relevance in the new milieu and the new Treaty evidently recognized the post-Cold War realities.

B. Moscow Declaration

During Prime Minister Rao's visit to Moscow in June 1994, two significant declarations were signed by Prime Minister Rao and President Yeltsin on 30 June 1994 – the Moscow Declaration on the Protection of the Interests of Pluralistic States and the Declaration on Further Development and Intensification of Cooperation between the Republic of India and the Russian Federation.

The Moscow Declaration categorically spelt out: "In particular, there is a growing threat from the forces of aggressive nationalism, religious and political extremism, terrorism and separatism, which strike at the unity of pluralistic states." India and Russia, being among the largest multi-ethnic, multi-lingual and multi-religious states, all the more "recognize their responsibility for opposing the threats to democracy and peace together with other members of the world community" on the basis of their "commitment" to "unity and diversity."

The other Declaration, first among others, urged "further *democratization*" of the United Nations Organization and prescribed that the United Nations system "should reflect the changing *realities of the contemporary* world to the *fullest extent.*" Second, both sides agreed in particular "to make every effort to facilitate the early conclusion of multilaterally negotiated comprehensive treaties on the universal ban of nuclear tests and cessation of production of fissile materials for weapons purpose."[54] The second point prompted *The Statesman* in its editorial to comment that it "shows Russia veering round to the Indian position on the NPT."[55]

Prime Minister Rao described the Moscow Declaration as "epoch-making" since it was a recognition of the "stark reality we face in the world today",[56] namely the conflicts resulting from religious exclusivism, political extremism, and terrorism. In his response to my question in 2003, ex-Prime Minister Rao commented on the background of the Moscow Declaration: "In a new relationship the parties have to identify new areas of agreement. This was such an instance."[57]

The two aforesaid Declarations are the first documents that signified the convergence of each one's national interests both regionally and globally.

C. Cryogenic Rocket Deal.

Under this 1990 deal between Russian agency Glavkosmos and Indian Space Research Organization (ISRO), India was to get two cryogenic rocket-engines with the corresponding technology for India's Geo-Stationary Launching Vehicle (GSLV) project. But the US put sanctions on both ISRO and Glavkosmos in May 1992 on the logic that these engines, along with the dual-use technology, can be considered as "production facilities" banned for transfer under norms of Missile Technology Control Regime (MTCR); also that such technology can help India build Inter-Continental Ballistic Missiles (ICBM). But both ISRO and Glavkosmos held the view that these engines use liquid hydrogen and oxygen at very low temperatures, too troublesome to be used for military purposes.

Hon'ble President A.P.J. Abdul Kalam in his written response to my faxed questionnaire, asserted, regarding my question – whether and how far the US logic stands in respect of cryogenic engine's usability in ICBMS to fall under MTCR norms – that: "Cryogenic Engine is not used normally in missile applications throughout the world for the reason of its storage problems and also volume."[58] The deal was finally cancelled in July 1993 and this revealed a number of hard facts.:

(i) Russia's vulnerability to the US pressure became significantly evident. It was reported that the US offered Russia, as compensation for cancelling the deal, bidding rights for launching nearly 12 commercial satellites in next 6 years at $40-70 million a piece and help for construction of the "Freedom" space project.[59] Foreign and Finance Ministers of G-7 countries also offered Russia an aid package of

$43,000 million in the G-7 Meet in Tokyo. At the Tokyo Summit on 10 July, President Yeltsin told Strobe Talbott that "he had decided to fire his chief negotiator, Alexander Shokhin, who had been stone-walling us over the Indian rocket sale, and replace him with Yuri Koptev, who was the head of the Russian space program and who therefore had an interest in removing any obstacle to US-Russian space cooperation. Koptev, said Yeltsin, would have instructions to come to agreement expeditiously, before American sanctions went into effect." Strobe Talbott recalled further: "Three days later, Koptev came to Washington and closed a deal on the rocket sale that obviated the need for American sanctions."[60] After the 10th July Meeting between the US President Clinton and President Yeltsin, Ronen Sen, the Indian ambassador to Russia, got the official backout notice by Glavkosmos, under the "force majeure" clause of the Agreement.[61] Russia justified its decision on grounds of the deal being inconsistent with the new Russian export control regime. India put it as a "significant development in Indo-Russian relations." Interestingly, Prime Minister Rao confirmed that President Yeltsin had written to him, stating his difficulties to continue with the deal, and wanted to present the cancellation of the deal as if done by mutual consent. Rao declined to budge.[62] Significantly, Russia agreed to join the MTCR in September 1993 and under the agreement, the US was to get full information on all Russian defence contracts since 1990.

(ii) Second, the fact that the US administration had cleared the same deal, of MTCR violation charge, for General Dynamics of the USA[63] only suggested that the US interest was not to allow Russia and a probable competitor, India, to enter the commercially lucrative space market, so far dominated by the US and the French-led European Consortium, Ariane Space. In May 1992, UR Rao, the ISRO Chief pointed out, "the proximity of the Sriharikota rocket launching centre to the equator and India's generally low-launch costs made it a potential threat in the multi-billion dollar space market."[64]

(iii) Third, the stated US logic against the deal failed to impress the concerned section of Russia. Though Yuri Koptev, Head

> of the Russian Space Agency, agreed with the US assessment of "dual-use" technology of cryogenic engines,[65] but NI Leontyev, Chief Designer of the Cryogenic Engines, insisted that "handing over this technology will develop the military might of India does not correspond to reality."[66] The staff of Glavkosmos also stated that these engines could not be used for defence purposes and held that the US goal was not to enhance international security but only to protect its own space industry from international competition.[67] Mikhail Maley, Advisor to the Russian government, declared that Russia – with its people suffering from severe economic crisis-could not afford to be more moral than western countries who sell their military products in the world market.[68] And Foreign Minister Kozyrev came under attack as Nikolai Semoyonov, Head of the International Department of Glavkosmos, stated that "Russian Foreign office does not understand the needs of Russia"[69] – referring to a statement by Kozyrev (a few days earlier in a public meeting at Krasnoyarsk) that "it was in the interest of Russia" not to sell the technology which might have proliferation effects. Ruslan Khasbulatov,[70] Speaker of the Russian Duma, and Alexander Dunayev,[71] Head of Glavkosmos, emphasized on the loss of goodwill for Russia as a supplier in case of the cancellation of the essentially commercial deal.

The intensive study of the international politics around the deal brings to the fore the emerging stark realities of the unipolar world – the evident US pressure and the vulnerabilities of Russia, consequent on its reduced stature in the international arena. For the first time, in India's relations with the erstwhile USSR and later Russia, the Russian President had to cancel the deal in July 1993, while he declared Russia's unconditional compliance to the deal during his January 1993 Delhi visit.

Significantly, the scope for manoeuvre in the new dispensation was also indicated by the instance of the deal. It was indicated by fact that Russia went the possible farthest point for compliance to accommodate India's needs for its space programme – and whatever its agreement with the US, the gesture was not unimportant. J.N. Dixit, in his interview to me, talked of the US pressure on Russia in cancelling the deal but at the same time, pointed out that "they (the Russians) gave us the drawings andz they sent us their engineers to help us manufacture (the engines)."[72] In my interview of Air Commodore Jasjit Singh, the ex-Director of the Institute of Defence Studies and Analyses (IDSA), he commented that "Cryogenic technology has no role for military purposes." He also noted that "Russia kept delaying the process (of banning the supply of engines) as they could, provided two cryoengines and provided as much of the design and, drawing as they could before the ban came."[73] It is also to be noted that both sides signed a new agreement in New Delhi in March 1994 which dropped the technology transfer provision but increased the number of engines to be supplied to India to seven.[74]

The significant trait of this early phase of Indo-Russian relations was the pre-dominance of the change factor, co-existent with an underlying continuity factor. The change factor was evident in ascribing lower priority to India in Russian foreign policy; in the initial uncertainties over the supply of arms and spares to India due to the near-collapse of Russia's infrastructure; in the deletion of the word "Peace" and Article IX in the 1993 Treaty; and in the cancellation of the cryogenic deal. India, significantly, was quite accommodative of the change, as pointed out by India's Prime Minister at the time, Narasimha Rao, in his written response to my question: "I think it (the change factor) only means that the other side encountered difficulties which we had to understand – which we did".[75]

At the same time, the underlying continuity factor was evident in the process of re-prioritizing India's worthiness in Russia's foreign policy perceptions as harped on by the old guard of the Russian foreign policy decision-making circle; and in the acknowledgment of the 1971 Treaty in the Preamble of the new Treaty of 1993.

The highlight of this early phase was, precisely, the realistic, down-to-earth (de-ideologized) assessment of the relationship from both ends. J.N. Dixit stated as much when he summed up both countries' viewpoints in this regard. In his interview to me, he noted that Kunadze, in his meeting with him in Moscow in January 1992, insisted that "Russia would have a matter of fact, down-to-earth approach in structuring its relations with different countries in the framework of the post-Cold War global scenario." And India's response was that "I (Dixit) further told Kunadze that the Government of India wished to establish new equations not on the basis of emotional or purely historical factors, but on a realistic basis."[76]

Second Phase (1996–1999)

The period was marked by Russia's two directions in perceptions and policies:

First, Russia's growing disillusionment with the US against all the required overtures from its end to accommodate, at its own cost, the US' perceived interests in Europe.

Second, Russia's policy perception to extend its circle of friends, primarily in Europe, that eventually includes Asia, i.e. Japan and China as well as its time-tested friend India.

A. In this context, two glaring moves by the West-NATO expansion and the Kosovo crisis – went decisively a long way toward Russia's disillusionment with the West.

On May 27, 1997, NATO Secretary-General Javier Solana and the Russian President Yeltsin were the first to sign in Paris the document "Founding Act on Mutual Relations, Cooperation and Security", hailed by the gathered leaders. The accord created a NATO-Russia Permanent Joint Council for consultation on European Security and enshrined close military and political cooperation between the former enemies, giving Russia a voice but not a veto in allied decisions. The US President Clinton said: the pact realized the goal of a "peaceful, democratic, undivided Europe .... In the twilight of the 20th century we look forward toward a new century with a new Russia and a new NATO working together in a new Europe of unlimited possibility."[77]

Beneath the euphoria, there were in Russia undercurrents of rancour against having been wronged. Sergei Baburin, Chairman of the anti-NATO commission in Russia, opined: "one has the growing impression that the NATO-Russia (Act), which is being prepared, is in its present form, a means for the West to deprive Russia of the will and time to oppose NATO's further expansion. The non-aggression pact did not prevent Germany's invasion of the Soviet Union in June 1941."[78]

Mikhail Gorbachev, who had introduced the concept of a "Common European Home" for Russia, raised a question in April 1997: "Why was not NATO expansion discussed in UN Security Council? It is a global problem concerning all countries. Europe needs integration and is ready for it. But the root of all evil is obsolete political stereotypes created by the long period of confrontation."[79]

NATO's war against Yugoslavia sharpened the differences in stance between the US-dominated NATO and Russia: Russia, opposed fragmentation of Yugoslavia, the West's recognition of Croatia and Bosnia as well as its explicit support for their secession and the NATO intervention. Nevertheless, Russia became a member of the Contact Group that negotiated a settlement for Bosnia. But Russia was eventually marginalized in the crisis scenario, when the US intervened in the conflict in 1995 and the peacekeeping task was shifted from the UN to NATO. President Yeltsin condemned NATO bombings on Yugoslavia during the Bosnia- Herzegovina crisis in 1995, drawing attention to the fact that the air strikes were without the UN approval and hence a violation of international law. NATO-Russia relations again deteriorated in 1998–99 when NATO started full-scale aggression on Serb targets following the Serbs' refusal to accept the Contact Group's formula of the Rambouillet Agreement, accepted by the Kosovo Liberation Army (KLA). In this context, NATO adopted, during its 50-th anniversary celebrations in Washington in April 1999, a new strategic doctrine that authorized NATO to intervene beyond the area of its traditional responsibility without seeking a UN mandate, presumably concerned by Russia's veto power in the Security Council. Russian Foreign Minister Igor Ivanov commented that NATO's military action in the Balkans violated the Russia-NATO Founding Act in letter and spirit.[80]

Russia's dilemma and hence, its oscillations, were strikingly demonstrated over Kosovo. On the one hand, Russia perceived that it was obliged to defend its traditional and time-tested ally Serbia (which represent a historical 1,500 year-long alliance) and on the other, it aspired to become an integral part of the Euro-Atlantic security community. Prior to and during the NATO air campaign against Serbia, Russia provided only humanitarian assistance to Yugoslavia.

The real danger, in Russian perceptions, stemmed from its apprehension that NATO's intervention in Kosovo would eventually lead to its embroilment in post-Soviet disputes: Azerbaijan, Georgia and Moldova feared NATO's role in Kosovo as a possible model for NATO intervention in their own disputes with separatist regions, as Moscow might then find itself in a position where "it could not help fighting and yet could not hope to win."[81] Significantly, Moscow shied away from availing itself of an opportunity offered by the Kosovo crisis. Moscow might have, as many Western analysts alleged, fostered a prolonged fight from Yugoslav President Milosevic's end that would necessitate a NATO-led ground offensive and the resultant casualties would embitter the relations between the US and Europe – portending a fateful future for NATO. Russia's compulsions for not to act that way stemmed partly from its economic dependence on the West, "in particular the United States administration's threat to vote against IMF lending"[82] and principally, perhaps from its adherence to Gorchakovian principles at this time – when Igor Ivanov was beginning to establish his own brand of policy on the Russian Ministry. These principles demanded non-aggressiveness to get a breathing space for domestic development-process, and were a refrain of the new Minister.

Simultaneously, cognizance of a real threat from the NATO grouping of allied forces was evidenced in the strategic military exercise conducted by Russia in June 1999 – codenamed "Zapad99" – after the Yugoslav War ended. A new strategic planning concept – "the regional group of forces" – was introduced in April 1999 to include Belarussian forces and its effectiveness was tested during the Exercise "Zapad 1999." The group's theatre of operations centred on Russia's north west including the *Kaliningrad* region and Belarus. The exercise's theme was the repelling of a massive space missile attack or powerful missile-and-bombing offensive by an armed coalition of Western countries against strategically important targets and economic regions in European Russia and Belarus.[83]

On the whole, the process of emergence of NATO in Russia's threat perceptions, among other driving forces, is crucial for understanding its resolve to stall the trend towards establishment of a unipolar structure, and to replace it with a multipolar system. Russia's 1993 Military Doctrine envisaged five situations that constituted a "military danger and an immediate threat" with no explicit reference to NATO.[84] But the November 1993 Russian Foreign Intelligence Service study characterized NATO as the "biggest military grouping in the world that possesses an enormous offensive potential", wedded to "the stereo types of bloc thinking."[85] The study was emphatic in its opposition to membership of NATO for the Central and East European countries. President Yeltsin's press spokesperson was categorical that the expansion of NATO in areas in "direct proximity to the Russian border" would lead to a "military-political destabilisation in the region."[86] The 1997 National Security Concept paper said, "The transition of NATO to the use of force (military force) beyond the zone of its responsibility and without the Sanction of the UN Security Council, which has been elevated to the level of a strategic doctrine, is fraught with the destabilization of the strategic situation in the World."[87] Russia's concern at the growing level and scales of threat was explicit in the 2000 National Security Concept paper also which identified NATO's eastward expansion as one of other specific threats to international security.[88]

B. During the period, Russia's thrust towards building friendly relations with significant power-centres of the world, other than and in addition to the US, was evidenced in its express efforts to validate a multipolar system replacing the trend towards establishing a unipolar one in global affairs, as well as to strengthen its case for deserving a rightful place in the post Cold War global arena.

Europe: Russia's entry in the Council of Europe (CE) on February 28, 1996 was a conscious strategic decision, made by Russia's leadership. Russia highly valued the accessibility to the experience and intellectual legacy of the CE as it continued the process of democratization in its domestic set-up as well as to lend Europe an access to and a better understanding of Russia. "We welcome the political declaration adopted by the Council's Ministerial Committee at the 104th session in Budapest – "Greater Europe without Dividing Lines"- which takes Europe closer to unification,"[89] as Igor Ivanov in his memoirs has been emphatic.

The Agreement of Partnership and Cooperation between Russia and the European Union (EU) went into effect in December 1997 and has had positive effects on Russia's ties with EU member-states. Russia sees multilateral cooperation with the EU as a priority and seeks to raise such cooperation to the level of a strategic partnership. The EU has been one of Russia's most important partners in political dialogue as well as in trade and economic interactions, finance and investments.

A Russian focus towards the East to assert its Eurasian identity, was another aspect of a fast-evolving disaffection from the US. The focus took shape evidently for geostrategic reasons to expand Russia's circle of friendly countries, where its presence was mostly restricted by Cold War logic of exclusivity of relations.

China: Russia signed on 25 April 1996 the Shanghai Agreement with China that resolved to develop a strategic 21st Century partnership. It was significant against the backdrop of US-Japan joint declaration of 17 April 1996 just 8 days ahead – that pledged an "alliance for the 21st Century." The Shanghai Agreement stopped short of forging a new alliance and shied away from creating a new axis, since the two countries harboured deep suspicions after a 25 year-long freeze in ties, ending only in the mid-1980s. The Agreement pledged to cooperate in a new world order, joining forces against NATO's eastward expansion toward Russia, described the Chechnya issue as an internal matter of Russia, while Russia reciprocated by identifying Tibet and Taiwan as internal matters for China. The bilateral "Joint Declaration on a Multipolar World and the Establishment of a New International Order" of April 1997 in Moscow established a partnership based on equality and mutual trust for the purpose of strategic interaction in the twenty-first century.[90]

Japan: The Prime Minister of Japan visited Moscow in November 1998 – the first in over a quarter of a century – to sign the Moscow Declaration on building a creative, long-term partnership between the two countries. It was a significant qualitative change in their bilateral relations.

During this period, the thrust of Yevgeny Primakov's argument for multipolarity in the world system, as reflected in a number of Russian official policy papers and statements, was the main driving force of Russian foreign policy, as he was the Foreign Minister since January 1996 and eventually the Prime Minister since September 1998. He was the main architect of the concept of multipolarity. A policy took shape on the basis of this notion even though multipolarity as a foreign policy concept was occasionally questioned by Russia's foreign policy elite. The latter is clear from a report by Russia's Foreign and Defence Policy Council in early 1998 arguing that the world is driving towards a fluid international system away from bipolarity, rather than towards a multipolar one. Primakov responded, while participating in the debate, that there was little difference between a fluid system and a multipolar one but the important thing is to avoid a unipolar system.[91]

Indo Russian Relations (1996-1999)

Indo-Russian relations acquired its main features from this context.

1996

In March 1996, both sides agreed to modernize 125 MiG–21 BIS planes under the programme Project MiG–21–93, which reflected a Russian turnabout towards India. Significantly, the entire MiG-21BIS modernization programme required 10 times less money than was being spent on the purchase of just one new-generation fighter. The entire overhaul and production effort would be centred in India, thereby helping to create new jobs and to keep local enterprises busy.[92]

The service-to-service cooperation agreement signed by Russian Defence Minister General Igor Rodionov and Defence Minister Mulayam Singh Yadav, envisaged, among other things, joint military exercises – the first in the long history of Indo-Soviet and Indo-Russian relations.[93] Also, a major acquisition contract was concluded with Russia in November 1996[94] for the supply of 40 SU–30 multi-purpose aircrafts for the IAF (a deal of $1.8 billion), with provisions for subsequent manufacturing in India. India became the first foreign buyer of this aircraft.

1997

Both sides agreed to a $1.5 billion deal for two Kilo-class submarines for Indian Navy.[95] During Prime Minister Deve Gowda's visit to Moscow in March 1997, both sides decided to continue their defence relationship beyond 2000.[96] The Russian $1 billion package to develop an integrated air defence system (ADS) envisaged the integration of Russian S–300 PMU with the indigeneous surface-to-air missile, Akash[97] India also agreed to purchase four Illyushin IL–78 aircrafts. During Defence Minister Mulayam Singh Yadav's visit to Moscow in October 1997, a third working group on joint development and modernization of land-based weapon systems like artillery, rocket guns etc was set up. The other two groups deal with aviation and shipbuilding.[98]

1998

During the visit of Indian defence delegation, led by Defence Secretary Ajit Kumar, to Moscow both sides reached an agreement on Russia's sale of six 9K81–300V mobile Air Defence Systems as well as Tunguska air defence systems to India.[99] Both sides decided to institutionalize their naval cooperation which would include operational doctrines also.[100] A significant bilateral agreement was signed during Prime Minister Yevgeny Primakov's New Delhi visit in December 1998: the "Long Term Agreement on Military-Technical Cooperation" that envisaged enhanced military cooperation upto the year 2010.[101]

1999

India and Russia signed a major defence protocol for joint manufacturing and licensed production of SU–30 combat jets, missiles, anti-missile systems, and submarines. They also agreed on Russia's sale of long-range bombers and AWACS (Airborne Warning and Control Systems). "For the first time, a comprehensive document involving all kinds of military cooperation between the two countries was signed", visiting Russian Deputy Prime Minister Ilya Klebanov commented.[102]

The major events of this phase are the Pokhran-II incident, the concept of 'Strategic Triangle' that was mooted by Yevgeny Primakov and the Kargil war.

1. Pokhran-II

Russian responses, after the May 1998 Pokhran nuclear blasts by India were of particular significance. On the one hand, President Yeltsin told an assembly of Russian diplomats at the Ministry of Foreign Affairs: "India let us down with this blast but I believe that more diplomatic efforts or a visit will adjust its policy."[103]

On the other hand, Parliamentary leaders like Gennadi Zyuganov of the Communist Party, Zhirinovsky of the Liberal Democratic Party and Gennady Seleznyov, the Speaker of the Russian Duma, all welcomed the Indian action. Russian military leaders also hailed the Indian move.[104]

Foreign Minister Primakov was worried, like President Yeltsin, and put forward a three-point proposal, the "Helsinki Initiative,[105] to diffuse tensions in the sub-continent. The Initiative proposed signing of the NPT (Non-proliferation Treaty) and CTBT (Comprehensive Test Ban Treaty) by both India and Pakistan, bilateral talks to resolve outstanding problems between India and Pakistan, and immediate interaction among P–5 members to workout a common strategy to curb the arms race in South Asia. The Initiative, at best, was evidenced in a reiteration of Russia's earlier calls for signing the NPT and CTBT, as was the January 1994 joint statement by the US and Russia which called on India and Pakistan to sign the NPT.

But Russia significantly ruled out the imposition of economic sanctions as an effective measure to make India and Pakistan fall in line. Also, Moscow defied US pressure to stop defence cooperation with New Delhi. A high ranking Russian official put the Russian stand thus: "any question of stopping defence cooperation with India has to be discussed in the context of the US military and technological cooperation with Israel, Saudi Arabia and its NATO allies in the close vicinity of the Russian border."[106] Also a sort of a discernible acquiescence was forthcoming when Moscow, as an act of defiance of the economic sanctions, amended (through a Supplement) the Indo-Soviet deal of November 1988, to actuate the $2.5 billion deal with New Delhi for the Koodankulam nuclear power station in June 1998 and signed in December 1998 the agreement on Military Technical Cooperation upto 2010.[107]

Russia went along with the multilateral consensus in condemning the nuclear test at the G–8 Summit, the P–5 conclave, the G–8 Foreign Ministers' Meet and at the UN Security Council and agreed with other P-5 members that India and Pakistan could not be recognized as Nuclear Weapon States (NWS). But, significantly, as it did not lead the charge against India, so it opposed sanctions against it, since such a measure of coercive diplomacy would be, to its view, counter-productive, eventually blocking collective sanctions against India. Even while voicing Russia's concerns about nuclear proliferation in the sub-continent, the Russian ambassador to India went as far as to state that his country was willing to recognize India as a nuclear weapons state if it signed the CTBT and NPT.[108] Individual views of commentators in Russian press are worth noting. Sergei Sokug interestingly pointed out, "Our country does not afford the luxury of refusing the Military Technical Cooperation with this country ... the most important peculiarity of Indo-Russian MTC is in the fact that today India is the sole country which not only buys arms from Russia but also finances our *scientific – research and experiment design works in the military field*"[109] He referred to the programme of building the multi-role fighter SU-30 MKI for the total value of $ 1 billion. Viktor Litovkin argued in the same vein that $2 billion earned annually from India in the context of the "present condition in Russia of economic instability", were not peanuts. He reeled off the figures to stress his point. In 1997 "India expressed its desire to purchase two diesel submarines like 'Kilo' from us, and three modern torpedo boats (worth $800 million), aircraft-carrier cruiser (worth nearly $2 billion), four refueller aircrafts IL–78 ($400 million) and Zenit missile complex S–300 PMU (value to be agreed upon) are some of the contracts already signed and are being fulfilled. And NATO demonstrates its disregard for Russian interests in the Balkans…."[110] This disregard for Russian interests by NATO was a recurring theme in the Russian press, in the context of Russian opposition against sanctions on India.

2. Strategic Triangle

Russian Prime Minister Primakov in his New Delhi visit in December 1998 mooted the idea of a Moscow-Beijing-New Delhi strategic triangle. The idea was a novel one in respect of earlier Soviet stance against China and of Soviet insistence on projecting China as inimical to Indian interests. The notion envisaged long term cooperation among the three countries in a changed perspective, not viable for short-term equations.[111] While New Delhi preferred to be non-committal, Beijing was unresponsive. *Novieye Izvestia* reported the proposal with a striking headline "Triangular embarrassment" and emphasized that "... he (Primakov) couched the proposal he had brought with him in a reply to a question from a reporter in his retinue. Moreover, the form of the proposal was noncommittal in the extreme: 'That would be very good."[112] Later Primakov has been explicit on the Russia strategy of the triangular cooperation in his memoirs: ".... Did this mean that we were playing with so-called "Indian" or "Chinese" cards? I have already written that such a view was widely circulated in the US. It is just crude, and it comes form the hubris of Americocentrism (the notion that everything revolves around the US and no more). The notion is doubly crude since it does not take account of the concern of the USSR and later Russia in active development of relations with these fast growing Asiatic giants, the population of which constitute half of humanity. Also, we could not and cannot disregard the fact that a diversification of links unconditionally strengthens our role as a great world power, even as regards the US ....."[113]

On the other hand, Indian foreign policy analysts and diplomats, I interviewed in December 2002, were unequivocal in their attitudes about the prospect of the idea, downplaying it as: "not viable"- K. Subrahmanyam, (ex-Chairman of National Security Advisory Board); "totally illogical" – J.N. Dixit; "makes no sense" – Brahma Chellaney (Security analyst); "not practical" – S.K. Lamba; and "a non-starter" – Air-Commodore Jasjit Singh.[114]

Kadakin, however, in September 2000, assessed the extent and scope of the "triangle" from this angle: "when the positions of the these powers coincide, as it was on the issues of strategic stability and the ABM Treaty, in denouncing the use of force under the guise of "humanitarian intervention", in combating international terrorism and the events in Chechnya, aggression against Yugoslavia, we should simply work together – not against somebody but for the sake of attaining positive goals." He stressed upon this formula for possible three-way cooperation.[115] Russian Foreign Minister, Igor Ivanov, brushed aside in December 2002 speculations about a "strategic triangle" while speaking in the weekly "Vremena" (Times) analytical programme of the "Channel" national TV network, and explained that India and China "simply enjoy prominence" in Russia's foreign policy and "this policy was not stimulated by the Balkan war" as his predecessor Yevgeny Primakov floated the idea of a trilateral cooperation in 1998, "after" NATO forces bombarded Yugoslavia." He, however, agreed that the combat against international terrorism, formation of a multipolar world, strengthening the role of the UN in global affairs and economic cooperation objectively bring the three countries together.[116]

Hon'ble Ex-Prime Minister Narasimha Rao, in his written response to my written question, "Is it (the idea) an admission, by implication, that national interests of the three countries converge at a point?" was categorical in his comment: "I think it is, by and large, the correct appreciation of the situation. Any look of tri-lateralisation would tend to create an image of 'ganging up." I think it is better avoided, in projection."[117]

3. The Kargil War

The Kargil crisis of 1999 brought the two countries nearer and was a factor to cement the ties. Voice of Russia denounced the Kargil infiltrators as "fundamentalists, extremists and separatists" receiving various kinds of support from Pakistan, in contrast to West's subtle criticism of Indian airstrikes and their stubborn silence over decades-old active military back-up of mercenaries by Pakistan. *Nezavisimaya Gazeta* noted India's concern over NATO airstrikes on Yugoslavia, on the pretext of human rights, in the context of Western attempts to seek internationalization of Kashmir problem and said, "in Delhi's view, it may mean for India a scenario quite similar to the Kosovo one, and that it is completely unacceptable to India, as so-called Kashmir problem is an exclusive concern of the people of the Indian sub-continent."[118]

While Russia was not the only country to have supported India over Kargil, no Western country officially referred to Jammu and Kashmir as an "Indian state", denounced Islamabad's action as "invasion", consistently opposed internationalization of the Kashmir problem and explicitly referred to the Shimla. Accord (1972) and the Lahore Declaration (1999) as the sole basis for resolving the problem, as Russia did.

Moscow demonstrated its solidarity with Delhi by stepping up defence supplies to India during the Kargil conflict. Russia shipped more SU–30 jets and Tunguska anti-aircraft systems to India, sent its newest T–90 Tanks for field trials and offered its unique artillery – tracking radar "Zoopark–1."[119] General Andrey Nikolaev, Chairman of the Committee on Defence of Russian Duma, commented: (during Kargil War) the Russians had been not only fully supportive of India's position on diplomatic and political fronts, "but very eager to assist in supplying urgently needed spare parts *even by stripping their own armed forces*."[120]

Professor Grigory Bondarevsky, a leading Russian expert on Asia, commented: "Russia's strong and unequivocal support for India throughout its two month-old conflict with Pakistan in Kargil goes to show that this country is perfectly serious about its declared goal of *building a strategic partnership with India*."[121]

Third Phase (2000–2002)

In this period Russia was predominantly occupied with the US decision to develop its National Missile Defence (NMD) systems, suggesting the US withdrawal from the 1972 Anti-Ballistic Missile (ABM) as well as with Russia's drive "to achieve a multipolar system of international relations," as enunciated in its 2000 Foreign policy concept.

NMD

The Clinton administration sought Russian agreement to amend the 1972 ABM treaty to accommodate a limited National Missile Defence (NMD). Russia opposed the idea, since it relied on its nuclear deterrent as a guarantee against possible onslaughts of Weapons of Mass Destruction (WMD), provided by the ABM treaty. The Russian Duma ratified the START-II on 14 April 2000 which reduces the number of nuclear weapons for each side from 6,000 to a maximum of 3,500 by the end of 2007 and it paved the way for bilateral negotiations on more reductions in each side's nuclear arsenals under the START-III accord. During the June 2000 meeting between Presidents Clinton and Putin, the Russian President deftly confronted the US move to develop NMD with his government's counter-strategy – i.e. to withdraw from all arms control agreements with the US and the West. The Bush administration's preferred solution to the problem in mid-November 2001 Crawford Summit was the simultaneous withdrawal of both sides from the ABM treaty as it was a relic of the Cold War – to promote the new agenda of cooperative defence and deep cuts in offensive forces. Putin refused to withdraw since his country regarded the ABM treaty as an important component of strategic stability. President Bush in his Rose Garden statement on 13 December 2001 was emphatic: "I have discussed with my friend President Vladimir Putin that the US was "moving beyond" the ABM treaty, thereby breaking free of "the grim theory" of mutual assured destruction and leaving behind "one of the last vestiges" of the Cold War."[122]

Within hours, President Putin released a statement, acknowledging that the US was within its right to withdraw, but pointed out that: "However, we consider the (US) decision to be a mistake ..... As is known, Russia, along with the US, as distinguished from other nuclear powers, has long had an effective system of overcoming anti-missile defenses. For this reason I can state with complete confidence that the decision taken by the President of the US presents no threat to the national security of the Russian Federation." Strobe Talbott has recalled: "In a single sentence, Putin had repudiated the numerous presentations I'd heard in 1999 and 2000 from General Nikolai Zlenko, who ... had argued vociferously and implacably that an American anti-missile system would neutralize Russia's strategic deterrent."[123] In the June 2000 Moscow Summit, President Putin had stressed the point "softly" to President Clinton: "But please believe me" that Russia was capable of an "adequate response" and always would be ... If NMD went forward, there would be reciprocal action – 'may be quite unexpected, probably asymmetrical' – that is, measures intended not to mimic American high-tech programmes but to thwart them. Whatever action Russia took would threaten the territory of the United States.'[124]

Drive Towards Multipolarity

EU: Since the European Union (EU) has a significant role in strengthening security and developing cooperation in Europe, President Putin in his message to the Federal Meeting of Russian Federation in 2001 emphasized that "Russia's course toward integration with Europe will become one of the key areas of Russian foreign policy."[125] The January 2000 Foreign Policy Doctrine of Russia also emphasized the importance of increased cooperation with the EU and stressed on Russia's particular interest in the European Security and Defence Policy as a possible counterbalance to NATO-centrism in Europe. Igor Ivanov, in his memoirs, noted: "The development of a unified policy for security and defence is a new direction for the EU ... Russia and the EU are natural partners in the search for joint responses to the new threats and challenges faced by European and international security."[126] The Joint Declaration on Strengthening Dialogue and Cooperation on Political and Security Matters in Europe, issued at the end of 30 October 2000 Russia-EU Summit in Paris was in tune with Russian Federation's June 2000 strategy for relations with the EU for the midrange future, approved by President Putin. Russia's strategy called for several initiatives that were subsequently adopted at the October Summit: expanding the format of political dialogue between Russia and the EU; developing mutual trade and joint investments as well as cooperation in finance; protecting Russia's interests as the EU expands; developing a pan-European structure for cooperation; increasing Russian – EU Cooperation in science and technology; expanding transnational and inter-regional ties; and bringing economic legislations and technical standards closer together. It was also resolved at the Summit to promote cooperation in operational crisis management and to examine mechanisms for Russia to contribute to the EU operations.

Russia has been watchful of the development of integration efforts within the EU, since Russia is not a disinterested by-stander as a fundamentally new structure for international relations is built in Europe. President Putin, while speaking at the EU Summit in Stockholm on 23 March 2001 pointed out that "joining the EU is not a goal for Russia, either now or in the foreseeable future. However, we cannot stand on the sidelines and simply watch the wide-scale integration of our continent."[127] Later on, President Putin suggestively pointed out in his Address to the German Bundestag on 25 September 2001: "I believe that Europe can, in the long-term, establish her reputation as a powerful, *independent* centre for global politics *only if* she combines her assets with the manpower, the territory and the natural resources of Russia and also with latter's economic, cultural and military potential."[128]

An eye to the East: Russia's relations with its largest neighbour China, came to focus on Russian foreign policy's "Strategic directions," as pointed out by Igor Ivanov.[129] President Putin visited Beijing in mid-2000 which was reciprocated by President Jiang Zemin in mid-2001 to sign a wide-ranging Treaty for Good-Neighbourliness, Friendship and Cooperation, that laid out the principles for long-term inter-governmental relations.

Russia was poised to develop long-term relations with Japan within a broad spectrum, that included closer coordination in international affairs, trade and expanded cooperation in economic interactions. President Putin visited Japan in September 2000 to issue, along with the Prime Minister of Japan for the first time in the history of their bilateral relations, a joint statement on cooperation between the two countries on international affairs, which included a declaration by Japan on the importance of Russia's entry into the WTO, and support from Russia of Japan's candidature for membership in the UN Security Council. There remained, however, the unresolved issue of bilateral agreements on the Southern Kurile Islands.

Indo-Russian Relations (2000-2002)

During this period, Indo-Russian relations took shape around concepts of "strategic partnership", as was evidenced in the Declaration on Strategic Partnership between the two countries in 2000, and reinforced in the Declaration on Further Consolidation of Strategic Partnership in 2002. Both agreements identified new areas of economic cooperation beyond the traditional areas and stressed commitments to cooperate, "as strategic partners," bilaterally and at the multilateral level on strategic issues for the development of a multipolar world "on a new cooperative security order."[130] However, such a notion of partnership coincided with increasingly intimate relations between India and the United States – witnessed in the support the US showed to India in dealing with cross-border terrorism (especially post 2001), in India's new position on NMD, as evolved over 2000-2001, and strong images of friendship promoted by Ambassador Blackwill in his time as Chief of US Mission in Delhi from 2001.

There were several important visits/bilateral contacts between the two countries during the period which included: External Affairs Minister Jaswant Singh's visit to Moscow in June 2000; President Putin's State Visit to India in October 2000; Foreign Minister Igor Ivanov's visit to India in May 2001; Defence and Foreign Minister Jaswant Singh's visit to Moscow in June 2001; Prime Minister Vajpayee's State Visit to Moscow from November 4-7, 2001; Foreign Minister Ivanov's visit to New Delhi from February 3-4, 2002; and President Putin's state visit to India from 3-5 December, 2002.

2000

Both sides agreed to upgrade their military cooperation (in respect of technology transfer and joint production) and set up a joint commission at the Defence Ministry level, after the meeting between Defence Minister George Fernandes and his counterpart Igor Sergeyev in Moscow in June 2000.[131] Earlier in April 2000, a Protocol was signed to establish a direct apex link between bilateral security establishments, with sub-groups on international terrorism and drug-trafficking. The Protocol would also look at economic, legal and ecological aspect of security.[132] During President Putin's visit in October 2000, Indo-Russian Inter-Governmental Commission on Military-Technical Cooperation was set up, and inter-governmental agreements were signed for acquisition of Admiral Gorshkov, MiG-29K fighters on board Gorshkov, KA-31 and KA-28 early warning helicopters, T-90S tanks, for licensed production of 140 SU-30 MKI and for lease of four TU-21M maritime reconnissnce bombers.[133]

2001-2002

During Foreign Minister Igor Ivanov's early May 2001 New Delhi visit,. Foreign Minister Jaswant Singh, in the Joint Press Conference, fully backed the Russian position on the Anti-Ballistic Missile (ABM) Treaty and opined that the ABM Treaty "should not be abrogated unilaterally; while welcoming President Bush's decision "to engage Russia in a dialogue" on Missile Defences. Foreign Minister Ivanov added that the approaches of India and Russia on missile defences "mostly coincide."[134] During the first meeting of the Joint Working Group (JWG) on Strategic Stability, both sides reaffirmed their opposition to any unilateral move to reshape global security architecture.[135] In the Joint Statement of India and Russia of 6 November 2001, issued in Moscow, "both sides expressed their support to preserving existing arms control and disarmament agreements, including the ABM Treaty." They reaffirmed their support for the UN Secretary General's proposal, noted by the Millennium Declaration for an International Conference to effectively eliminate nuclear dangers. As original states-parties to the Chemical Weapons Convention, both sides stressed their commitment to ensure that the provisions of the Convention are effectively implemented and emphasized on concluding a legally binding protocol to strengthen the Biological & Toxic Weapons Convention (BTWC) of 1972.

Major issues in this period were: the Strategic Partnership Declaration, NMD, and the 2002 Declaration.

Declaration on Strategic Partnership

Declaration on Strategic Partnership between India and Russia was signed by Prime Minister Vajpayee and visiting President Vladimir Putin in New Delhi on 3rd October 2000 and it pronounced that both the countries were "convinced that the further comprehensive development of their bilateral ties would promote progress and prosperity in both states and the consolidation of positive trends in the world as a whole." They declared their partnership in view of "seeking to impart a qualitatively new character and long-term perspective to their multi-faceted bilateral relations and to actively develop them in political, economic, trade, scientific, technological, cultural and other fields, in the years ahead and into the 21st century."

The near-strategic partnership of 1971 was redefined in 1993, shorn of its Cold-War context. The 2000 Declaration demonstrated a meeting-ground of their common interests – the word "strategic", bereft of its Cold-War connotation, meant a long-term and "comprehensive" development of the bilateral relationship. The Declaration continued to imply a paradigm shift from the 1971 context when the dominant perception was that the USSR would help deter any probable American and Chinese adventurism. The Declaration, like the 1993 treaty, steered clear of forming any sort of "axis": "The strategic partnership between the sides is *not directed* against any other state or group of states, and does not need to create *a military – political alliance*."[136] President Putin explained what Russian perception precisely meant to imply by Strategic Partnership: "when we say strategic, we mean long-term partnership in keeping with the pragmatic national interests of our two countries, especially in this time of globalisation and increasing competition on the world scene. I'm not talking about military competition, but economic, scientific and technological competition."[137] Strategic partnership, in the Russian diplomatic vocabulary, is used to denote various dimensions of close cooperation in politico-economic and defence fields that prompted it to sign a Strategic Partnership with China way back in 1996.

Strategic partnership is an oft-used new term in the post-Cold War international relations. Pertinently, China and the US have had a "Strategic Partnership" since November 1997. Not necessarily directed against any third country, prevalent strategic partnerships essentially bring into sharp focus the shared long-term interests of bilateral relationships. But India and Russia have institutionalized their relations with an Indo-Russian Joint Working Group on Afghanistan as well as with other sixteen agreements and memoranda, supplementing and substantiating the Declaration that include a package of documents in military-technical field, a MOU on peaceful uses of nuclear energy (breaching a long-standing international blockade against India) and an Integrated Long-Term Programme (ILTP) of scientific and technological cooperation. Notably, the Declaration "has formalised what had already existed in practice between our two countries -- the broad-based coincidence or proximity of fundamental national interests, the deeply rooted national consensus regarding high priority of comprehensive enhancement of our bilateral ties."[138] The Declaration included countering the spread of international terrorism and illicit drug and arms trafficking, making consistent steps in curbing the proliferation of the weapons of mass destruction with the ultimate goal of their total elimination and taking efforts in establishing a just and multipolar world.

The new meaning put to strategic partnership by Russian perceptions has been *persistently* hinted at: on October 22, 1995 during the UN anniversary celebrations, President Yeltsin, in a discussion with Prime Minister Rao, referred to the "strategic partnership" existing between the two countries;[139] during the March 1997 visit of Prime Minister Deve Gowda to Moscow, both countries resolved "to upgrade their relationship to the level of strategic partnership";[140] in the Joint Statement during Prime Minister Primakov's visit to India in 1998, the two sides declared "to move towards strategic partnership";[141] and in July 1999 Russian Foreign Minister Igor Ivanov communicated to his counterpart, Jaswant Singh in Singapore during the multilateral conference under the auspices of ASEAN, that the stage could now be set for the formation of a "strategic partnership." The persistent reiteration of intentions to upgrade the bilateral relationship to a strategic partnership revealed precisely the growing importance of each in the perceptions of respective national interests of the two countries. Pertinently, Prof. Felix N. Yurlov of the Moscow Institute of Oriental Studies in mid-2000 (a few months ahead of the signing of the Declaration on Strategic Partnership) urged its immediate conclusion: "The history of their relations and their geopolitical positions in the world should convince Russia and India that they are *natural strategic partners*. Indeed, never before they had any conflicts or serious contradictions. For many decades, Soviet-Indian ... cooperation has been perceived as a continuous interaction between equals.... With the emergence of a new President of the Russian Federation, it (Russia) has to strengthen its eastern policy by making it more concrete, more substantial, and more dynamic. Russian-Indian bilateral relations, and international cooperation between the two countries must be a very important part of this policy. The signing of the Declaration on Strategic Partnership between Russia and India should not be further delayed."[142]

S.K. Lamba, India's ambassador to Moscow during the period, in his interview to me, specified the impact of the Declaration: "The signing of Strategic Declaration in October 2000 was a *turning point* (in our relations). The highlights of bilateral relations that I see during the three years of my work (there), on the political side, is the signing of Strategic Partnership and the resultant resumption of high-level contacts between Heads of Government."[143]

Again, Air-Commodore Jasjit Singh, when I interviewed him, pointed out: "India needs Russia and Russia needs India, so there is the Strategic Partnership."[144]

Indo-Russian Responses to NMD

By the end of 2002, both Russia and India had decided *independently* that NMD could not be prevented. On this, the sides had *relatively different* views. India now "welcomed" NMD as it heralded an era of moving away from the hair-trigger alerts, associated with the prevailing nuclear orthodoxies and thought that there was a strategic and technological "inevitability" in stepping away from a world, held hostage by the doctrine of Mutually Assured Destruction (MAD) to a "Cooperative defensive transition", underpinned by further cuts and a de-alert of nuclear forces. But according to the Russian First Dy. Chief of General Staff, Valery Manilov, the NMD had three serious shortcomings: it is costly; it has exceptionally complex mechanism to guarantee 100 per cent protection from missile attacks; and the decision on creating a national missile shield would trigger a new outbreak of the arms race, since the existing parity between the offensive and the defensive weapons would be broken.[145]

Delhi Declaration on Further Consolidation of Strategic Partnership

It was signed during President Putin's visit to India on 3-5 December 2002, gave priority to "elevate" their strategic partnership to a "qualitatively new level in both bilateral and international arenas." The two most significant points, stressed by this Declaration, were: first, their commitment to work towards "a new cooperative security order that recognizes the legitimate security interests of all countries", and second, the recognition of the threat of terrorism, as it emanates from their "common neighbourhood", i.e., Afghanistan and Central Asia.[146]

We will, now, discuss bilateral cooperation in three significant fields—defence, nuclear energy and anti-terrorism, during the decade.

Defence Cooperation

Of all the fields of cooperation, envisaged in the Strategic Partnership Declaration, the defence-relationship has utilized the potentials in this field relatively more fruitfully than others. India's need for defence cooperation with Russia is primarily for two reasons:

(i) The Russian (and the Soviet) connection in Indian defence sector is predominant. The data shows that: for the army, half the tanks, 90 per cent of armoured infantry vehicles and surface-to-surface missiles, two-thirds of artillery pieces and assorted guns; for the Navy, all destroyers, 80 per cent of submarines, 40 per cent of frigates, entire corvette fleet and missile boats; for the Air Force 36 of 48 fighter and ground attack squadrons, 80 per cent of transport and helicopter squadrons are supplied by Russia.[147] It highlights India's dependency on Russian spare parts as well as the advantages, associated with traditional links.[148]

(ii) Second, Russian products are still cheaper than products from other sources and Russia is more willing to supply related-technology and to involve in joint production.

The issue of arms sales was an important area where Russia vigorously pursued its foreign policy agenda against the opposition from the West. Total Soviet and Russian arms sales continued to decline from around $12 billion annually in the early 1980's to $ 7.8 billion in 1991, $ 3 billion in 1992 and $ 2.5 billion in 1993. This decline cost Russia dear in terms of hard currency earnings and job security for millions employed in the arms sector. This continued decline also threatened Russia's technological and skilled base in the arms manufacturing sector, which was of great strategic importance to Russia. Stephen Blank has categorized reasons for Russia's arms sale policy thus – the need for cash, the need to keep production facilities, the advantage of keeping technicians and scientists employed lest massive unemployment and falling investments ruin that sector and undermine its readiness and technological competitiveness, resentment over the loss of markets, in particular, to the US and the desire to reassert Russia's standing as a great power.[149]

To increase arms production and sales, Russia's Military Doctrine of 1993 adopted the concept of "economic foundations" and to achieve this, a three-pronged policy of conversion, privatization and corporatization was undertaken by the Russian government. To prevent the collapse of the defence industry, a new State Agency for export of armaments – Rosvoorouzhenie – was established and in 2000, Putin signed a decree to merge Rosvoorouzhenie and Promexport to a single entity – Rosoboronexport – for better management.

Yeltsin's strategy of increasing arms sales to China and India since 1993 was in close consonance with the "Russia First" idea of closer cooperation with the East. India again shored up in Russian military thinking as it was one of the biggest markets for Russian military hardware and as it offered the best prospects for a *major new base* for export of licensed manufactured equipment to other Asia-Pacific states.

Here are some significant weapon – acquisitions of India from Russia in view of their importance for India's defence-capabilities.

The first and foremost is the PJ–10 Brahmos Air-to-Surface missile (ASM), the first product of Indo-Russian joint ventures in defence field, and the agreement for it was signed in 1998 in Moscow at the fifth meeting of the Russian-Indian Working Group on Military and Technical Cooperation. It can be launched from multiple launch platforms, can carry multiple warheads and has a speed of 280 kilometers within 300 seconds. The acquisition of this level of technology would boost India's capacity to *indigenously* develop advanced cruise missiles.[150] It is a joint venture between Russia's State-owned NPO Mashinostroyenia and India's DRDO (Defence Research Development Organization). It was first test-fired on 12 June 2001.

Second is the SU–30 MKI, a multi-role combat aircraft, designed for specific Indian needs and will have equipments from five countries like France, India, South Africa, Israel and Britain. For the *first time* in their bilateral relations, a Russian product will incorporate so many equipments from various countries to produce an India-specific product. It will serve as the force-multiplier of the IAF as it operates long-range precision-guided air-to-surface missile-systems and can engage several targets simultaneously.[151] Under the $ 3.3 billion contract, India will undertake licensed production of 140 SU-30 MKI jets in the next 15 years, which will be in addition to the 32 SU-30 MKIs produced in Russia, which will join the IAF in a phased manner.

The third is the T–90S tanks which will better serve Indian Army's needs than the existing T–72 tanks. T–90S tanks have a range of 500 kms; have "Refleks" anti-tank guided missile systems, infra-red jammer, laser warning systems, air-defence machine guns and improved mobility – all these give it a critical advantage in combat. Like the bilateral contract for SU–30 MKI, the contract for these tanks also has built-in clauses for technology-transfer and joint production. India will buy 310 sophisticated T-90S MBTs under a $700 million deal signed during the Russian Dy. Prime Minister Iliya Klebanov's visit on 15 February 2001.

Fourth is Admiral Gorshkov, the 44,000 tonne former Soviet aircraft carrier, carrying 30 aircrafts that include 24 MIG-29K fighters and 6 helicopters like KA-31. Carriers are crucial for Indian Navy like other navies of the world that base their entire maritime strategy on *sea-control* which these *floating* airfields provide. Defence Minister George Fernandes elaborated on the need for Gorshkov: "Our aircraft carrier is going for a refit. Refitting and equipping it is going to take a long time. And it will take another eight years to build our own aircraft-carrier. Viraat is also to be phased out in the next ten years. India cannot be without aircraft carriers. Therefore, Gorshkov is important for us."[152] Gorshkov's innards will be replaced with equipments procured from a number of countries – Russian propulsion system, Italian radars and Israeli electronics.[153] Indian Naval Chief Admiral Madhavendra Singh, said it will be "70 percent new." The aircraft on board will take off from a relatively short runway using the STOBAR (Short Take Off But Arrested Recovery) technique. Vice-Admiral Madanjit Singh commented: "Acquisition of the Gorshkov will give us strategic capability in the entire Indian Ocean region." Admiral Jayant Nadkarni, former chief of Naval staff, warned: "It will be good only for 10-15 years." Even that, say the officials of the Indian Navy, is good enough since "The price is three times cheaper than the market rate", as pointed out by Admiral Madhavendra Singh.[154]

The Indian Navy acquired two submarines – Sindhurakshak and Sindhushastra from Russia. Sindhushastra is a force multiplier, armed with Klub cruise missiles that can attack targets on both land and sea and is the first -submarine in Indian Navy that can fire cruise missiles even when submerged. Under the billion-dollar deal signed in 1997, Russia is building three multi-purpose "stealth" (Krivak-class) frigates for Indian Navy-INS Talwar, Trishul and Tabar. The stealth feature allows these frigates to "tiptoe" across the Indian Ocean and these frigates are meant for anti-submarine warfare and air defence of warship groups. Equipped with two-stage anti-ship Klub cruise missile, Shtil-1 SAM, Kashtan gun-missile system and a mini-AWACS radar, mounted on KA-31 AEW helicopter, INS Talwar will form the *cutting edge* of Indian fleet for targets on land. The signature reduction devices or "stealth" feature adds to its lethality.[155]

The discussion was held between Defence Minister Fernandes and his counterpart Ivanov during Fernandes' April 2002 Moscow visit, for the new project on the Fifth-generation striker aircraft, which would be the most ambitious and sophisticated *joint defence project* undertaken by both countries so far. Russian officials said the new aircraft would replace the SU-30 and MiG-29 (the fourth-generation jets) and would rival the joint strike Force Fighter, to be built in the US by Lockheed-Martin.[156] Alexei Fedorov, the President of the Irkutsk Aviation Industrial Association, in his interview to *Indian Express* opined: "We have to remember that it is not a plane just for India and Russia. It will be available for any country that has those aviation needs...... For our needs – India and Russia – it will probably be ready for 2015-2020.[157]

For air defence systems, India signed a one-year lease for Russian S–300 PMU systems in 2000. Its targeting and guidance radar can guide a single-stage interceptor missile against counter attacks by aircrafts, cruise and ballistic missiles. Significantly, the US, like the banning of cryogenic engines, barred Russia from the lease of supersonic Tu–22 long-range bombers to India despite Moscow's claim that these are sub-strategic weapons. India will get Kh–22 cruise missiles with conventional warheads.[158]

That both the states "have long-standing mutually beneficial relations in the field of defence within the overall framework of their time-tested ties which are characterised by continuity, trust and mutual understanding, have been corroborated by the above facts."[159]

India's Indigenization Programme

Notwithstanding the stable defence relations between India and the Soviet Union, there was a perceptible drive towards India's self-reliance in the 1980's through its programmes of Main Battle Tank (MBT), Light Combat Aircraft (LCA) and Integrated Guided Missile Development Programme (IGMDP). The Indian drive was reinforced by an urgency in the 1992-95 period when Russia – the "successor-state" to the USSR – was *not responsive*, due to a resultant overall disarray in its defence establishment following the Soviet disintegration, even to comply with the spare parts requirements of India for the Soviet – supplied defence equipments. The urgency was express in the 1995 Indian Policy Statement that predicated a 70 per cent indigeneous procurement rate for defence equipments by 2005. Yet, Indian imports of major conventional weapons from Russia as a percentage of total Indian arms imported during the 1991–95 period figured as 69 per cent.[160] Imports of major conventional weapons by India increased by 72 per cent, in 2002, to the highest level since 1998. India accounted for 5 per cent of all imports of major arms at the global level in 1998–2002, giving it the third place and 10 per cent in 2002, making it the second largest recipient in that year. Russia was India's major arms supplier.[161]

Against the background of the fact that "Indian defense industry floundered for over half a century in its attempts to become 'self-reliant'",[162] India's drive towards indigeneous development of advanced technologies for the nation's defence was evidenced throughout the 1983–2002 period in two fields: A. the two indigenous projects of developing the Arjun Main Battle Tank (approved in 1974) and the Light Combat Aircraft (initiated in 1983) – the former as a replacement for the Soviet-supplied T-55 tanks and the latter as a replacement for the Soviet-supplied MiG-21; and B. the IGMDP, initiated in July 1983, after the successful launch of satellite named Rohini, using the indigenously built SLV-3, India's first Satellite Lauch Vehicle.

A. The MBT Project

Though the Arjun tank was scheduled to be deployed in 1985, the procurement of the highly capable Soviet T-72 main battle tanks (1700 in number) and their indigeneous production slowed down fielding of Arjun's first two prototypes until March 1993.[163] The "Project Rhino" of the mid-1990's for upgrading 1500 of India's T-72 MI tanks to extend their service life until 2015 further delayed the Arjun tank's production, until the Indian government eventually approved in 1997 the serial production of 124 Arjun tanks.[164]

But the main snags with the Arjun tank has been its fifty-eight-ton weight which raises its transportation cost on Indian railways by 150 percent over the normal tank transportation cost[165] and its width extending nine centimeters beyond the sides of Indian tank-carrying flatbed railcars.[166] In addition, its fire control system, developed jointly by a Netherland company and two State-owned companies has revealed inconsistent accuracy during field tests and reportedly "reached its development limit" and is not responsive to further technical inputs; its armour skin lacks protective containers for its on board ammunition; and one of the greatest obstacles is its engine, which was originally the German MTU 838 1,400 hp diesel, and which continually underwent overheating during trials in the desert.[167] MTU eventually offered a new engine to India that increased the end cost of the tank from Rs. 15 crores to Rs. 20 crores.[168] Additionally, since its imported content rose from 27 percent in 1987 to 60 percent in its pre-production prototypes, its projected cost underwent a hike making its final delivery cost presumably between $4.7–$5.3 million each.[169]

The LCA Project

India's Light Combat Aircraft programme (LCA), initiated in 1983 to replace the Soviet-supplied MiG -21, was subjected to an eventual delay due to a major programme to modernize 125 MIG–21BIS planes under project MIG-21 – 93 in March 1996.[170] Its first Phase-1 model did not roll out until 1995.[171] Foreign collaboration in this project had a significant role, as the design of a digital fly-by-wire flight control system was jointly designed by the US based Lockheed Martin and the Hindustan Aeronautics Limited (HAL). The foreign collaboration proved crucial in slowing down its process of development when ten Indian scientists had to leave the Lockheed Martin research facility, under US sanctions[172] post-Pokhran-II tests, without the digital flight control computer. Similarly, the delivery of US-based General Electric F-404 turbofan engines was also discontinued.[173] Consequently, India was under compulsions to accelerate the progress of its indigenous Kaveri GTX-35VS engine project to motivate the production series of the LCA, which is expected to be operational after 2010.[174] Chris Smith argued in 1994: "Although there are many claims to indigenization, in reality foreign technology is present in many of the systems produced in India. Thus, although export prospects are often used as one justification for the LCA, there will be several foreign government to persuade before a sale can be approved, not least the USA if India fails to develop an indigenous engine."[175] A few western analysts have "overestimated" the import-content of the LCA prototype "as high as 70 per cent." But in the West too, aircraft design and manufacturing companies "depend entirely on specialist designers cum manufacturers within the country or outside. Since India has no IDC (or even NIDC e.g. Russia or Israel) as political "ally", India is obliged to obtain supplies of these items of specialist nature from non-allies like the USA, France, Germany etc."[176]

So, the above two projects, initiated to attenuate India's dependence on the Soviet Union/Russia in terms of military hardware, run well behind schedule due to technical snags, acquisitions of superior versions (thus diluting the urgency), modernization programme of the existing version and the sanctions of the foreign collaborator country. "The job of exploring the possibility of bringing about a defense R & D collaboration is, by itself, a difficult task for India in view of the fact that most of the NIDCs and all of the IDCS are US allies, and therefore, unlikely candidates for such a partnership with ..... In any case, from all evidence India continues to single-handedly pursue efforts to bring the development of a MBT, the LCA and the remaining missiles of the IGMDP to a successful completion."[177]

B. The Integrated Guided Missile Development Programme (IGMDP)

The IGMDP was formally launched on 27 July 1983 to develop, instead of making missiles in phases, weapon systems: Prithvi – surface-to-surface defence system; Trishul—the Tactical Core Vehicle System; Nag – the anti-tank missile project; Akash – the Surface to Air defence System and Agni – the Intermediate Range Ballistic Missile Project with the formulation of the Re-Entry Experiment (REX).

During India's temporary suspension of the Agni missile programme, India continued to obtain crucial technology for its ballistic missile programme from its continued development of its space programme: "India's successful test of its polar satellite launch vehicle (PSLV) in March 1996 enables New Delhi to build an ICBM .... The

PSLV is understood to provide the foundation for India's next two long-range ballistic missiles, the Agni-3, which is designed to have a range of 3,700 kilometers and the 4,000 to 5,000 kilometer – range Agni-4, which is also referred to as the Surya."[178] This was substantiated with a longer range prospect (12,000 kilometers) by press reports in May 2000.[179] "Clearly, India's nuclear capability could transcend minimum deterrence and become a significant strategic force, comparable in range to that of the original five nuclear powers."[180]

Against the backdrop of the constraints of foreign collaboration that has proved crucial towards the development of the MBT and the LCA, India's self-reliance in the development of indigenous *technologies*, specific to India's *needs* and *capabilities*, has been perceptible in the instance of IGMDP: the accuracy of 50 meter circular error probable (CEP) in the case of Prithvi defence system; imaging infra red (IIR) as well as millimetric wave (MMW) and the competence in the crucial area of re-entry experiment (REX) technology in the instance of Agni, and radar technology for the Nag missile system have secured India's place in the context of international R & D efforts in missile technology. The perspective of the IGMDP as well as India's compulsions for attaining self-reliance in the technological field have been articulated by the – then director of the DRDO, who masterminded the entire programme:

> 'The multi-project environment of the programme provided a challenge, for five advanced missile systems had to be simultaneously developed... We borrowed ideas that had been developed elsewhere, but adapted them in the light of what we knew were our strengths and what we recognised as the constraints we would be compelled to work under.... The Technology management philosophy of IGMDP is not exclusive to missile development. It represents the national urge to succeed and an awareness that the world is never again to be directed by muscle or money power. In fact, both these powers will flow through technological excellence. Only nations with technological superiority will enjoy freedom and sovereignty."[181]

This discussion highlights the ultimate point of argument that though Indian import of major conventional arms during 1991-95 came around 69 per cent and increased to 72 per cent in 2000, and though there have been high-technology interactions between the two countries since 1997, there are limitations to the Indo-Russian defence cooperation that hardly allow an excessive preoccupation in view of: India's drive towards self-reliance to lessen/alternate its dependence on Russia as exemplified in its efforts to develop the MBT and the LCA, which have been as yet less than successful; and India's efforts to develop indigenous technologies, attuned to its needs and capabilities, to secure a meaningful place in the international R & D efforts in missile technology that have fairly materialized. Moreover, Indo-Russian cooperation in this significant field is in no way exclusive and allows for India's quest for diversification as in a moment of crisis, so in preparations to avert a crisis. Relatedly, to replenish a deficit in ordnance supplies and basic army equipments, India turned to South Africa and Israel both during and after the Kargil War.[182] India made use of Israeli "Litening Pods" that contained an infra-red camera and were installed on Mirage-2000 fighters to conduct night-time attacks and Israel – made Griffen laser guidance kits to precision – guide Spanish – made 250 kilogram bombs to targets.[183] At the end of the Kargil Crisis, India made provisions to buy grenade – launchers from Bulagaria and Russia, lightweight flak jackets from Germany, target acquisition gear from South Africa and Israel, and Russian flame throwers with a 300-400 meters range.[184] The Indian Navy also opted for purchasing Israeli equipments, including Barak ship-defence system.[185]

Nuclear Cooperation

The terms of the Supplementary Agreement, signed in New Delhi in June 1998, were *radically different* from those of the November 1988 Inter-Government Agreement (IGA) for the construction of two light-water VVER-1000 units at Koodankulam: under the Supplementary Agreement, the Russians were to provide the reactor designs and supply the equipments; the NPCIL (Nuclear Power Corporation of India Limited) would build the reactors; Russia would supply enriched uranium for the entire life of the reactors; and *unlike* in the earlier 1988 IGA, India would keep the spent fuel with it under IAEA safeguards. SK Agrawal, Project Director of the Koodankulam Nuclear Power Project (KKNPP) has elaborated: "The entire supply of all the major equipment that will go into this is from the Russian Federation. This is because the soft loan extended by the Russian government is in the form of the supply of material ...the Russian Minister, who was here, was hopeful when he told the press that .... the world will know how safe and efficient these reactors are and he was confident that more units will be built."[186] Subsequent induction of a new light water reactor, based on the latest technology, was contemplated as that would enable the project to produce another additional 6,000 M we of nuclear power by 2020.[187]

The 2000 Declaration envisaged cooperation "in the peaceful use of nuclear energy." The Russian decision to cooperate appeared to be part of an artfully designed nuclear initiative that was unfolded by President Putin at the Millenium Summit of the UN in September 2000. He stressed on two broad themes at the summit: First, the relevance of nuclear technology in the context of expanding global energy requirements as well as of concerns about global warming, largely born of excessive use of coal and other carbon-based fuels. Second, he challenged the orthodox view head-on that greater use of atomic energy would result in proliferation of nuclear weapons, since the "policy of restrictions on nuclear technology transfers to other countries and enhanced international control proved to be insufficient to bar nuclear proliferation."[188] Putin's new approach to nuclear non-proliferation was driven by the new technologies that allow the creation of an "inherently safe" and "proliferation-resistant" civilian nuclear power programmes, pointed out insistently by the Russian Minister for Atomic Energy, Evgeny Adamov in the annual General Conference of the International Atomic Energy Agency (IAEA) of 2000. The IAEA itself was considering a proposal to set up a task force on the "Role of Innovative Nuclear Reactors and Fuel cycles for Sustainable Development."[189] This new approach, significantly, are attuned to India's own approach to nuclear issues.

Russian nuclear cooperation with India are prompted with an eye on seizing a large share in an expanding Indian market for nuclear energy, since it is poised to increase its nuclear energy output to 20,000 MW by 2020. Russian compulsions to exploit the potential for nuclear exports to revive its own nuclear industry were revealed when the Director-General of Russian Electric Power Company, that operates 29 nuclear power plants, admitted on April 12, 1999 that his enterprise "lacks money to pay workers, perform maintenance and repairs, inspect crucial pipes and even buy fuel."[190]

Indo-Russian nuclear cooperation is also *inversely-related* to the state of US – Russian relations. In fact, the Nuclear Suppliers Group (NSG) guidelines were drafted primarily on an American initiative. In a similar context, the Russian interest in reprocessing spent fuel for other countries in face of US opposition, was evidenced in the US offer to release $75 million, contingent on Russia's halting the reprocessing of spent fuel, out of a total of $100 million US aid for joint research in civilian reactors and fuel. Adamov, Russian Minister for Atomic Energy, insisted that Russia can hardly abandon its reprocessing plans in view of the fact that the venture is well-poised to bring in $20 billion over the next 20 years.[191]

India, after Pokhran II, does not technically fit into either category of Non-Nuclear Weapons State (NNWS) or Nuclear Weapons States (NWS) which prompted the Director of Minatom (the Russian Ministry of Atomic Energy) to place India's position as "awkward" and to recommend to the Russian government that nuclear exports to India might be sought without the application of Full-Scale Safeguards (FSS), since it is *technically* neither and in the event of its being accepted as NWS, then even under the NSG, it can escape the FSS anyway.

Russia's continuing and professed nuclear cooperation with India was a *signal* of its emerging assertiveness in the international arena: the contract for supply of 58 tonnes of low-enriched uranium fuel for the US-built Tarapur nuclear power plant was followed by a separate but classified Indo-Russian agreement signed during Putin's 2000 visit to India to cooperate on peaceful uses of nuclear energy. This Russian decision to come to Tarapur's rescue in view of the grave situation, threatening disruption of electricity to India's main industrial belt of Bombay, underlined Russia's *crucial* importance for Indian interests. The US State Department, in a strongly-worded Statement, spoke of Russia's "disregard" of its commitments as a member of the (39-nation) Nuclear Suppliers Group and asked it to "live up to its non-proliferation obligations" in view of Russia's shipment of nuclear fuel to India's Tarapur nuclear power reactors and demanded its cancellation. The tenor of the Statement came close on the heels of an uncharitable remark about India by the US Secretary of Defence Donald Rumsfeld, who, in a TV programme, virtually clubbed India with the likes of Iran and North Korea, while targeting "proliferator" Russia for helping these countries with technologies of destruction.[192] Nikolai Uspensky, Head of the International Security Department of the Russian National Security Council stated that proposed tightening of export control in his country would not affect Russian nuclear supplies to India, despite objections from the US: "we did our best to re-assure our Indian colleagues that we saw no reason for halting nuclear fuel supplies: it is an absolutely clean contract as regards our international obligations."

President Putin stressed that export controls "must become an instrument of protecting Russia's economic interests."[193] Putin's tour of the Bhabha Atomic Research – an unprecedented Indian gesture to a foreign dignitary – substantiated, to quote President Putin, "the special nature" of Indo-Russian ties.

Notably, in the revised guidelines of the IAEA, Para 4(e) has been added to read, "Suppliers reserve the right to apply additional conditions of supply as a matter of national policy"; second, it is also stipulated in para 4(d) that FSS would not be required in case of transfers made to NNWS in "exceptional cases", meaning if the transfer is deemed essential for the safe operation of existing facilities or to contracts drawn prior to April 3, 1992. It is under these *two provisions* that cooperation between India and Russia got under way. The Russian decision to build two 1000 MW light water reactors in Koodankulam is premised on the logic that the contract was made before the cut-off date. Russia's decision to supply low-enriched uranium for Tarapur was made on the logic that it came within Putin's decree to allow supply of nuclear materials in "extraordinary" situations.[194] And the fact that this bilateral nuclear cooperation got momentum during a period, when India was under the sanctions, bears testimony to the depth of mutual understanding—the core basis of their relationship.

Terrorism

In the 1994 Declaration on Further Development and Intensification of Cooperation, India and Russia noted with concern: "Aggressive Nationalism, religious and political extremism, terrorism and separatism present a special threat to territorial integrity and unity of sovereign states and international peace and stability." Mindful of this, both the states were prompted to adopt the Moscow Declaration on Protection of Interests of Pluralistic States that noted with conviction: "...destabilization of relations between ethnic or religious groups, efforts to forcibly displace them, ethnic cleansing and promotion of internal and transborder terrorism, motivated by vested interests, lead to annihilation of all the positive and constructive elements accumulated by mankind during the many thousands of years of its existence." The problems and conflicts India and Russia faced, in Kashmir and Chechnya respectively, got sufficient exposure in both the declarations.

This study would confine the focus to the shared concerns of both the states from international terrorism.

Kashmir

The Soviet disintegration in 1991 and the eventual end of the cold-war rivalry of the two superpowers made India face new security challenges. Afghanistan was the theatre of superpower rivalry for 10 years (1979–89) and the eventual Soviet pull-out (1989), the disintegration of the USSR (1991) and the emergence of new states of Central Asia along its borders have *redefined the nature and scope* of Afghanistan's battle-ground. The political vacuum created after the Soviet pull-out, the inter ethnic war, the failure of mujahedeens in building some form of political stability, the alarming growth of drug-trafficking, the proliferation of small arms leading to "Kalashnikov culture" and a devastated economy – all helped create an ideal atmosphere for militant religious extremism to flourish in Afghanistan.

India fell victim to the destabilizing forces of international terrorism, religious extremism, separatism and secessionism, transborder organized crime and illicit traffic in arms and drugs from their *epicentre* in Afghanistan and their *centre* in Pakistan-occupied Kashmir (PoK). Significantly, Vince Cannistraro, a former CIA (Central Intelligence Agency) Chief of counter terrorism operations and Charles Santos, a fellow intelligence analyst opined in a testimony before the House International Relations Committee on 30 October 2001 that Pakistan's support to the Taliban enabled it to re-locate its training camps for Kashmiri separatists to Afghanistan, thus benefitting from extremist networks in Afghanistan, and getting a *plausible deniability*.[195]

The factors culminated to impact on the spurt in the influx of mercenaries and terrorists from states like Afghanistan, Saudi Arabia, Pakistan, Sudan etc, to Kashmir. In the process, Kashmiri militant outfits like Jammu-Kashmir Liberation Front (JKLF) was marginalized by terrorist groups like Hizbul Mujaheedin, Harkat-ul-Mujaheedin, Tehrik-i-Ahyuay-Khilafat, Lashkar-e-Toiba, Jaish-e-Mohammed (affiliated with the infamous Al Qaeda) etc. The involvement of foreign marcenaries in Kashmir can be gauged from the data that the number of foreign marcenaries killed in Kashmir went up from a meagre 3 in 1991 to 258 in 1997,[196] as well as the number of foreign infiltrators were 436 in 2002, while the number of locals were 175.[197]

Extremists' goal of isolating the people in Kashmir through intimidation was largely achieved as was evidenced in occasional bandhs of long duration imposed on the people by militant outfits, peoples' forbearance taken for granted as a sequel to an innumerable toll of

Kashmiri lives and of Kashmiri leaders, who were considered non-cooperative to their dictates and goals.

The hijacking of the Indian Airlines Flight IC-814 on 24 December 1999 and the following Kandahar deal highlighted the fact that India was held *under siege* by the terrorist forces to compel it to submit to their own terms. A few significant terrorist attacks, among others, in India are: suicide attack on Jammu and Kashmir state Assembly on 10 October 2001; attack on Indian Parliament on 13 December 2001; attack on United States Information Service in Kolkata on 22 January 2002; and suicide attack on Raghunath Temple in Jammu, 30 March 2002.

Chechnya

The crisis in Chechnya started with the November 1991 Decree, by the Chechen leader Dzokhar Dudayev, on the sovereignty of Chechnya, virtually demanding its secession from the Russian Federation. After the Soviet disintegration, the general instability in Russia, lawlessness and weak central power led to the criminalization of the socio-politico-economic situation in Chechnya. The growing conflict between the Russian authoritarian leadership and the militant nationalist leadership of Chechnya catapulted into the Chechen War of 1994–96. The Peace Treaty of 1996 visualized a final agreement on the political status of Chechnya after 2001. But a number of events, e.g., the formation of the Congress of Peoples of Chechnya and Daghestan in April 1998 to form a theocratic state by an alliance of radical religious leaders from Chechnya under the leadership of Chechen leader Shamil Basayev, leaders from Daghestan and a group of mujaheedins under Ibn-Ul-Khattab; the invasion of Daghestan in August 1999 and bombing in Moscow in September 1999 by Chechen rebels-shattered the fragile peace process in Chechnya.[198] The Russian Prime Minister Victor Chernomyrdin in his December 1994 New Delhi visit pointed to the fact that in Chechnya the battle was not between the Chechen and Russian forces, but between Russian forces and mercenaries, mostly from Pakistan and Afghanistan.[199] Mercenaries operating in and around Chechnya believed that if the Mujaheedeens could defeat the Soviet army in Afghanistan, there is no reason why they cannot repeat the same in Chechnya.

The problems the two states face are largely akin in nature as has been pointed out by J.N. Dixit:

> In his interview, granted to me, he asserted: "We are pluralistic societies, we face internal centrifugal forces challenging the

> state structure and we face externally inspired divisive tendencies within our territory."[200]

President Putin, in his address to the Indian Parliament, pointed to another common aspect of the problem: Basing himself on "absolutely true and verified information," he said "the same individuals, the same terrorist organisations are organising and participate in organising, in conducting and igniting terrorist acts from the Philippines to Kosovo, including Kashmir, Afghanistan and Russia's northern Caucasus."[201]

The Russian concerns were inclined towards the grave probability that if terrorists' gameplans were allowed to succeed in Chechnya and in Daghestan, internal tensions aided and abetted by external forces in its five Muslim-majority Caucasian republics-Adygea, Karachay-Cherkessia, Kabardino-Balkaria, North Ossetia and Ingusethia might come to dangerous propertions to threaten the state structure of Russia. Alexander Kadakin, Russian ambassador to India, referred to this point[202] : "As President Putin said, for us the most important thing is to prevent this territory from being used as a bridgehead for attack on Russia and for rocking it from within." Pertinently, Russian Special Services confirmed[203] that M. Khamza, emissary of Osama Bin Laden, met O. Firzani, the head of the "Information Center of Ichkeria" in Copenhagen in 1999 when the latter asked for diverting the end-point of anti-tank guided missiles, mortars and modern firearms, originally intended for the religious extremists in Kosovo, to Chechnya where Arab participants of the Afghan war were invited as instructors. President Putin categorically pointed to President Clinton, when they met on 12 September 1999 in Auckland Summit of the Asia-Pacific Economic Cooperation (APEC) forum: "..... what had happened in Daghestan in August (1999) was not just a resumption of the war that had gone into suspension three years before – it was the beginning of an invasion of Russia. And an invasion not just by Chechen bandits but by the forces of international Islamic terrorism."[204]

Also, Russia's economic stakes are high in Chechnya and Daghestan[205] : Daghestan commands 70 per cent of Russia's Caspian Sea coast, and its capital Makhachkala is Russia's only all-weather port on the Caspian Sea, and, more critically, the oil pipeline from Baku traverses through Daghestan before crossing Chechnya to reach Russia's Black Sea Port of Novorossisk. Instability in this region has already threatened millions of dollars annually to Russia's exchequer.

Equally, terrorists' gameplan in Kashmir challenges India's security as well as undermines India's secular polity: the forced displacement of "almost entire Kashmir Pandit indigenous minority" from Jammu and Kashmir brings out a unique case of ethno-religious cleansing that has long-term implications for the composite socio-cultural set-up and secular polity of J & K, which has been traditionally nurtured through the "Kashmiriyat" mores.

Bilateral Moves

Following the 11 September 2001 incident, senior diplomats from India, Russia, Iran and some Central Asian Republics met in Dushanbe to discuss assistance to the Northern Alliance.[206] The Russian Foreign Ministry Communique on the conversation between the two Foreign Ministers of Russia and India stated, "Russia and India, have reaffirmed to closely coordinate, in the spirit of strategic partnership, joint efforts aimed at curbing the threat of terrorism and religious extremism.[207] Indian Security Advisor to the Prime Minister, Brajesh Mishra discussed, during his mid-September 2001 Moscow visit, current security situation with his Russian counterpart General Vladimir Rusilailo, Defence Minister Sergei Ivanov and Foreign Minister Igor Ivanov and stated, "we are for combating terrorism in a global framework which would include Chechnya and Kashmir. We have an eye on the effect of US military action against the Taliban on India and Russia."[208] According to Russian Foreign Ministry officials, Tehran and New Delhi had special role in shoring up the Northern Alliance.[209] Foreign Minister Jaswant Singh, in his early October 2001 Moscow visit, spoke to his counterpart on the evolving situation in Afghanistan and its fallout. He stated that India was in touch with the Northern Alliance which would play a significant role now and in the future. Briefing the media, a representative of Russian Defence Ministry, stated that the US strikes on Taliban strongholds were likely to "energise" the Northern Alliance.[210] Visiting Dy. Prime Minister Klebanov in mid-October 2001 stated, after his meetings with Indian Defence Minister, Foreign Minister and Principal Advisor to the Prime Minister Brajesh Mishra that while Russia did not join the military action against Osama Bin Laden, "It's very much engaged in other aspects, including the humanitarian assistance. In this regard, we have had the closest contact with India." Both sides also considered ways for a "broad-based, multi-ethnic establishment in the war-torn country which represents the aspirations of all ethnic groups."[211] After his one-day visit to Moscow in early June 2002 to attend the celebration of the 10th anniversary of the Russian Security Council, Brajesh Mishra stated that "we are heartened by the understanding and sympathy from our Russian friends in our fight against cross-border terrorism." Foreign Minister Ivanov stated that Russia was greatly concerned over cross-border terrorism in Kashmir because "Kashmir lies in the middle of the "arch of stability" Russia wants to build from Vancouver to Vladivostok."[212]

The tragedy involving hostage-taking in Moscow in October 2002 as well as the wave of terrorist attacks in India and other countries demonstrate that the international community is faced with an extensive threat by the forces of international terrorism. The India-Russia Joint-Statement of 4 December 2002, following President Putin's New Delhi visit in December 3–5 2002, firmly rejected and condemned "all types of terrorism, based on any ground-political, religious or ideological – and wherever it may exist." It recommended that countermeasures against this menace "should be directed also against those states, entities and individuals who support, fund or abet terrorists or provide them shelter or asylum to engage in cross-border terrorism. There should be no double-standards in the fight against terrorism." Both sides re-affirmed the relevance of the Moscow Declaration on International Terrorism of 6 November 2001, of UN Security Council Resolution 1373 on the fight against terrorism, the need to intensify efforts to finalize in the UN the draft International Convention for the Suppression of Acts of Nuclear Terrorism and the draft Comprehensive Convention against International Terrorism. Their resolve to fight terrorism was reaffirmed by the signing of the Memorandum of Understanding on Combating International Terrorism during the Summit. Both also made positive assessments of the continuing utility of their Joint Working Group (JWG) on Afghanistan, established during President Putin's October 2000 New Delhi visit.[213]

Influence of Gorchakovism in Russia's Foreign Policy Orientations Since 1997

This study has dwelt upon Russia's "looking to the West" policy as well as on Eurasianism, the theory of "Russia First", and Realism as acting and counter-acting influences, all of which moulded Russian foreign policy perceptions at the early phase (1992–95). Students of Russian foreign policy noted that in recent years, Foreign Minister of Tsar Alexander II, Aleksandr Gorchakov (1798–1883) was prominently reinstated in Russian Foreign policy thinking. At one of the many Gorchakov conferences, discussing the principles of his diplomatic efforts, the Russian Foreign Minister Igor Ivanov explained that "the main thing is that we have started *not only to interpret*, but also to *implement his legacy* which is remarkably suited to (our) current tasks ..."[214] The wide currency of Gorchakovism in Russia today has to be explained by the largely identical international challenges, faced by Moscow in the post-Cold War years, to the problems encountered by St. Petersburg after the Crimean War in the post-1856 era. Both eras had to confront *unfavourable* changes in the international distribution of power and the changes were largely the outcome of *inferior* Russian economic system.

The foreign-policy concepts of Gorchakov or Gorchakovism, consisted of three pillars: First, a temporary reversal of the foreign – domestic dichotomy of the preceding decades to lay stress on domestic reforms to be at par with other leading powers of the time; Second, to ensure the domestic development process, Gorchakovism prescribed a foreign policy based on the twin principles of *predictability* as opposed to uncertainty and *non-aggressiveness* as opposed to open hostility; and the Third was a more *cautious* foreign policy principle – a policy of revisionism to secure a return to the old order. The contextual reference was to annul the most harmful clause of the Paris Peace Treaty of 1856, the demilitarization of the Black Sea.

It must be clear that the main thrust of the currency of Gorchakovism in Russia today is directed towards the West, towards facilitating a significant *rift* between the NATO and the OSCE, the CE and the EU – a strategy to *overturn* the unipolar trend in the international system. The relevance of this Russian strategy for Indo-Russian relations is evident in both countries' Declarations and Joint Statements towards the establishment of a "multipolar world based on the sovereign equality of all states," as in Indo-Russian Joint Statement of 22 December, 1998 and in the Declaration of Strategic Partnership in 2000; and towards strengthening the "role of the *United Nations* organization" as well as "the efficiency and further *democratization of this organization*" (Declaration on Further Development and Intensification of Cooperation ...of 30 June 1994). Russia's adherence to the Gorchakovian foreign policy principle of non-aggressiveness is evidenced in the 2000 Declaration: "The strategic partnership between the two sides is not directed against any other state or group of states, and does not need to create a military political alliance." This policy is well-attuned to India's traditional stance and is more relevant in the context of post-Cold War realities. Another Gorchakovian foreign policy principle of predictability is apparent in Russia's transparency about its close relations with the US and its partnership with China, while seeking India's cooperation as a partner.

So far our discussion has broadly noted the currents and cross-currents in the bilateral relationship from initial uncertainties towards a stable one that culminated in the Strategic Partnership Declaration, while accommodating each other's compulsions in the perspective of post-Cold War realities. In this sphere of political and strategic dimension, the relationship was broadly one of undeterred growth, *unlike* in the sphere of economic relations.

The continuity factor in Indo-Russian relations, as we have noted earlier, is persistently present despite the preponderance of the Russian "Looking to the West" policy in initial years: both countries draw upon "their rich and fruitful tradition of cooperation in various fields accumulated over half a century", and emphasize the fundamental and lasting importance of the 1993 Treaty of Friendship and Cooperation "which was a *continuation* of the bilateral Treaty of Peace, Friendship and Cooperation of 9 August 1971."

Continuity is evident in two key areas of India's interests:

> "One is military cooperation – a very vital area. Another is Kashmir, Russia has continued the Soviet legacy of supporting India's position on Kashmir", as Dr. Jayantanuja Bandyopadhyay pointed out in his interview granted to me.[215]

Both the countries have taken into serious and active consideration the change factor also, while striving for a mature relationship: "… it's clear that both we and Indian partners have to take into consideration the fact that the world has changed, Russia has changed, the balance of force in the world has changed and so have some of our priorities"[216] – President Putin reiterated prior to his New Delhi visit in 2000. But notable is the fact that both countries started the process of searching out the *islands* of commonalities of interests in the *sea-change* of post-Cold War realities.

Ex-Prime Minister Narasimha Rao did take note of the change as well as the continuity factors, while answering to my relevant question:

> "On the whole I would say that we did not have any insurmountable difficulties in *changing over*, in view of the *traditional* friendly relations between the two countries, as such. To the extent the system on the other side changed completely, necessary adjustments had to be made, and they were made, after a short initial groping."

He too stressed on areas of common interests in the perspective of change and on common task:

> "For instance, it was realised very early that we had a common task in the management of pluralities. We had a lot of interaction on this subject. Thus we lost no time in *identifying common areas of dialogue* and endeavour in the new situation."[217]

There was, and remains, a national consensus in both countries on the fundamentals of the bilateral relationship. President Putin stressed in his October 2000 New Delhi visit on the fact that the two countries have never clashed even once nor has there ever been any serious dispute or contradiction. In the 37th Munich Conference on Security Policy, in February 2-4, 2001, Brajesh Mishra, National Security Advisor and Principal Secretary to the Prime Minister of India, stated on "Indo-Russia Relations:

> "A number of objective factors have shaped the congruence of outlook and shared concerns, which have determined the course of Indo-Russia relations:

- ... There is a compelling geostrategic logic for close Indo-Russian relations, which has been clearly grasped by every leadership of both our countries, regardless of its political or economic ideology.
- The two countries have a common interest in the development of a multi-polar world based on a cooperative security order. In fact, even in the bipolar construct of the Cold War, the development of India's relations with the Soviet Union was perhaps one of the *first expressions of multipolarity*.
- We do not share a border, but we do share neighbours and a number of security threats from across our borders ... We understand Russia's real security concerns in Europe, *Central Asia and the Caucasus* and about the destabilizing effects of

undermining existing arms control and arms limitation treaties. We receive the *same understanding from Russia on our concerns.*

- Russia's "National Security Concept" of January 2000 and its "Foreign Policy Concept" of June 2000 enunciate a worldview similar to that of India."[218]

We conclude this chapter with an answer to the view on Indo-Russian relations that the relationship only comes down to Declarations and that only Declarations may not mean too much:

(but) "What really matters is experience. Russia is a tried and tested friend of India"[219] Brahma Chellaney was categorical on the valid ground of the relationship, in his interview.

Notes and References

1. *Mikhail Gorbachev, Perestroika: New Thinking for our country and the world*, harper and Row, New York, 1998, p. 134.
2. *New York Times*, 18 June, 1992. emphasis added.
3. Paul Marantz, "Russia's Foreign Policy During Yeltsin's second Term" *Communist and Post — Communist Studies*, Vol. 30, No. 4, 1997, pp.345-351.
4. Hari Vasudevan, "Perspectives on Disintegration and Integration in the CIS : Andrei Kozyrev and the Making of Russian Foreign Policy", in Arun Banerjee (ed.) *Integration, Disintegration and the World Order*, School of International Relations and Strategic Studies, Jadavpur University, Kolkata, 1995, p. 92.
5. *Rossiskaia Gazeta*, 1994 cited in Marantz. *op. cit.*
6. *Nezavisimaya Gazeta*, 28 March, 1992. See Alexander Rahr, "Atlanticists' versus 'Eurasians'" in Russian Foreign Policy," *RFE/RL Research Report*, Vol. 1, No. 22, 29 May. 1992, *www.referl.org*
7. See Alexander Rahr-Joachim Krause, *Russia's New Foreign Policy*. Deutsche Gesellchaft Fur Auswartige Politike, Bonn, 1995, p. 8.
8. Dmitry V. Shlapentokh, "Eurasianism: Past and Present", *Communist and Post — Communist Studies*, Vol. 30, No. 2, 1997, pp. 129-1517.
9. Madhavan K. Palat, "Eurasianism as an Ideology for Russia's Future", *EPW* Special Number, 18 December 1993, pp. 2799-2828. For details on prevalent ideologies in contemporary Russia, see MK Palat, *Ideological Choices in Post — Soviet Russia*, Delhi Policy Group, New Delhi, 1997.
10. See Joseph L. Nogee — R. Judson Mitchell, *Russian Politics: The Struggle for a New Order*, Allyn and Bacon, London, Boston, 1997. p. 157.

11. *CDPSP, Vol. XIIV,* No. 13, 29 April, 1992, p. 2.
12. Alexander Rahr — Joachim Krause, *op. cit.*, p. 9.
13. Cited in Vasudevan, *op. cit.*, p. 96.
14. See Pavel K. Baev, *The Russian Army in a Time of Troubles,* International Peace Research Institute, Oslo, SAGE Publications, London, 1996, p. 30.
15. P. Truscott, *"Russia First: Breaking With West", op. cit.*, P. 37. See Chapter-2, fn. 8.
16. *CDPSP,* Vol. XLIX, No. 32, 9 September, 1992, p. 5.
17. Neil Malcolm "Russian Foreign Policy Decision—Making", in Peter Shearman (ed.) *"Russian Foreign Policy Since 1990"* Westview Press, Boulder, 1995, p. 41.
18. *Independent,* 24th March, 1995.
19. Truscott, *"Russia First", Op. cit.*
20. *"Russia's New Foreign Policy", Op. cit. p. 21.*
21. Hari Vasudevan, "Russian Foreign Policy and India's Response after Pokhran II", in Anindya Majumdar (ed.) *Nuclear India Into the New Millennium.* Lancer's Books, New Delhi, 2000, p. 307.
22. J.N. Dixit, *"My South Bloc Years",* P. 215. See Chapter 2, fn. 46.
23. Anita Inder Singh, "India's Relations with Russia and Central Asia", *International Affairs,* Vol. 71, No. 1, 1995, p. 72, Note 14.
24. *Hindustan Times,* 27th January 1993.
25. Andrei Kozyrev, *Preobrazheniia,* Moscow, 1995, pp. 248-49, cited in Hari Vasudevan, *Russia — India — China Cooperation. The shaping of a Notion in Russia Foreign Policy,* Paper presented at the Seminar on "Building a New Asia : Problems and prospects of Regional and Pan — Asian Cooperation" for Maulana Abul Kalam Azad Institute of Asian Studies (MAKAIAS), Kolkata on 29-31 March 2004.
26. Shams Ud-Din Bhaswati Sarkar "Indo-Russian Relations An Overview" in Shams Uddin (ed.). *"India and Russia"* p. 2. See Chapter 2, fn. 2.
27. Cited in Girish Mathur, " New Russian Elite Reviews Ties with India" *Patriot,* 27 April, 1992.
28. *The Hindu,* 3 August, 1992.
29. *Indian Express,* 5 January 1992.
30. *The Hindu,* 3 May, 1992.
31. Dixit, *op. cit.*, p. 210.
32. Cited in *Patriot,* 10 September, 1992.
33. BBC, Short Wave Broadcasts (SWB) SU/WO, 215 A/3, 31 June, 1992.
34. *(SWB) FE/1372 A1/2,* 5 May 1992.
35. BBC, *SWB, SU/1484 C2/5,* 12 September, 1992.
36. BBC, *SWB, SU/1483/ A1/3,* 11 September, 1992.
37. BBC, *SWB, SU/1511, A1/2,* 14 October, *Su 1513 C2/3,* 6 October, *Su/1516, A1/3,* 20 October, 1992.
38. Yuri Sigov, VEK Journal, 6 October, 1992, Cited in AG Noorani, "Boris in India : No Time for Sweet Talk", *Statement,* 22 January 1993.

39. *Asian Defence Journal*, January 1993, p. 154.
40. Ednond Dantes, "An Indepth Look at the Asia—Pacific Air Force and Future Procurement", *Asian Defence Journal*, January 1993. p. 23.
41. BBC, *SWB, FE/1600, A1/4*, 30 January 1993 and *FE/1601 C1/7*, 1 February, 1993.
42. *SWB, FE 1601, C1/7*, 1 February, 1993.
43. *Annual Report* of the Ministry of Defence, 1992-93.
44. Arundhati Roy, "Indo—Russian Military Ties in the Post—Cold War Period: some Observation", *Jadavpur Journal of International Relations*, Vol. 2, 1996, p. 167.
45. *Annual Report*, Ministry of Defence (MOD), 1994-95.
46. Lt. general R.K. Jasbir Singh, (ed.) *Indian Defence Yearbook*, 1998-99 Gay Printers, New Delhi.
47. *MOD Report*, 1994-95.
48. Dixit, *op. cit.*, p. 215.
49. *Ibid.*
50. My Interview of J.N. Dixit on 17-12-2002, in India International Centre, New Delhi.
51. My interview of Dixit, *op. cit.*
52. *The Hindu*, 30 January 1993.
53. *The Hindu*, 26 January 1993.
54. Text is from *www.meadev.nic.in*, Emphasis added.
55. *The Statesman*, "Special Relationship", Editorial, 9 July, 1994.
56. *The Hindu*, 3 July 1994.
57. I met Hon'ble ex-prime Minister Narsimha Rao at his New Delhi residence on 7, December 2002 with a questionnaire and he sent me his written responses.
58. His letter dated 12th September, 2003.
59. Izvestia, cited in *Hindu*, 5 July 1993.
60. Strobe Talbott, *The Russia Hand*, *op. cit.*, p. 83. See Introduction.
61. *Hindu*, 18 July, 1993.
62. *The Telegraph*, 19 August 1993. Also see Maya Chadda, "Indo-Russian Relations in the Post-Cold War Era", in Hafeez Malik ed. in *The Roles of the US, Russia and China in the New World Order* Macmillan, London, 1997, p. 114.
63. Glavkosmos officials claimed that Indian government possessed a two-year old letter from the US administration, clearly explaining that the project did not violated MTCR norms and cleared participation for General Dynamics. V. Radyuhin "Trade War Now?" *Hindu*, 26 April 1992. See Atul Aneja, "In Defence of Cartels", *Hindu*, 24 April 1992.
64. Cited in Ramesh Thakur, *The Politics and Economics of India's Foreign Policy*, Oxford University Press, New Delhi, 1994, N. 42, p. 141.
65. Jyotirmoy Banerjee, "Indo-Russian Relations. The Cryogenic Rocket Deal" *Jadavpur Journal of International Relations*, Vol. 1, 1995, pp. 121-129.

66. BBC, *SWB, SU/1795, S1/2*, 16 September, 1993.
67. BBC, *SWB, SU/WO 230 A/8*, 15 May, 1992.
68. *Ibid, A/17*, 15 May, 1992.
69. *Hindustan Times*, 9 August, 1992.
70. *BBC, SWB, SU/1747i*, 22 July, 1993.
71. *BBC, SWB, SU/1749 A1/2*, 24 July 1993.
72. My interview of Dixit, *op. cit.*
73. My interview of Jasjit Singh in Indian Express Office in New Delhi, on 12.12.2002.
74. *BBC, SWB, SU/1959 S1/5*, 30 March, 1994.
75. In his written response to me.
76. Dixit, *op. cit.*, p. 216.
77. Reuter Report, *Statesman*, 28 May 1997.
78. Sergei Baburin, "NATO Expansion: Greatest Threat to Russia", *Statesman*, 23 June 1997.
79. Mikhail Gorbachev, "NATO Expansion-A Losing Proposition", UNI Report, cited in *Statesman* , 16 April 1997.
80. *SWB, SU/3679 B/5*, 30 October 1999.
81. Anatol Lieven, "Ham-Fisted Hegemon: The Clinton Administration and Russia", *Current History*, October 1999, pp. 307-315.
82. *Ibid.*
83. Victor Gobarev, "Russia-NATO Relations after, the Kosovo Crisis: Strategic Implications", *The Journal of Slavic Military Studies*, Vol. 12. no. 3 (September 1999). reproduced in *Strategic Digest*, February 2000, pp. 147-158.
84. *FBIS-USR-93-037*, 25 March 1993.
85. Izvestia, 26 November 1993, cited in. Hannes Adomeit, "Russia as a 'great power' in world affairs: images and reality", *International Affairs.* (71.1), 1995, pp. 35-68.
86. ITAR-TASS, 5 January 1994, Cited in *ibid.*
87. The text provided by the Information Department of the Russian Embassy in New Delhi. Emphasis added.
88. *Ibid.*
89. Igor S. Ivanov, *The New Russian Diplomacy,*" The Nixon Center and Brookings Institution Press, Washington DC, 2002. p. 100.
90. *Keesing's Record of 'World Events*, 1996 and 1997.
91. Igor Khripunov and Anupam Srivastava, "Contending with the "Bearish" Arms Market: US-Indian Strategic Cooperation and Russia" in Garry K. Bertsch (ed.) *Engaging India: US Strategic Relations with the World's Largest Democracy*, Routledge, New York, 1999, p. 243.
92. *Indian Defence Yearbook*, 1998–99.
93. *Ibid.*
94. *MoD Report*, 1996–97.
95. Defence News, cited in *Telegraph*, 9 January, 1997.

96. *Yearbook*, 1998–99.
97. *Ibid.*
98. *Statesman*, *Indian Express*, 20 June 1998.
99. *Indian Express*, 12 June 1998.
100. *Hindustan Times*, 30 July 1998.
101. Joint statement after Primakov visit, text is from *www.meadev.nic.in*
102. *Times of India*, 6 November, 1999.
103. Boris Yeltsin "President Yeltsin's Address to Russian Diplomats", (The Text), *International Affairs*, Vol. 44. No. 3, 1998, pp. 1–6.
104. H. Vasudevan "Russia Foreign Policy and India's Response after Pokhran-II", *op. cit.*
105. *Hindustan Times*, 4 June 1998.
106. *Statesman*, 3 September 1998.
107. *Indian Express*, 12 November, 1998.
108. Sumitra Rajagopalan, "India is Now a Power in Russia's Vision of a Multipolar World", *Times of India*, 12 June 1998.
109. Nezavisimaya Gazeta, 15 May 1998, cited in A.G. Noorani, "Russian Views–I", *Statesman*, 7 January 2000, emphasis added.
110. Izvestia, 17 June 1998, cited in "Russian Views–II", *Statesman*, 8 January 2000.
111. It is worth mentioning that leading scholars like Professor Ma Jiali of China, Professor Devendra Kaushik of India and Dr. R. Rybykov of Russia, among others, founded on July 30, 1999 in New Delhi the "Triangular association" – a non–governmental group–that pledged itself "to develop mutual understanding and cooperation among the three nations." Mary Bradman, "Eurasian Cooperation: The Future for Humanity" in J.K. Roy (ed), *Asia Annual 2000* Maulana Abul Kalam Azad Institute of Asian Studies, Calcutta, 2000.
112. *CDPSP*, Vol. 50, No. 51, 1998, p. 25–26.
113. Evgenii Primakov, *Gody v bol'shoi politike*, Moscow, 1999, pp. 207ff., cited in Hari Vasudevan *op. cit.* 2004.
114. My interviews taken in New Delhi of: K. Subrahmanyam at his residence on 7.12.2002; J.N. Dixit, at Indian International Centre on 17.12.2002. Brahma Chellaney, at Centre for Policy Research, on 11.12.02. Jasjit Singh, at Indian Express office, on 12.12.2002.
115. A.M. Kadakin "Russian-Indian Relations: A View into the Third Millenium in V.D. Chopra (ed.) "*Indo-Russian Relations.*" See Chapter 2 , fn. 137.
116. Moscow, December 23, 2002 (PTI) *www.defenceindia.com*
117. My interview of Hon'ble Ex-Prime Minister Narsimha Rao, *op. cit.*
118. Both quotations cited in *Times of India*, 29 May 1999.
119. Vladimir Radyuhin, Hindu, 10 July 1999.
120. A. Nikolayev, "Indo-Russian Cooperation in the 21st Century," *Indian Defence Review*, January–March 2002, Vol. 17(1), p. 32. Emphasis added.
121. Cited in Radyuhin, *op. cit.* Emphasis added.

122. Strobe Talbott, *Russia Hand, op. cit.*, p. 418.
123. *Ibid.* p. 419.
124. *Ibid.* p. 396.
125. Cited in Igor Ivanov, *The New Russian Diplomacy, op. cit.*, p. 102.
126. *Ibid.*, p. 103.
127. *Ibid.*, p. 104.
128. Cited in Henri De Grossouvre, "Paris, Berlin, Moscow: Prospects for Eurasian Cooperation", *World Affairs*, Vol. 8, No. 1, January-March 2004, (pp. 44-56). [Translated by Come Corpentier de Gourdon]. p. 52, emphasis added.
129. Ivanov, *op. cit.*, p. 122.
130. Joint Statement on Strategic Issues, 6 November 2001. *http://www.meadev.nic.in/speeches*
131. *Hindu*, 28 June 2000.
132. *Hindu*, 29 April 2000.
133. Baidya Bikash Basu, "Putin's visit and Future of Indo-Russian Defence Cooperation," *Strategic Analysis*, December 2000, pp. 1763-1769.
134. *The Statesman*, 5 May 2001.
135. *Hindu*, 22 June 2001.
136. Text of the Declaration *www.meadev.nic* in Emphasis added.
137. The interview *www.india-today.com*
138. Alexander M. Kadakin, "Indo-Russian Relations", *op. cit.*, p. 374.
139. *Statesman*, 17 April, 1996.
140. *Indian Defence Yearbook* 1998-99.
141. The text of Joint Statement *www.meadev.nic.in*
142. Felix N. Yurlov, "Russia: Problems of Security in the Post-Cold War World." *World Affairs*, Vol. 4, No. 2, April-June 2000, pp. 42-56. Emphasis added.
143. My interview of S.K. Lamba, 2002.
144. My interview of Jasjit Singh, 2002.
145. *Statesman*, 2 June 2001.
146. Text is from *http://meaindia.nic.in/event/2002.*
147. *Indian Defence Yearbook*, 1998–99.
148. In my discussions with Ex-Defence Secretary N.N. Vohra in New Delhi in December 2002, he stressed on this point of India's dependence on defence supplies from Russia, which is unlikely to change in the near future.
149. See Stephen Blank, "*Challenging the New World Order: The Arms Transfer Policies of the Russian Republic*", Strategic Studies Institute, U.S. Army War College, October, 1993. p. 13.
150. *Defence Yearbook*, 2002.
151. From *www.globalsecurity.org/military/world/russia*
152. George Fernandes's interview in October 2000. *www.india_today.com*
153. Technical data on Gorshkov are from *www.globalsecurity.org/military/world/russia.*

154. Quotations are from *India Today*, 15 December 2003, Gorshkov deal has been signed on 20 January, 2004.
155 . Technical data are from *www.defenceindia.com/navy.html*
156. *Hindu*, 8 November 2001.
157. *Indian Express*, 23 April 2002.
158. *Defence Yearbook*, 2002.
159. *MoD Annual Report*, 1999–2000.
160. SIPRI Yearbook: *Armaments, Disarmament and International Security"*, Oxford University Press, New York, 1996, p. 482, Table 11.8.
161. *SIPRI year book 2003*, p. 446.
162. Jerome M. Conley, *Indo-Russian Military and Nuclear Cooperation: Lessons and Options for US Policy in South Asia*, Lexington Books, New York, 2001, p. 65.
163. Eric Arnett (ed.) *Military Capacity and the Risk of War: China, India, Pakistan and Iran*, OUP for SIPRI, 1997, p. 266.
164. Rahul Bedi, "Purchase of Latest T-905 will kill the Arjun Tank", *Asian Age*, 4 November 1999.
165. *Ibid.*
166. Rahul Bedi "Mixed Fortunes for India's Defence Industrial Revolution" in *Jane's International Defence Review*, May 1999, p. 24.
167. Rahul Bedi, "Indian Army's Tanks Requirements Viewed," *Asian Age*, 13 July, 1999.
168. Rahul Bedi, *Asian Age*, 4 November 1999.
169. Rahul Bedi, *Jane's International Defence Review*, May 1999, p. 24.
170. *Indian Defence Yearbook*, 1998-99.
171. Wg. Cdr. N.K. Pant, "Light Combat Aircraft Unduly Long Wait", IPCS Article no. 257, 6 Sept. 1999, *http://www.ipcs.org/issues/articles.*
172. Rahul Bedi, May 1999, p. 27.
173. Wg. Cdr. N.K. Pant, *op. cit.*
174. Rahul Bedi, May 1999, p. 27.
175. Chris Smith, *India's Ad-hoc Arsenal*, SIPRI, 1994, p. 143.
176. Air Vice-Marshall Samir K. Sen, *Military Technology and Defence Industrialization: The Indian Experience*, Manas Publications, New Delhi 2000, p. 176, n.18 (IDC, i.e. Industrially Developed Country and NIDC-Newly Industrially Developed Country).
177. *Ibid.*, p. 154.
178. Raju G.C. Thomas, *India's Nuclear Security*, Lynne Rienner/SAGE, 2000.
179. "India Set to Test Launch ICBM, says Reports", 5 may, 2001 *http://www.timesofindia.com*
180. Raju G.C. Thomas, *op. cit.*, p. 178.
181. APJ Abdul Kalam, *Wings of Fire*, Orient Longman, Universities Press, New Delhi, 1999, p. 174.
182. K.P. Nayar, "Merchants of Death Descend on Delhi", *Telegraph*, 11 October 1999.

183. Atul Aneja, "Israeli Night Fighting Pods for IAF", *Hindu*, 13 October, 1999.
184. V.P. Malik, *Statesman*, 14 October 1999 and Keith Flory-Srinjoy Chowdhury, *Statesman*, 21 October 1999.
185. Atul Aneja, *Hindu*, 4 September 1999.
186. Excerpts from an interview of S.K. Agrawal, to T.S. Subramnian in his office at the KKNPP site on 13 March 2004; *Frontline*, 23 April 2004. p. 110-111. The Data are from T.S. Subramanian, "Setting standards", *Ibid.*
187. P.L. Dash, "Indo-Russian Relations", *Economic and Political Weekly*, 18 January, 2003, p. 193.
188. Cited in C. Raja Mohan, "Russian nuclear exports: a new approach," *The Hindu*, 10 October 2000.
189. *Ibid.*
190. Cited in Manpreet Sethi, "Indo-Russian Nuclear Cooperation: Opportunities And challenges", *Strategic Analysis*, Vol. XXIV, No. 9, 2000, pp. 1757-1761.
191. *Nuclear Engineering International*, April 2000, cited in *Ibid.*
192. *Hindustan Times*, 18 February, 2001.
193. *Hindu*, 24 February, 2001.
194. Sethi, *op. cit.*
195. *Times of India*, 5 October 2001.
196. K. Warikoo, "Islamist Mercenaries and Terrorism in Kashmir" in *Himalayan and Central Asian Studies*, Vol. 21, No. 2, April–June 1998, pp. 35–57.
197. K. Santhanam-Sreedhar, *Jihadis in Jammu and Kashmir: A Portrait Gallery*, IDSA, New Delhi, 2003, p. 34.
198. See Anatol Lieven, "Through a Distorted Lens: Chechnya and the Western Media", *Current History*, October 2000, pp. 321-328.
199. *Asian Recorder*, Vol. XXXX, 1994. In his interterview granted to me, Prof. Felix N. Yurlov also stressed on this fact, as well as on the inseparability of Chechnya from the Russian Federation. I took his interview on 31 March, 2004, Kolkata.
200. My interview of Dixit, *op. cit.*
201. *Visit of the President of the Russian Federation to India* October 2.5.2000, Ministry of External affairs, New Delhi.
202. A.M. Kadakin "Indo-Russian Relations" *Journal of Indian Ocean Studies*, December, 2001.
203. Cited in Irina Koudryashova, "Terrorism in Chechnya Components and Ideology" in Om Prakash Mishra-Sucheta Ghosh (eds.) *Terrorism and Low Intensity Conflict in South Asian Region*, Manak Publishers, New Delhi, 2003, p. 127.
204. Strobe Talbott, *Russia Hand*, *op. cit*, p. 359.

205. See Rajan Menon-G.E. Fuller, "Russia's Ruinous Chechen War," *Foreign Affairs*, March-April 2000, pp. 32-44.
206. *Hindu*, 16 September 2001.
207. *Ibid.*, 18 September 2001.
208. *Hindustan Times*, 19 September 2001.
209. *Hindu*, 1 October 2001.
210. *Ibid.*, 9 October 2001.
211. *Statesman*, 16 October 2001.
212. *Hindu*, 6 June 2002.
213. India-Russia Joint Statement, New Delhi-December 04, 2002 *http://meaindia.nic.in/event/2002*
214. Igor Ivanov, *Rossiya, i lmir na rubezhe tysyacheleti*, presentation delivered at the MGIMO Gorchakov Lectures, Moscow, 23 May 2000, cited in Flemming Splidsboel–Hansen, "Past and Future Meet: "Aleksander Gorchakov and Russian Foreign Policy," *Europe–Asia Studies*, Vol 54, No. 3 2002, pp. 377–396. Emphasis added.
215. My interview of Dr. Bandyopadhyay, Emeritus Professor, in the Department of International Relations, Jadavpur University, Kolkata in March, 2003.
216. Putin's interview in *www.india_today.com*
217. In his written response to my questionnaire, emphasis added.
218. Text is from *www.meadev.nic.in/ speeches* (emphasis added).
219. In his interview to me.

Chapter 4

Central Asia: The Meeting Ground

Russia, India and the Central Asian States: Common Political Orientations

To start with, it must be duly noted that focalization of the Central Asian region as a centre of gravitation for geostrategic goals, that include geopolitical and geoeconomic interests of major global and regional powers, was activated as and when the five erstwhile Soviet Republics of Kazakhstan, Kyrgyzstan, Tajikistan, Uzbekistan and Turkmenistan were virtually pushed to become new independent entities, that were ill-prepared for their new uncertain identities. The post-Soviet decade for Russia was primarily characterized by salvage- operations on its part, to rescue, the remnants of past influences in the post-Soviet space as well as to stall "intrusions" of external forces in the process.

The extent and levels of Russia's interests and stakes in its "near abroad" are overwhelmingly much larger and more intensive than India's because they were a part of a common entity for well over a century since these regions were included in the domain of the Czarist Russia in the later part of the 18th century. India's vital interests in the region were largely safeguarded by its friendly relations with the Soviet Union and consequent on its disintegration, altogether new dimensions of threats to its integrity are thrust upon India that relate it vitally to Russia's threat perceptions vis-à-vis forces of destabilization emanating from the Afghan imbroglio that engulf the Central Asian region.

Central Asia in Russia's Security Perspective

Russia remains a centripetal force for the newly independent republics of Central Asia (CARs) in view of the long tradition of their dependencies on Russia in fields of economic activities and security. Its very presence "impacts massively", as Zbigniew Brezezinski has noted, on the CARs within the vast post-Soviet Eurasian space. Another noted analyst has determined Russia's Near Abroad as a "unipolar" region in view of the overwhelming preponderance of Russia, characterized by "asymmetric interdependence." He indicates the propensity of the dominant strategy of the regional states toward Russia will be "'bandwagoning' (accommodation), not 'balancing' (resistance)", emphasizing that even in their efforts to diversify economic and political transactions to attenuate their dependence on Russia, their guidelines will be that they inhabit a zone that Russia considers vital for its national security.[1]

Initially, Russia ignored Central Asia's relevance to its overall security perspective, since it was made to believe that its security was likely to be more guaranteed by the western powers, in lieu of its favourable gestures towards their interests. It ultimately led to the resultant *dismal shrinkage* of its previous area of influence in the post-Soviet space. Russian think tanks even questioned the prospect of the CARs to become partners of Russia on its way towards economic transformation: the specialists of the Russian think tank MGIMO viewed that a Russo-Asian Union was undesirable because of the "'danger of the proclaimed' alliance for reform" degenerating into an anti-reform alliance, with the Conservative elites remaining in power in Central Asia.[2]

Russia underwent a process of disillusionment with the West, having been continually denied of expected reciprocal gestures from them towards its claim to be treated on an equal footing in every sphere of global interactions.

There was an almost *simultaneous pattern* of reawakening to its vital stakes, specifically in its southern near abroad, in view of three incidents: the outbreak of the Moldova-Transdniestria war and the Georgian Civil War in early 1992 and in both the cases the opposition, constituted of Communists and nationalists, supported in Duma the Transdniestrians over the Moldovan government and Abkhaz population over the Georgian government.

The third one is the Tajik civil war that broke out in May 1992 and the ouster of President Nabiyev by opposition forces there. By then, the Russian political elite consolidated their stance on the pragmatic nationalistic idea that Russia should retain influence in the near abroad and take responsibility for ending the conflict, that may necessitate military action.

Here lay several overriding reasons for Russia's taking cognizance of the stakes involved:

(a) Russia's role in Eurasia "consists, above all, in stabilising herself and the contiguous states whose equal and intensive cooperation . . . will restore to the continent the missing 'critical mass' of stability."[3]

(b) The presence of 10 million ethnic Russians in the CARs requires Russia to retain a special role for itself in this "zone of responsibility."[4] It is not solely an internal affair of regional governments but a legitimate concern of the Russian Federation for reasons both "symbolic and tangible." The limits of Russia's zone of "vital interests' are dictated essentially by its own assessments of the state of affairs in its southern near abroad, as has been emphatically pointed out by Andrannik Migranyan.[5] Menon also noted that the post-Soviet space "constitutes Russia's geostrategic, as opposed to legal, boundary."[6]

(c) Russia's apprehension of an eventual vacuum in its southern peripheries has been due to "Asiaticism"(sic): "We must prevent a drift to "Asiaticism" or we may risk, say, allowing Islamic fundamentalism or other extremists in the region to bring Central Asia under their sway."[7] Three methods have been identified towards this end: (i) by manipulating the economic dependence of some republics, the presence of ethnic Russians and Russian army on the territory of other republics, and in still others, the inter-republican ethno-political and border conflicts;[8] (ii) by peaceful integration, since the modern world is an interdependent world, Russia must learn the art of integration from the EU,[9] and (iii) by a balanced admixture of the two, while the newly independent republics should be drawn "into the OSCE process with all its lofty principles", yet Russia reserves "the use of forcible methods; economic and military."[10]

(d) Russia's apprehension of a continual shrinkage of its vital interest-zones was largely motivated by the West's NATO enlargement moves in Eastern Europe and in the Baltics that would bring the Atlantic Alliance to its Kaliningrad frontier and within 150-kilometers of St. Petersburg. An analysis by the Russian Foreign Intelligence denoted NATO as a defence alliance, with massive offensive capabilities wedded to a bloc mentality.[11] Russia's process of disillusionment with the West started when categorical assurances by James Baker, the then US Secretary of State, to President Gorbachev and Foreign Minister Shevardnadze on February 9, 1990[12]: "If we maintain a presence in Germany, there would be no extension of NATO's jurisdiction for forces of NATO one inch to the east" was eventually belied. The disillusionment impacted enormously towards Russia's drives towards its southern near-abroad to fortify its stakes there.

(e) It should be noted that the British Petroleum Statistical Review of World Energy and the U.S. Geological Survey World Petroleum suggest that Central Asian states of Kazakhstàn, Turkmenistan and Uzbekistan together possess proven reserves of 17 billion barrels of oil and 5 trillion cubic meters of gas.[12A] And control over the lifelines of energy networks, i.e., oil and gas pipelines, is at the core of energy diplomacy and is more strategically significant than exploration and production of oil and natural gas. Russia, in its present status, has lost many significant accesses to the sea and has lost control over some oil and gas pipelines to other CIS countries. But Russia still tries to be relevant in regard to three new pipeline-projects – the CPC pipeline is totally dependent on Russia, as it traverses entirely through Russia, after leaving Kazakhstan; similarly the Baku-Novorossisk line passes entirely through Russia to reach the Russian port, after it crosses the Azerbaijan-Russian border. Regarding the Baku-Supsa project, Rajan Menon[13] opined that as Russia places itself as the "decisive outside power" in assuming Georgia's stability and is "crucial to the continuation of peace" in the Nagorno-Karabakh dispute, Russia will retain a considerable command in determining the viability of this project also.

(f) Economic integration with the CARs promises to prove instrumental in making a breakthrough in Russia's economic modernization programme. Russia has been importing 85% of its total need for cotton, 70% of barley and till recently 54% of wheat from the CARs. Notwithstanding its trade relations with the CARs, based primarily on traditional agricultural items, Russia is set to concentrate more on hydropower, oil and gas, gold, silver, polymetallic ores, aluminum, boron and other mineral resources of the region.

(g) The region's geostrategic potentials and Russia's compulsions for their use to preserve its status of a world power are unavoidable imperatives: the Baikanour space—launch complex in Kazakhstan provides for 70% of Russia's space—launches; the Sary—Shagan anti-missile test ground, together with Russian radar—stations on the shores of Lake Balkhash, have been of immense strategic importance to Russia that it can ill-afford to part with; and the long-range communication point of Russian navy in Kyrgyzstan and the recently opened optical electronic—surveillance station in the Pamirfoothills in Tajikistan that belongs to Russia's global system of space control, are cases in point.[13A]

India Emerges as an Actor in Central Asia

India's age-old historical, cultural and economic ties with Central Asia make sense in the present context in emphasizing the absence of any form of *rooted resistance* in the psyche of the peoples of the region to come close to India that verily transcend the question of religion – India being preponderently a non-Muslim country – in view of the intimate relationship sustained from pre-Islamic days to the end of the Soviet era.

This is uniquely significant for India in the context of the advantages that Turkey has over Central Asia on ethno-linguistic grounds or Iran has over Tajikistan on a common ground of Persian culture or Saudi Arabia or Pakistan has on common religious grounds of Sunni beliefs, preponderent in Central Asia. India has none of the advantages but still retains acceptability among the peoples of the region on grounds of:

(a) A sense of toleration, both having been the meeting grounds and *melting-pots* of various civilizations and cultures like Persian, Greek, Kushan, Hun and Islamic, making both, resultantly, more receptive and more tolerant.

(b) Absence of any perception of threat in the region from India both in the historical context or in the contemporary scenario; and the tradition of long-sustained Indo-Soviet friendship imparted in their perceptions of India an embedded intimacy that still lingers, when they are confined to the security logic of a regional sub-system, having been disintegrated from the security logic of a global system of a superpower.

Growth of India-CARs Political and Trade Relations

Kazakhstan

R.L. Bhatia, the Indian Minister of State for External Affairs was the first Indian Minister to visit Kazakhstan, in October 1992, yet the real boost for bilateral relations came during Prime Minister Narasimha Rao's visit in May 1993 when cooperation and joint ventures were envisaged in areas like peaceful uses of atomic energy and space, telecommunications, trade and commerce, pharmaceuticals, ecology etc. The important bilateral visits that followed were: Minister of State for External Affairs, Salman Khurshid's visit in 1994; Kazakh Defence Minister S.K. Nurmagambelov's visit to India in 1995; Vice-President K.R. Narayanan's visit in September 1996, followed by President Nursultan Nazarbayev's visit to India in December 1996; Minister for External Affairs Jaswant Singh's visit in Almaty in September 1999 to attend the CICA meet; Prime Minister A.B. Vajpayee's visit in June 2002 and President Nazarbayev's visit to New Delhi in February 2002.[14]

Bilateral economic relations started with the signing of Indian Technical and Economic Cooperation (ITEC) with Kazakhstan and India's lending of a credit line of $ 10 million in 1992 and another $ 10 million in 1993. Indo-Kazakh trade consists mainly of traditional items as India imports iron, gold and silver, non-ferrous metals, machinery (except for electrical and electronics goods) and exports tea, pharmaceuticals, cosmetics, machinery and instruments, readymade garments, consumer goods etc.[15] The Report of Confederation of Indian Industries' (CII) Industrial Mission to Central Asia in 1993 suggested four priority areas for collaboration[16] – fuel and energy, mining and mineral processing, food processing and consumer goods, and communications, though not much have been fruitfully ventured upon.

Some private Indian business enterprises became involved in Kazakh economy, e.g., Ispat International Consortium took over the Karagonda Metal Plant and the new ISPAT-KARMET company came to export 90 per cent of its products to India; Kazakhstan Pharma was another joint venture in pharmaceuticals sector; Larsen and Toubro also is involved in a number of joint ventures with the Kazakh government.[17]

Both sides took steps to boost up bilateral economic relations as time went on – in February 2002 a bilateral Protocol on Trade, Economic, Scientific, Technological, Industrial and Cultural Cooperation was signed, and in April 2002,[18] Indian Minister of State for small-scale industries visited Kazakhstan to attend "Eurasia Summit" and "Enterprise-India 2002"[19] and inter-alia discussions were held on cooperation in small-scale industry sector.

Indo-Kazakh Trade Figures

(*in Rs. Lakhs*)

Years	*India's Imports*	*India's Export*
1993–94	663.06	846.76
1994–95	1261.96	2561.77
1995–96	2656.97	2986.69
1996–97	4461.18	1558.78
1997–98	15685.4	5623.61
1998–99	5229.28	15986.31
1999–2000	4670.30	12116.23
2000–2001	6412.81	22878.97
2001–2002	3525.73	21795.87

Uzbekistan

India maintained its only consulate in Central Asia in Tashkent, during the Soviet era, where the famous Tashkent Agreement was signed between India and Pakistan in 1965. Notably, Uzbek President Karimov visited India in August 1991 – the first visit by any President of the Republics, yet to become independent.

Some important bilateral visits that followed were Prime Minister Rao's visit to Tashkent in May 1993; President Islam Karimov's visit to India in January 1994; Minister for External Affairs Pranab Mukherjee's visit in March 1996 and Uzbek Foreign Minister Abdulaziz Kamilov's visit to India in August 1996; Minister for External Affairs Jaswant Singh's visit in May 1999; President Karimov's visit in India in May 2000; and Minister for External Affairs Yashwant Sinha's visit in February 2002.[20]

Indo-Uzbek economic relations started with the October 1992 agreement on the establishment of a Joint Commission for Technical and Economic Cooperation, which was hailed by the Uzbek Foreign

Minister Abdur Razakov as the first such agreement to be signed by Uzbekistan since its independence and "would serve as a model for Uzbek cooperation with other countries." India granted a credit line of $ 10 million in 1992, another $ 10 million in 1993 and again $ 10 million in 1999 under the ITEC programme.[21]

Indo-Uzbek Trade Figures

(*in Rs. Lakhs*)

Years	*India's Imports*	*India's Export*
1993–94	2618.37	469.26
1994–95	2618.37	2213.31
1995–96	3590.63	2502.50
1996–97	923.94	2888.32
1997–98	1006.42	6538.31
1998–99	701.28	5399.71
1999–2000	5535.93	4445.50
2000–2001	4835.43	4291.95
2001–2002	8235.99	3116.39

India's main import items from Uzbekistan came to be raw cotton, non-ferrous metals, raw silk and raw wool, whereas India's main export items have been tea, pharmaceuticals, machinery and instruments, chemicals, cosmetics, paper and wood products etc. The Joint Commission identified agriculture, science and technology, civil aviation and tourism as promising areas for bilateral cooperation, whereas CII Report earmarked energy sector, pharmaceuticals, hotel and transport, textiles and cotton/wool processing for joint investments. The Bilateral Investment Protection Agreement (BIPA) of 1999 was an important move to augment low bilateral investment scenario.

Turkmenistan

President Saparmurad Niyazov visited India, for the first time, in April 1992 and during the visit, two Protocols on establishment of diplomatic and consular relations, apart from agreements on cooperation in economy, education, science, art and culture, tourism and others were signed. Important bilateral visits that followed were: visit of Salman Khurshid, the Minister of State for External Affairs in late 1992, Prime Minister Rao's visit in September 1995; Turkmen Deputy Prime Minister and Foreign Minister Boris Shikhmuradov's visit to India in

July 1996; President Niyazov's visit to India in February 1997; Shikhmuradov's visit to India in April 1997; Minister for External Affairs Jaswant Singh's visit in May 1999; the visit in September 1999 by Ministry of External Affairs and Ministry of Defence' joint team to Ashghabat for cooperation in defence training; and Turkmen Deputy Defence Minister's visit in October 1999 to participate in the Defence Expo, in New Delhi.[22]

India provided a credit line of $5 million in March 1995 and another $ 10 million in September 1995. Main import items for India are raw cotton and leather while Turkmenistan mainly imports pharmaceuticals, readymade garments and machinery from India.

Indo-Turkmen Trade Figures

(*in Rs. Lakhs*)

Years	*India's Imports*	*India's Export*
1993–94	3352.57	479.41
1994–95	3344.26	166.25
1995–96	919.86	391.64
1996–97	94.63	490.26
1997–98	13.38	632.23
1998–99	44.50	810.61
1999–2000	169.65	2683.14
2000–2001	512.74	1238.64
2001–2002	927.73	2075.48

Tajikistan

Salman Khurshid, the Minister of State for External Affairs, was the first Indian Minister to visit Tajikistan in June 1994. During President Rakhmanov's visit to India in December 1995, agreements on bilateral Joint Commission and bilateral investment protection, among others were signed. This was followed by President Imomali Rakhmanov's second visit in February 1999; his third visit in May 2001; and Defence Minister George Fernandes' visit in April 2002.[23]

Tajikistan was a beneficiary of ITEC programme and India offered a credit-line of $ 5 million in 1994 and another $ 5 million in 2001. Bilateral agreements on long-term cooperation in trade, economy and industry were signed during President Rakhmanov's visit in May 2001; the first session of the Indo-Tajik Joint Commission was held in December 2001 and the first-ever exclusive trade show "Enterprise-

India 2002" was held in Tajikistan (and also in Kyrgyzstan) in August 2002.[24] India imports mainly textile yarns and non-ferrous metals from Tajikistan and exports pharmaceuticals, RMG wool and cotton, cosmetics, cotton yarns etc. to Tajikistan.

Indo-Tajik Trade Figures

(*in Rs. Lakhs*)

Years	*India's Imports*	*India's Export*
1993–94	241.00	344.73
1994–95	648.51	31.78
1995–96	1115.13	1631.80
1996–97	285.57	257.52
1997–98	65.57	415.21
1998–99	1064.62	213.68
1999–2000	1017.84	1375.21
2000–2001	248.47	1623.47
2001–2002	637.94	584.10

Kyrgyzstan

Kyrgyz President A. Akayev visited India in March 1992 for the first time. This was followed by bilateral visits, e.g., Salman Khurshid's visit to Bishkek in June 1994; Prime Minister Rao's visit in September 1995; Kyrgyz Deputy Foreign Minister T. Chinetov's visit to New Delhi in 1995; Vice-President K.R. Narayan's visit in September 1996; Kyrgyz Prime Minister Apas Jumagulov's visit in May 1997; Kyrgyz President Akaev's visit to New Delhi in April 1999; Vice-President Krishna Kant's visit in August-September 1999; and President Akayev's third visit in August 2002.[25]

Kyrgyzstan also was a beneficiary of Indian ITEC programme and received a credit-line of $ 5 million from India. The CII Report earmarked potential areas of Indo-Kyrgyz economic cooperation as food processing, engineering and mining, pharmaceuticals, textiles, hotels and tourism, consumer goods, computers, road transport and conversion of military plants into consumer goods – manufacturing units.

India's main import items from Kyrgyzstan are organic chemicals, silver, textile yarns, raw hides etc. and main export items are pharmaceuticals, readymade garments, leather goods, jewellery, cosmetics etc.

Indo-Kyrgyz Trade Figures

(*in Rs. Lakhs*)[26]

Years	*India's Imports*	*India's Export*
1993–94	NA (Not available)	118.35
1994–95	NA	NA
1995–96	8.33	13.55
1996–97	406.07	346.21
1997–98	32.35	4008.41
1998–99	42.60	3662.19
1999–2000	857.20	6215.00
2000–2001	2023.84	8036.73
2001–2002	265.44	5230.58

In 2002, India participated in 10 trade fairs and trade negotiations with Central Asian partners that included expositions in Dushanbe and Almaty to exhibit the quality of Indian textiles, electronics, food processing and pharmaceutical industries. India supplied around 30 per cent of Central Asia's pharmaceutical needs in 2002.[27]

But bilateral economic relations are still in the nascent stage – India has not yet been able to exploit vast reserves of minerals and other natural resources of the region. Apart from government-level initiatives, Indian private sector also has not been able to make a strong presence there due to various constraints: lack of direct and established land- and sea-channels of transportation; severe liquidity constraints on the part of Central Asian entrepreneurs; lack of development in banking sector and of clear taxation policies; quota system pursued by the CARs in granting trade in specific items; inter-republican problems that often lead to denial of access to transport facilities by one Republic to another; and the pervasive economic crisis and administrative disarray leading to corrupt practices that restrict profit-returns of private foreign investors.[28]

As regards the constraint of transportation, the Trilateral Agreement on international transit of goods among India, Iran and Turkmenistan was signed in February 1997 to provide a legal framework for the multi-modal movement of goods from India to Turkmenistan and other CARs through Iran. The project provides India an access to Central Asia and Turkmenistan, and similar opportunities for the CARs to reach South Asia. Kyrgyzstan later offered to join in this initiative.[29]

India's Quest for Energy Security: Relevance of Central Asia

Compulsions of energy requirements that operate on India

India has come to be the seventh largest consumer of oil in the world – and it produces just about 30 per cent of its consumption requirements. During the decade 1991-2001, India's oil consumption increased by 68 per cent to touch 2.07 million barrels per day. It is estimated that India's fuel requirements will rise to 3.2 million barrels per day by 2010 and in the process, India will emerge as the fourth largest consumer of oil after the US, China, and Japan.[30]

Currently, India consumes approximately 26 billion cubic meters (bcm) of natural gas annually and is running at a gap of 6-8 bcm between demand and supply. According to the US Department of Energy estimate, India, which is the home of 20 per cent of humanity, will need 37 bcm by 2005, rising to 51 bcm by 2010, and 145 bcm by 2025.[31]

Despite the much-hyped new oil strikes in Rajasthan and discovery of gas at the Krishna-Godavari basin off the Andhra Pradesh coast, the fact remains that India will probably never be in a position to produce more than 30 per cent of its energy needs from the oil fields and gas reserves within its territorial boundaries. S.N. Jha, Chairman of ONGIO – International, a venture between ONGC and IOC, has pointed out: "The country needs to have equity oil to the tune of 40 per cent, domestic supply of 30 per cent and the balance 30 per cent should be met through imports. If not, the country will have to face price fluctuations.[32]

In this context, "India Hydrocarbons Vision – 2025" under the Chairmanship of Finance Minister Yashwant Sinha (delivered on 20 February 2000) focused, among five Key areas, on securing of acreages in identified countries for long-term supplies.[33] Central Asia came to draw India's interest in these circumstances, and the consequences have been clear and evident.

A rather belated recognition of the fact that "energy is the most critical imperative, and the most critical link in the strategic linkages" between India and the Central Asian region, as pointed out by a senior Indian policy advisor in the CII,[34] prompted New Delhi to adopt high level diplomatic initiatives on energy. There were reports that the Indian company ONGC-Videsh Ltd. (OVL) got a five year license for oil exploration over an area of 9,085 sq. km. in Pavlodar in Kazakhstan and a 15 per cent holding in Kazakhstan's Alibekmola oil fields as well as a 10 per cent holding in Kurmangazy fields there. 'Water-rich' Tajikistan and Kyrgyzstan have also offered India hydro-power projects.[35]

There are also pipeline projects, under Indian consideration, to link India and Central Asia: Though the 1995 UNOCAL initiative to construct gas pipeline from Turkmenistan's Daulatabad gas fields across Afghanistan and Pakistan to reach Indian markets were eventually shelved in 1998, the first Trilateral Steering Committee meeting of Afghanistan, Pakistan and Turkmenistan to implement the intergovernmental agreement on the construction of TAGP project was held in Ashghabat on July 9-10, 2002 with the participation of the American Deputy Chief of Mission and officials of the Asian Development Bank (ADB) as observers. The Steering Committee of the TAGP considered constructing the pipeline initially upto Pakistani port of Gwadar and would consider the extension of this pipeline to India via Multan in Pakistan. Though the Indian ambassador M.N. Roy in Ashgabat welcomed the project on 24 July, 2002, India was apprehensive of its likely usability to India-given the continuance of inter-ethnic clashes and the potentials of the Taliban resurgence in Afghanistan as well as the increasing hold of terrorist elements in Pakistan. India can hardly opt to be held a hostage in respect of its energy security.

From the Indian point of view, accessibility to the Central Asian oil and gas remains a central question and its prohibitive costs through the existing transport-system has been a major issue of consideration. Offers of oil swap deals by Turkmenistan – to lend Iran oil from the Caspian in the north expectedly to be delivered to India in the south – has been seriously considered. The Joint Working Group (JWG) on energy relations with Turkmenistan was set up in this regard.

OVL proposed in mid-2002 the "Energy Highway" project to construct a Russia-China-India (RCI) pipeline, stretching from Russia through Turkmenistan, Uzbekistan, Kazakhstan to Kashgarh in China's Xin-Jiang province and then to enter into Kashmir via Ladakh, crossing the Siachen glacier and the India-China Line of Control (or alternatively through Himachal Pradesh) to supply gas to northern India. During the SCO conference in Almaty, delegates of Russia, Uzbekistan, Kazakhstan and China suggested that the viability of the pipeline be studied. The RCI proposal is propelled to avoid the Pakistani route. According to OVL, the economic and technical aspects of the proposal remain undetermined.[36]

Central Asia's Place in India's Security Perceptions

Yashwant Sinha, Indian Minister of External Affairs noted: "For India Central Asia is the *immediate and strategic neighbourhood*."[37] Two related factors predominantly determined Central Asian Republics' relevance in India's security perceptions following their independent status: the practicability for forces of religious extremism, under the prevailing conditions, to take roots in the CARs; and relatedly, the projected reach of the forces of destabilization[37A] (manifest in the alarming growth of drug-trafficking and proliferation of small arms) to engulf the whole region including South Asia. The epicentre of the twin forces was Afghanistan where India was ill-disposed to resist their motivations. Significantly, India's apprehensions were about the North-bound advance of these forces to overwhelm the Central Asian region, only to reverberate with added intensity on India, already a victim to their infiltrations in Kashmir, simultaneously from their epicentre in Afghanistan and their centre in Pakistan – occupied Kashmir (PoK). This portended an extended formation of an arc of instability from Pakistan through Afghanistan into Central Asia to impact massively on India's integrity and its secular underpinnings.

India's apprehensions were alarmingly vindicated and hence intensified by such candid declarations like Quazi Hussain Ahmed's (Chief of Jamat-i-Islami) in February 1992: "a great Islamic state, spread from Kashmir to Central Asia would emerge after the independence of Kashmir."[38]

Bilateral stance vis-a-vis Terrorism

Though India has been the victim of terrorist scourges since 1989[39], the extent and reach of the terrorist onslaughts on the CARs have been highlighted through the explosions in February 1999, the Batken events in mid-1999 and the IMU raids in 2000 through Kyrgyzstan to Uzbekistan.

The growing terrorist threats in the region impel the CARs to reinforce cooperation among themselves as well as to seek material assistance from a country, like India, with common concerns and having the experience and expertise to combat terrorism. Bilateral contacts at the highest level have underscored the fact that "negative influences like religious extremism, terrorism, ethnic conflicts and the crisis in Afghanistan have a detrimental effect on the security of the region as a whole."[40]

During Kyrgyz President Askar Akayev's April 1999 visit to New Delhi, India's stance on terrorism was proclaimed as in tune with Bishkek. During Akayev's next visit to New Delhi in August 2002, an intergovernmental JWG to combat international terrorism and related crimes was formed.

During Uzbek President Karimov's May 2000 New Delhi visit, extradition of criminals, recognition of religious extremism, drug smuggling and organized crime as common threats as well as instruments of terrorism were emphasized. President Karimov's visit was part of the diplomatic initiatives of the CARs to engage India inclusively in their efforts to mobilize a multinational coalition in isolating the destabilizing forces emanating from Afghanistan. During Foreign Minister Jaswant Singh's May 2000 Tashkent visit, his counterpart A. Kamilov proposed "regular and topic-related political consultations" along the lines of joint economic commission, that was readily welcomed by Singh, who proposed relatedly, to enlarge the number of Uzbek specialists for training courses under the Indian Technical programme and welcomed Uzbek servicemen to join practical courses at Indian military colleges.[41] Muhammad M. Yukbov of the Institute of Strategic and Regional Studies in Uzbekistan was categorical in assessing India's role in the regional fight against terrorism: "India is quite experienced in handling fundamentalism and religious extremism, and since we are faced with almost identical problems, we will be glad to have the benefit of its knowledge."[42] He suggested regional cooperation to evolve a mechanism to this end.

During Kazakh President Nursultan Nazarbayev's February 2002 New Delhi visit, President Nazarbayev denounced the terrorists' assault on the Indian Parliament on 13 December 2001, while committing his support for a "global, all-encompassing, and consistent" struggle with terrorism till its complete eradication. The negotiations concluded with an agreement on the creation of a JWG to fight international terrorism. To help forward the initiatives, a Joint Declaration on fighting terrorism was signed during Prime Minister Vajpayee's June 2002 Astana visit.

The Tajik President Emomali Rakhmanov summoned India's help and influence to accelerate a peaceful settlement in Afghanistan on several occasions. During his May 2001 visit to New Delhi, particular attention was focused on enhancing bilateral cooperation in maintaining regional security, in stalling as well as eradicating international terrorism and its instruments like religious extremism and drug trafficking. In December 2001, both sides signed a memorandum on exchange of informations regarding terrorism-related matters.[43]

During the first summit of CICA in Almaty on 3-5 June 2002, the Declaration on Terrorism was endorsed which condemned all forms and manifestations of terrorism, specifying that no consideration whatsoever can be invoked to justify it. The Declaration categorically identified "separatism" as one of the main challenges to security and stability in the region indicating its bindingness upon the member-states not to support any separatist movement on the territory of other member-states. The commitments in the Declaration are in tune with the UN Charter that address issues of illicit arms and drug-trafficking and support the efforts for global elimination of all weapons of mass destruction as well as for prevention of nuclear, chemical and biological weapons proliferation.[44] According to Igor Ivanov, Russian Foreign Minister, CICA may contribute to fighting terrorist threats, while its ultimate goal is to form a secure zone throughout the Asian continent.[45]

Defence Cooperation

Within the framework of the international war on terrorism, India has been upgrading its strategic and military profile in Central Asia through establishing military cooperation with the CARs. Z. Siroev[46], a representative of the Tajik Ministry of Defence, noted that the matter concerned military exercises. Joint military exercises have been held with both Tajikistan and Uzbekistan.

In 2002, India started repair work on an air base at Ayni, about six miles away from the Tajik capital Dushanbe. Indian technicians and engineers are involved in the training of Tajik defence personnel (including English language courses), and the servicing and repairing of Russian-built military equipments, they prevalently use.

Kazakh President Nazarbayev proposed India's participation in the regional security alliance – the Shanghai Cooperation Organization: "considering India's geographical proximity in the neighbourhood, and its active participation in regional and global matters of cooperation, India's membership of SCO would add to the strength of that organization."[47] Kyrgyz President Akayev was in tune with his Kazakh counterpart when in his New Delhi visit in August 2002, he pointed out: "participation of India in SCO would contribute to the growth of this organization's potential.[48] Tajikistan and Russia also welcomed India's entry.

During Prime Minister Vajpayee's visit in June 2002 to attend the CICA Meet in Astana, India and Kazakhstan signed a MoU on Military and Technical Cooperation.[49]

Till 2000, India's policy orientations towards Central Asia were more or less *uncoordinated, under focalized and lacked an overall strategy*. The decade-long terrorist campaign in Kashmir since 1989, under a *regional pattern* of nearly simultaneous operations engulfing Central Asia and Southern Russian regions of Chechnya and Daghestan, came under sharp global focus with the events of 11 September 2001 leading to an international war on terrorism. India's active gestures, attuned to the international efforts, were responded with terrorist attacks on Indian Parliament and on the J & K Assembly in December 2001, which urged for an Indian imperative to devise a comprehensive strategy to stabilize Central Asia and Afghanistan from the clout of the forces of destabilization.

The process of stabilization in the region needed a concerted effort that must, India urgently felt at this juncture, take into account *in its inclusiveness* the significant role of India to make it a success. Sodyq Salikhovich Safoev, Foreign Minister of Uzbekistan, acknowledged: "The issues of security and integration in Central Asia have been strongly supported and initiated by Uzbekistan's reliable and tested partners like India."[50] On the other hand, India's participation in the process was driven by its eagerness in securing an established place for itself in Central Asia including Afghanistan instead of being left behind other major players who saw the process primarily as a "game." That needed a unified strategy to subsume its quest for energy, its search for a transport corridor, its efforts to forestall a resurgence of disruptive forces as well as to gain an effective influence through power-projection capabilities.

A favourable view of India in the CARs often led them to resent India's under involvement in both commercial as well as security sectors. A high-level non-official American delegation – the Atlantic Council – that visited Central Asia in mid-1998 subscribed to the view, while in New Delhi, that a large and a more visible Indian presence in the region would be very welcome there: "We have come to New Delhi by way of Beijing, Bishkek, Dushanbe, Tashkent and Islamabad ... and wherever we went (in Central Asia), we found there was high regard for India, which had maintained contacts with them all through the Soviet period ..." said former US Assistant Secretary of Defence Chas W. Freeman, now Vice-Chairman of the Atlantic Council, a leading American think

– tank.[51] Indian assistance would also be welcome by the Republics to train and modernize their armed forces, added the Atlantic Council Team, particularly as all of them use Soviet-made equipments, with which the Indian military is familiar.

India's belated arrival in the Central Asian arena is sufficiently compensated by the strength of its very large and rapidly growing economy that projects a large and prospective market for the Central Asian energy so much so that viability of southern routes of oil and gas pipelines are weighed against their feasibility to reach the Indian market. At the same time the huge Central Asian market for consumer goods promises reciprocal consolidation of economic interactions between them to build up meaningful strategic linkages.

Common Cultural Bonds

In July 1999, Indian Prime Minister Atal Bihari Vajpayee in New Delhi made a plea to the peoples of South Asia and Central Asia for taking the only possible route of "Peace, Friendship and Cooperation" among the countries of the region, since the peoples of the region belong to a "geocultural family of which we were, and continue to be, members."[52]

Uzbek President Karimov's as well as Kazakh President Nazarbayev's ideological programmes in 2000 – "national idea" and "national ideology" respectively – steadfastly refer to *non-Islamic* and *pre-Islamic* religions as part of their national heritage, while their Islamic heritage is focused on Sufism, noted for its tolerance and general human values.

Tajikistan's projected gesture in restoring the reclining 42 ft. long and 9 ft. high Buddha statue, the most notable in Central Asia,[53] indicated the country's high esteem of their national heritage, linked to a common civilizational bond with India as well as the country's (along with the region's) urge for *a quest of an identity* related to their long past history. The gesture was conspicuous against the Taliban's demolition of Bamyan Buddha in 2001. Relatedly, Buddhism acted as a binding force to bring the peoples of Kashmir, Afghanistan and Central Asia together towards the end of 3rd century BC. During the Kushana Emperor Kanishka's reign, an intimate liaison was established among these three regions.

Excavations by archaeologists have brought out a great wealth of Stupas, Viharas, sculptures and murals from ancient cities, buried under sands, on the routes north and south of the Takla Makan desert. Chinese travellers like Fa-Hien, Che Mong, Fa-Yong, Hieun Tsang and others, who came to India via Central Asia, wrote fascinating accounts of the state of Buddhism in places like Turfan, Kucha, Kashgarh, Bharuka, Agnidesh or Karashahar, Yarkand, Khotan and Niya in their travelogues that attested the role of Kashmir in promoting the religio-cultural and trade (through the Great Silk Route) relations between India and Central Asia. The cave complexes of eastern Turkestan, Kyzyl, Bezekilk, Kucha, Khotan-have their *prototypes* in the Hindu-Buddhist cave art of India, and the monumental sculptures are akin to the Gandhara Bamyan Buddhas.[54]

Cultural diplomacy, bereft of a key focus, has been regarded belatedly by India as an effective instrument to reach out to Central Asia. Indian cultural centres were opened in Tashkent and Almaty. The Indian government created one chair each at the University of World Economics and Diplomacy in Tashkent and at the University of Osh in Kyrgyzstan to conduct courses on "Indian Civilization-Study in Continuity and Change: Unity in Diversity."[55]

A significant aspect of their growing relationship is the close affinity the Central Asians feel for India partly due to the civilizational and historical links between them as well as partly due to their proven craze for Bollywood films that may very well form the basis, in the contemporary context, of India's cultural diplomacy.

Common Ground with Russia: The Concern with Terrorism

Before 11th September 2001

A network of common interests came to bind India and Russia in the Central Asian region in the circumstances, as projected by the post-Cold War security scenario in the central and south Asian regions. The focus was the uncertainty that the environment of the CARs came to throw up for the politics of the broad neighbourhood – the activities of the large number of terrorist organizations, stimulated by the narcotics trade and various adventurous initiatives of those who supported Islamic extremism. Just as the Russian Federation considered that the state of affairs in the CARs was increasingly beginning to affect the internal security of Russia, Moscow also understood that India was concerned about the way it would affect the situation in Kashmir – aided and abetted by the Taliban government in Kabul and important figures in Pakistani society and government.

India and Russia's support for the United Front for the Liberation of Afghanistan or the Northern Alliance, essentially the army of the Rabbani government, crystallized when the Taliban captured the western city of Herat in September 1995. While Russia had been providing sporadic exports of military equipments to Rabbani's government, India started sending non-military supplies through Iran.[56] In early 1996, Russia upgraded the Alliance's airbase in Taloqan, close to the Tajik-Afghan border to establish an airbridge between Taloqan and Kolub, a Russian airbase in southern Tajikistan, which the Alliance was allowed to use for the resupply and basing of its airwing.

The hijacking of the Air India Flight IC-814 in December 1999 by the Kashmiri militants and the hijacker's eventual asylum inside Afghanistan granted by the Taliban regime, pushed New Delhi with an added impetus toward the Northern Alliance. India's assistance was crucial in the Alliance's upkeep of its airwing: about 30 Indian aeronautical technicians were reportedly engaged in the maintenance of the Alliance's tiny collection of Soviet-made MI-17 and MI-35 attack helicopters. Indian military advisers also assisted the Alliance with training in high altitude warfare techniques and specialized equipments for that purpose (military hardwares to the tune of around US $8 million altogether were supplied).[57]

To help going both countries' concerted efforts to sufficiently strengthen the Northern alliance vis-a-vis the Taliban, India stepped up its non-lethal military assistance to the Alliance in early 2001. In response to a request by Ahmed Shah Massoud, India provided four transport helicopters against Massoud's insistence for 20 and arranged the lease of five AN-32 "Cline" freighters. New Delhi also sent engineers to south Badakhshan to renovate an airfield.[58]

Against this backdrop, Indo-Russian strategy to support the Northern Alliance, particularly helped the Alliance survive aganist the Taliban's overwhelming superiority. The coalition air assault led by the US in November 2001 provided the military breakthrough for the Alliance forces to occupy over half the country, including the capital Kabul and the city of Mazar-i-Sharif in less than a week. Russia's and India's concerted strategy over these years to reinforce the Northern Alliance to confront the Taliban had almost certainly saved Washington and London, post-11th September 2001, from deploying large number of ground troops[59] – a costly invasion – to dislodge the Taliban from power and to close Al Qaeda Camps.

Another point to note is that both countries' strategy did not develop along a *unilinear* course, it had involved risks to the extent of a *gamble* to support a weak side, occupying between 5-10 per cent of the country. Often they were even blamed for prolonging the war, since the defeat of the Alliance might, at least, hasten peace in the country. At a certain point of time when Massoud, viewed to be the sole figure to coordinate the Alliance vis-a-vis the Taliban, was killed on 9 September 2001, the gamble was perceived to be finished with the apprehension of bitter infighting among the various factions of the Alliance.

Pakistan and Iran operated as two way "linkage states" between internal and external actors: Pakistan functioned as a linkage between the Taliban and the external states, such as the US and Saudi Arabia, when Iran served as the linkage between the Northern Alliance and the two Central Asian neighbours, Uzbekistan and Tajikistan, including the non-regional countries – Russia and India.

The Telegraph[60] lauded India's stance: "India has prudently stuck by the Alliance for the last five years and has continued to recognize the government of Mr. Burhanuddin Rabbani. It has, therefore, at present considerable leverage and influence..."

After 11th September 2001

The common ground between India and Russia over Central Asia as a breeding ground for terror, and their interest in the future of the region developed a new dimension in their relationship following the attacks on the World Trade building in New York on 11th September.

The Implications of the Afghan War

The terrorist attack on the US on 11th September 2001 implied not only the beginning of a new series of distinctive developments in global politics but also a *new dimension* in the existing competitive scenario of political and strategic interests of various actors in Central Asia. Though any long-term changes in the balance of power and in the regional security system were not unmistakably clear till this point of time, significant changes in the postures of major actors as well as of the Central Asian Republics were embarrassingly discernible.

The inevitable prioritization of Central Asia from the periphery to the very centre of US strategic perception *essentially altered* the balance of the two major players – the US and Russia in the region. Russia had obvious reasons to be worried over the following developments: an accentuation in the US military presence in the region, a protracted war against terrorists in Afghanistan and an expansion of the zone of conflict into Central Asia.

The first US strategic move in the changed situation was to cultivate Pakistan and Uzbekistan, the key countries, to its military operations in Afghanistan. President Karimov, by the agreement of 7th October 2001, provided the US with extended use of its Khanabad airbase, the biggest in Central Asia, for flying humanitarian and 'search and rescue missions' directed to Afghanistan. The bombing campaign in Afghanistan began on October 7, 2001, from Karshi-Khanabad airbase, literally an hour after Uzbekistan and the US signed the Status of Forces Agreement.[61]

Russia defined its position almost immediately: on 24 September President Putin offered close cooperation with Washington on several levels – intelligence sharing, use of Russian air corridors for humanitarian deliveries, increased support for the Northern Alliance, endorsement of decisions by the CARs to grant the US forces access to their military bases and airfields, and participation in international operations of a search and rescue character.[62]

This was essentially an overt posture towards strengthening resistance against international terrorism that Russia had persistently asked for since mid-1990's in the context of the outreach of the terrorists in Russia. Russia, significantly, stopped short of direct participation in military campaigns, and was not asked to do so by the U.S, for its own reasons and perceptions. Russian Policy makers were guided by Russia's own problems in Chechnya and the possible repercussions of getting further embroiled in a war, evidently laden with anti-Islamic overtones. They were also motivated by the USSR's past experience, that such a war would hardly permit a simple conclusion of a triumph over international terrorism.

Throughout October 2001, the US gestures implied that it sought to create a sort of a political alliance in the region that would include Pakistan and Uzbekistan, isolating in the process any future roles for Russia, Iran and China. But the effectiveness of air strikes having been proved less than adequate, the increasing need for ground operations prompted the US to reach a compromise with regional powers on matters of strategic interest. Subsequently, it took the first move towards a compromise when President Bush met President Putin and Chinese President Jiang Zemin at the Summit of the Asia-Pacific Economic Cooperation (APEC) forum in Shanghai. The latter two leaders, in general, expressed their support for the US military campaign against the Taliban with an obvious rider appended, while clarifying their positions at private talks with President Bush: Russia, alongwith Iran, preferred the largest possible representation of the national minorities that are closely linked to Moscow and Tehran, in any future post-Taliban government. The rider was evidenced in 2 November 2001 Dushanbe Declaration by a joint Russian-American working group which categorically denied any role of the Taliban in the future government of Afghanistan.

Significantly, Russia initiated a *tactical* move at this juncture in objective terms: while categorically denying itself any direct involvement in the US-led military campaign, it reinforced its ties with the Rabbani government – which, until the ascendancy of Hamid Karzai as the interim President, conducted all the diplomatic offices of Afghanistan around the world – through a strenuous and enhanced military support to the Northern Alliance. This approach restricted its risks and expenses to a minimum, while effecting a leading role for itself in the post-Taliban re-allocation of power in Afghanistan. The establishment of American military bases in Uzbekistan and Tajikistan drew the US into a peculiar position: it was forcefully compelled to manoeuvre between its strategic goal of resolving the Afghan conflict with the elimination of the Taliban and its tactical compulsion of raising a bulwark there to defend its interests which, in effect, implied that it must recognize the interests of Russia and Iran, while seeking the assistance of the Northern Alliance to actuate such a bulwark.

US and NATO military installations on the territory of the CARs were instrumental in providing logistics support for multinational forces[63] and their operations. The US and NATO substantially asserted themselves at Uzbek, Kyrgyz and Tajik bases, e.g., Manas (Bishkek), Karshi, Kulyab, Kokaidy and Termez.

The political elite in Russia, despite the government's express overtures towards the US-led initiatives against international terrorism, were increasingly concerned about the virtual *re-division* of sphere of influence taking place in the post-Soviet space. Kostantin Zalutin, Head of the Institute of CIS states, speaking at a Moscow seminar on 14 March 2002, pointed out that Russia faced a new US geopolitical challenge in Central Asia and that the US military presence in the region posed a threat to both the CIS and Collective Security Member countries.[64]

Significantly, after 11 September 2001 terrorist strikes on the US, India, Russia, Iran, Uzbekistan, Tajikistan and representatives of the

Northern Alliance met in Dushanbe on 13 September to chalk out a common strategy. The Moscow Declaration (6 November 2001) by India and Russia on International Terrorism was extolled by the Indian press: "For once Indian diplomacy can be applauded. The Joint Statement issued in Moscow is just what the situation demanded."[65]

The July 2002 meeting of Indo-Russian Joint Working Group in New Delhi highlighted the shared perception that US military presence in Afghanistan as well as in the Central Asian Republics was justified within the parameters of the "war on terror"[66] – suggesting *by implication* that once the goal was achieved, there would hardly be any further justification for *prolongating* the US military presence in the region.

The united stand of both countries against transnational terrorism was reiterated in the Delhi Declaration on Further Consolidation of Strategic Partnership on 4 December 2002: "Situation in our common neighbourhood – Afghanistan and Central Asia – is of vital security interest to both the countries ... India and Russia agree to cooperate closely in the reconstruction efforts in Afghanistan and agreed that these should be driven by *Afghan priorities*... Both sides have a vital interest in maintaining security, stability and a secular order in the Central Asian region."[67]

The bilateral Agreements and Protocols signed since November 1996 to April 2000 were aimed at providing teeth to their mutual cooperation in combating terrorism and allied threats. India and Russia achieved a common understanding that new additional opportunities were found to promote their anti-terrorist stance in the UN, e.g., the Indian draft of the Comprehensive Convention on International Terrorism as well as the Russian draft of the Convention for the Suppression of Acts of Nuclear Terrorism. That underlined their togetherness in building a global system of countering the threats on an international legal basis.

New Delhi's Special Envoy for Afghanistan, SK Lamba, attended the G-21 meeting in New York for the reconstruction of post-war Afghanistan. India, however, was excluded from the group of countries- which include six neighbours of Afghanistan together with Russia and the US – that was given the primary responsibility by the UN to evolve a peace plan for Afghanistan.

At the UN sponsored Bonn Conference (2001) on Afghanistan, attended by India, Pakistan, Russia, the US and others, the countries put across their proposals through their respective representatives of friendly Afghan groups invited by the UN. Indian Special Envoy Mr.

S.K. Lamba, in his interview confided to me about Indo-Russian close cooperation at Bonn for a *favourable* outcome to mutual interests.[68]

Russia and India have coordinated their policy approach towards Afghanistan which have helped *solidification* of their strategic partnership: as in strengthening the Northern Alliance against the Taliban, so in extending "full support to the Karzai Administration, aimed at promoting national reconciliation, economic reconstruction, rebuilding of Afghan institutions, including indigenous security structures according to Afghan needs and priorities and to bring back Afghanistan on to its feet so that it is able to defeat internal and external threats."[69]

Relatedly, Trenin has noted that "Russia did have an urge to play a lead role in the Afghan reconstruction effort, but that its history in Afghanistan and its limited financial resources prevented it from doing so."[70]

In the context of intimate traditional relations between Indian and Afghan peoples and that of Afghanistan's emergent compulsions of wide-ranging reconstruction drive that preponderantly exceeds the negative impact of Indian "neutrality" on Afghan people during the Soviet invasion, India played a significant role in the reconstruction process of Afghanistan: The Tokyo international conference (January 2002) on "Reconstruction of Afghanistan" pledged an assistance of US $4.8 billion that included India's commitment of US $100 million, and an additional 1 million tonnes of wheat worth about $ 100 million was also pledged by India. During November 2001-February 2002, India supplied about 140 tonnes of medicine; during Afghan President Hamid Karzai's New Delhi visit on 26–27 February 2002, India announced a grant of $ 10 million for immediate utilization for reconstruction purposes and offered assistance in areas like rebuilding educational and health infrastructure, setting up computer training and maintenance facilities with computer hardware and software support to various ministries, providing 50 buses and other material support to help rebuild public transport system in Kabul, rehabilitation and construction of the existing and a new industrial park, imparting training to officials of various ministries at Indian Institutes related to capacity building and human resources development, and sending a composite Indian team to undertake feasibility studies of projects, related to water and power sectors. Additionally, Indian Ministry of Civil Aviation gifted in 2002 three Air India Airbus-300-B4 aircrafts worth $7 million to Ariana airlines and the Construction Industry Development Council of India came out with a four-point action plan that included setting up of a communication network through satellite imagery and creating civic maps and municipal records through web-enabled information systems. Also, a LAN system with internet access was established in the office of the Afghan Foreign Ministry.[71]

India's initiatives were primarily intended to nourish the pre-conditions for lasting peace in Afghanistan by removing land mines, providing immunization against communicable diseases and securing access to food. The Telegraph suggested: "The poor state of Kabul's over-stretched medical facilities is well known, and Indian medical specialists can play a vital role in re-establishing the traditional bonding of affection and respect that was shared by Afghans and Indians… (The liaison office must) also reach out to Pashtun groups, particularly those that did not form the core of the Taliban."[72]

Significantly, the CARs extolled the Indian initiatives in the reconstruction of Afghanistan's basic needs of the hour with all its infrastructureal expertise in view of their own economic deficiencies to lend a meaningful assistance.

The Meeting Ground

The crucial importance of the Central Asian region for Russia has been clearly defined in this study. Also, both Russia's and India's stakes in combating forces of destabilization that have engulfed the Central Asian region, Chechnya and Kashmir from their epicentre in Afghanistan have been dwelt upon. India has found material grounds in the region, as this study has revealed, to substantiate its quest for a befitting relevance in Asia beyond its confinement in the South Asian context. It must be noted that Russia's stakes and interests in the region are far more compelling in intensity and scope than India's. This study now seeks to establish that Russia's favourable perception of India's importance in the region stems from its view that India is an *unobtrusive* actor in the region and is more a *partner* than a competitor to outshine Russia's strongholds there, even in a limited scale.

Russia has a fundamental clash of interests with the US in the region in view of the US Eurasian geostrategic goals. In March 1992, the post-Cold War US global strategy was spelt out in definitive terms by a US Defence Department Planning document -

(a) "to prevent the reemergence of a new rival either on *the territory of the former Soviet Union*, or elsewhere …";

(b) "to prevent any hostile power from dominating a region whose resources would, *under consolidated* control, be sufficient to (its status) as a global power"; and

(c) "to maintain the mechanism for determining potential competitors from aspiring to a larger regional or global role."[72A]

The pointed reference to the post-Soviet space, that includes Central Asia, can hardly be missed.

Russia has similar conflicts of interests in the region with some of the neighbouring regional countries which have proceeded to get a sizable share of the region's energy resources as well as to manipulate the CARs' vulnerabilities to their geostrategic aims in the region, helped by the so-called doctrine of "Eurasia's geopolitical pluralism" to balance the prevalence of a single dominant power:

The Pan-Turkic ideology and its associated political ambitions drive Turkey's initiatives towards the CARs, yet it views its strong ethno-linguistic ties with the region not as a goal in itself but only as a means to make Ankara more indispensable to the West as the most important component of NATO on its southern flank and as a dependable key country to offer an alternative energy route to bypass Russia to reach Europe. So there has been an essential conflict of interests between Russia and Turkey in the region, since Turkey can only gain ground in the region so far as it can successfully erode Russian influence there.

On the other hand, there is a convergence in the Iranian and Russian positions in arms supplies and civilian nuclear cooperation as well as in bolstering the Northern Alliance to restore a balance of power in Afghanistan. But at the same time, Iran has endeavoured to strengthen ties with the Persian-speaking world, which includes only Tajikistan among the CARs, in seeking to contest the "Turkic arc." But equally important has been Tehran's policy regarding the division of the Caspian Sea bed where the conflicts of interests between Russia and Iran have been consistent. Tehran has also opposed, in particular, the creation of a regional security system under the aegis of Russia, since that would restrict its role in the region.

Though the commonality of threat perceptions and actual challenges from international terrorism and regional extremism have helped establish mutual solidarity among Russia, China, Kazakhstan, Kyrgyzstan, Tajikistan and Uzbekistan through the Shanghai Cooperation Organization (SCO), Russia has been pushing more strongly its own Collective Security Treaty Organization (CSTO) with the CARs. The SCO was supposed to become a vehicle to stall further US inroads into Central Asia and a centrepiece of Sino-Russian collaboration, yet all this can hardly screen China's ambitions to outshine Russia in the region on the strength of its dynamic economic potentials and a vast energy market. Morris Rossabi has noted that China "harbours aspirations of replacing Russia as the dominant economic force in Central Asia..."[73] Also, China's decision to provide military supplies for the Kyrgyz army has helped to demonstrate to the CARs that military-technical cooperation with China is no better than with Russia. Russian analysts have noted the facts, as Dmitri Trenin, Deputy Director of the Carnegie Centre, Moscow, while pointing out Moscow's drive towards the creation of "geopolitical coalitions under the flag of a political struggle against American hegemony", argued that "Having refused to become the junior partner of the United States, Russia can become the vassal of China."[74] There has been a latent urge on the part of China to oustrip Russia in the region in view of its geostrategic aims as "China... sees itself as an undisputed regional leader."[75] So there has been inherently an *abeyant* rivalry between the two in the region.[76]

Energy politics around the Central Asian States' proven and potential energy resources is another area where Russia has a definite clash of interest with these powers. While the U.S. follows the so-called "multiple export" policy, meaning providing a choice of multiple pipeline routes to the west for export of energy to the Central Asian States, by passing Russia, China offers an alternative eastern transport route to an emerging energy market to the CARs. Turkey, Iran and Pakistan also offer alternative routes as well as markets to the CARs.

On the other hand, the convergence of interests of Russia and India in the Central Asian region is reinforced by a notable fact – India poses no threat whatsoever, in short-term and long-term perspective, to Russia's own security interests there. So, Russia wanted to engage India in Central Asian affairs without any sort of reservation: Russia favoured inclusion of India in the Tajik peace process in 1994 where Russia, the CARs as well as Iran and Pakistan participated. The latter two countries, however, opposed India's participation.[77] Later, in the Dushanbe Summit of the SCO (2000), President Putin expressed the view that the grouping could be converted into a Shanghai Forum in which Uzbekistan, India and Iran too could participate to create a comprehensive mechanism against the scourge of international terrorism.[78] Simultaneously, India poses no threat to Russia's commercial interests in the region as India offers aid and investments in the exclusive fields of information technology, pharmaceutical expertise and biotechnology, where Russia has little to tender.

Dmitri Trenin, pertinently, pointed out: "There is *no fundamental clash of interests* between India and Russia preventing a *real partnership* between the two nations" and this provided a "stark contrast to its (Russia's) troubled relations with Turkey, Iran and Pakistan, the other major players in the (Central Asian) region."[79]

Similarly, there have been certain irritants in the relations between the CARs and the major regional players: Turkey's projection of its image as "elder brother" of the CARs clashed with Uzbekistan's aspirations to a leadership role in the region. The CARs also viewed the activist policy of Turkish Islamists as a threat to their national security. The ruling elite of most of the CARs have been also apprehensive of Iran for their perception that Iran's clerical elite supports and arms the Tajik Islamists in an effort to expand their presence in the region. The domestic political and economic problems of Pakistan have diminished its capacity and attractiveness to the CARs as a viable partner for cooperative efforts. Islamabad's overall support for the Taliban regime have elicited irritation, bordering on a threat-perception, among the CARs, except Turkmenistan. China's billion-dollar Project 635 to divert 5 per cent to 15 per cent of the flow of the Irtysh river for the needs of its Karamai oilfields and for the irrigation of 1,40,000 hectares of its land, led Russian and Kazakh specialists to conclude that this diversion would exacerbate serious desertification in the Irtysh basins of both the states.[80] Moreover, Kazakhstan alleged that China had plans to divert the Ili river, in the south of the Irtysh, threatening to turn Kazakhstan's Lake Balkhash into another Aral Sea.[81] Moreover, China's March 2000 plan for "the large-scale development of the West" clearly proposed to resettle Han Chinese population in the Xinjiang-Uigher Autonomous regions,[82] and this portended ethnic strife as in that case ethnic Uighurs (7.5 millions) and Kazakhs (1.3 millions) there would be pushed to the bordering Central Asian region, with enormous socio-economic and political repurcussions for the latter. Notably, while in the 1989 census no Chinese were counted, it was estimated that some 300,000–350,000 Chinese lived in Kazakhstan in 1994.[83] Also, despite China's assurance to Kazakhstan on 8 February 1995 that "it would never use nuclear weapons against it,"[84] the real threat of an immediate nuclear neighbour "prevents Kazakhstan and other Central Asian states from distancing itself (sic.) too much from the Russian army."[85]

Contrarily, India has secured a place in the Central Asian region that is not resented but greeted welcomingly by the CARs for their perceived advantages and, specifically, in absence of any threat-perception from India, as was evidenced in the historical perspective, so in the contemporary context and in the near-future scenario. Against the backdrop of over-enthused stampede of countries and multi-national energy companies to get a chunk of the energy resources of the region and the wild rush of the neighbouring countries of the region and beyond to effectively exploit the vulnerabilities of the CARs to their own geostrategic aims in the region, India *stands out singularly* unenthusiastic to join the rush, save and except when the developments in the region touch its security-perceptions palpably. India's role is increasingly perceived by the CARs as a dependable friend, extending helpful assistance in times of need, as is evidenced in its concerted efforts, with Russia, the CARs and Iran to assist the Northern Alliance against the Taliban, and in its reconstruction drive in war-torn Afghanistan.

It is established, through the discussions so far, that stakes and interests of both Russia and India in Central Asia tend to converge. The Central Asian Republics too correspond invitingly to their postures and involvements in the region – thus imparting a *trilateral dimension* to a correlation in various processes of development in the area: when both Russia and India confront, in their security interests, destabilizing forces from their epicentre in Afghanistan, their postures have been invariably in tune with the region's security interests; or when trade routes are ventured/opened to reach the European markets via Russia or to reach India and the South East Asia, the primary beneficiary is deemed to be the Central Asian region for promotion of its commercial interests.

Notes and References

1. Rajan Menon, 'After Empire: Russia and the Southern "Near Abroad" in M. Mandelbaum (ed.) *The New Russian Foreign Policy*, Council on Foreign Relations, New York, 1998.
2. "The Commonwealth of Independent States: processes and perspectives", MGIMO, Moscow, September 1992, p. 7, cited in Irina D. Zviagelskaya, "Russia's Policy Options in Central Asia", in G. Chufrin (ed.) *Russia and Asia*, SIPRI, OUP, London, 1999, p. 124.

3. A. Bogaturov, "The Eurasian Support of the World Stability", *International Affairs*, Moscow, February 1993, p. 42.
4. *Ibid.*
5. A. Migranyan, "Near abroad Is Vital to Russia, "*CDPSP*, Vol. XIVI, No. 7, 6 March 1994, p. 11.
6. R. Menon, *op. cit.*
7. A. Kozyrev, "What Foreign Policy Russia should Pursue", *International Affairs*, Moscow, February 1993, p. 4.
8. A.G. Arbatov, "Russia's Foreign Policy Alternatives", *International Security*, Vol. 18, No. 2 (Fall 1993), p. 30.
9. A. Zagorsky, "The Commonwealth: One year on" *International Affairs*, Moscow, February 1993, p. 46.
10. Kozyrev, *op. cit.*, p. 5.
11. Cited in Hannes Adomeit, "Russia as great power in world affairs: images and reality", *International Affairs*, 71: 1, 1995, p. 49.
12. Cited in Strobe Tabott, "*The Russia Hand A Memoir of Presidential Diplomacy*", Random House, USA, May 2003. n.1, p. 441.

12A. Jen H. Kalicki, "Caspian Energy at the crossroads", *Foreign Affairs*, Vol. 80, No. 5, September-October 2001, p. 123.

13. Rajan Memon, *op. cit*, p. 123.

13A. See Dmitri Trofimov, "Russia and the United States in Central Asia: Problems, Prospects and Interests", *Central Asia and the Caucasus.* 1(19)2003, pp. 72-82.

14. Data on bilateral visits compiled from *Annual Report*, Ministry of External Affairs, for respective years.
15. Data on bilateral import and export items among India and the CARS, collected from Dr. Gulshan Sachdeva, *Theme Paper* for the Seminar on "*Growth Through Partnership-Doing Business with CIS*", 5 March 2002, New Delhi, organised by FICCI and Ministry of Commerce, Government of India.
16. "*Industrial Mission to Central Asia: A Report*", 9-19 March 1993, CII.
17. Meena Singh Roy, "India-Kazakhstan: Emerging Ties", *Strategic Analysis*, January-March 2002, pp. 48-64.
18. *Ibid.*
19. *MEA Report*, 2002-03, pp. 43-44.
20. Data compiled from *MEA Annual Reports* of respective years.
21. Notably, India also maintains an impressive relation in the sphere of science and technology with Uzbekistan
22. Data compiled from *MEA Annual Reports* of respective years.
23. *Ibid.*
24. *MEA Annual Report*, 2002-03, pp. 43-44.
25. Data compiled from *MEA Annual Reports* of respective years.
26. All data on India's annual trade with the CARs: for 1993-94 from Madan Mohan Puri "Central Asian Geopolitics: The Indian View", *Central*

Asian Survey, 16(2), 1997, pp. 237-268; from 1994-95 till 1999-2000 are taken from Shri Prakash "India-Uzbekistan Relations during the 1990s and Future Prospects," *Contemporary Central Asia*, Vol. V No. 1, 2001, pp. 58-65, Data for 2000-01 and 2001-02 taken from *http://dgft.delhi.nic.in*

27. Rahul Bedi, "India and Central Asia," *Frontline*, 14-27 September 2002.
28. See M. Puri, *op. cit.* and Haji Umarov, "Tajik-Indian Economic Relations: Difficulties, Problems and Obstacles" in Mahabir Singh (ed.) "*India and Tajikistan: Revitalising A Traditional Relationship*" MAKAIAS, Anamika Publishers, Kolkata, 2003.
29. Two other transport corridors are proposed, which are doubly significant for India: they provide alternative access points to reach Afghanistan and Central Asia as well as they promise to reinforce overall economic development of both Afghanistan and Central Asia, crucial for India's stakes in the entire region. A trilateral agreement among India, Iran and Afghanistan stipulates in January 2003 that Iran has accepted to build a new transit route that connects the Melak region in its south-west to Zaranji in Afghanistan. India is entrusted with construction of a 210 km long road connecting Zaranji and Delaram. The Melak-Zaranji-Delaram route will connect Iran's Sistan province to Nimruz, Farah, Helmand and Kandahar in Afghanistan. India and Iran have further signed a protocol to develop the existing Chahbahar route, passing through Melak-Zaranji-Delaram and connect it to the Iran's nationwide railroad network to reach Central Asia (in www.iranexport.com/2003). Relatedly, another agreement among Iran, Afghanistan and Uzbekistan on transport corridor was signed in June 2003 to connect Termez (Uzbekistan)-Mazar-e-Sharif-Herat (Afghanistan)-Bander Abbas-Chahbahar (Iran).
30. See Anup Jayaram – Rajeev Dubey, "India's Oil Hunt", *Business World*, 14 July 2003, p. 31.
31. Cited in Aftab Kazi-Tariq Saeedi, "India and the Politics of the Trans-Afghan Gas Pipeline", *Central Asia – Caucasus Analyst*, 28 August, 2002.
32. Cited in *Business World, op. cit.*
33. The concept of securing acreages abroad or equity oil-prompted OVL to pick up a 20 per cent stake in the Sakhalin I project in Russia in February 2001 for $ 1.7 billion. In March 2003, it signed up for a 25 per cent stake in the Greater Nile project in Sudan. It is also involved in exploration efforts in Myanmar, Iran, Iraq, Libya and Syria. Besides, it is looking for acquiring blocks in Sri Lanka, Kuwait, Abu Dhabi, Nigeria, Angola and Tanzania. [See N.K. Nayyar, Director (Planning and Business Development)] IOC, *Business World, op. cit.* p. 34.
34. Cited in A. Blua "Central Asia: India Keen on expanding its influence", *RFE/RL*, 23 August, 2002.
35. According to a January 2003 Report by Johns Hopkins University

Central Asia-Caucasus Institute, India would like to put down a minimum 20 per cent stake in Uzbekistan's oil and gas fields.

36. See Aftab Kazi, *Central Asia-Caucasus Analyst*, 13 January 2003, *www.cacianalyst.org*.
37. See Yashwant Sinha, "India and Central Asia in the Emerging Security Environment" in K. Santharam – R. Dwivedi (ed.) *India and Central Asia: Advancing the Common Interest*, Anamaya Publishers, New Delhi, 2004, p. 7.
37A. According to the UN Regional Representative Office for Drug Control and Crime Prevention, approximately 65% of drugs from Afghanistan follow this route: Afghanistan-Tajikistan-Kyrgyzstan-Kazakhstan-Russia-Europe. A 2002 U.S. State Department Report mentioned another route: Afghanistan-Turkmenistan-Uzbekistan-Kazakhstan-Europe.
See "International Narcotics Control Strategy Report 2002", www.state.gov/g/int./rls.
38. Riyaz Punjabi, cited in K. Warikoo, "Islamist Mercenaries and Terrorism in Kashmir", *Himalayan and Central Asian Studies*, Vol. 2. No. 2, April-June 1998, pp. 35-57.
39. According to Delhi representative at the "International Conference on Ensuring Security and Stability in Central Asia" held in Bishkek in December 2001, more than 8,500 Servicemen and 61,000 civilians have been killed as a result of terrorist onslaughts in India over the decade. Cited in Irina Komissina, "India: Cooperation with the Central Asian Countries in Regional Security", *Central Asia and the Caucasus*, No. 6(24) 2003, p. 16, no.11.
40. *MoD Annual Report*, 1997-98, p. 4.
41. *Indian Express*, 19 May 2000; in February 2003 an agreement was signed on creating an Indo-Uzbek JWG to combat terrorism, Associated Press, 3 February 2003, *http://www.ap.com*
42. *The Hindu*, 17 July, 2000.
43. Relatedly, Indo-Tajik agreement to set up Joint Task Force for combating international terrorism was signed in January 2003. *www.meadev.nic.in/govt./loksabha/February26*.
44. Text of "Declaration on Eliminating Terrorism and promoting Dialogue among Civilizations."
45. Sergei Blagov, "Post-Soviet diplomacy faces check of Asian realities", >*http://www.atimes.com/c-asia*.
46. "India is going Through Tajikistan to Central Asia" German Wave Radio, 13 April 2003, cited in Irina Komissina, *op. cit.*
47. "Joint Declaration-India and Kazakhstan" *http://meadev.nic.in/foreign/jt-dect-indo-Kazakh.htm* Notably. India attended the Shanghai-5 Meet in 1999 as an observer. See Barktaybek Beshimov (Ambassador of the Kyrgyz Republic to India), "Security Concern of Central Asia," *ICCCI*

Newsletter, August 2000, p. 3. India ultimately joined the SCO as an observer in 2005, along with Iran and Pakistan.

48. *MEA Report*, 2002–2003. p. 44
49. *www.indianembassy.org/special/cabinet/primeminister/2002.*
50. See S.S. Safoev "Regional and International Security" in K. Santhanam (ed.) *op. cit.* p. 4.
51. Cited in Kaushik Mitter, "India Can do well in Central Asia's Great Game", *Asian Age*, 8 July, 1998.
52. *Contemporary Central Asia*, Vol. III No. 1 1999.
53. *The Times of India*, 15 February 2001.
54. See B.B. Kumar, "Central Asia: The Indian Links", *Dialogue*, Vol. 3, No. 4, April-June 2002, pp. 175-181.
55. Information rendered by Ms. U. Rawal, Senior Programme Director (ICC&C), vide her Letter No. ICC/MIS/2002-03 26 November 2002) cited in Surendra Gopal in his Paper "The Role of Indo-Central Asians Relations in Making a New Asia", presented at the international seminar on "*Building a New Asia: Problems and Prospects of Regional and Pan-Asian Cooperation for Security and Development*", Kolkata, March 2003 (MAKAIAS).
56. See Thomas Withington, (College London), "The Other Allies: Russia, India and Afghanistan's United Front", *Current History*, January 2002, p. 42
57. Rahul Bedi, "India and Central Asia", *Frontline*, 14-27 September 2002.
58. Withington, *op. cit.* p. 43
59. *Ibid.* p. 44.
60. *The Telegraph*, First Editorial, 23 November 2001.
61. *Fact Sheet*, Bureau of European and Eurasian Affairs, U.S. Department of state, 27 November, 2002, www.state.gov/p/eur/rls
62. *http://www.ntv.ru* 24 September 2001.
63. International Security Assistance Force (ISAF) in Afghanistan for 'Operation Enduring Freedom" comprised, till 2002, the following national troop contingents "Great Britain, 2000 soldiers; France, 500 soldiers; Germany, 900 soldiers; Norway, 100 soldiers; Italy, 100 soldiers; Turkey, 2000 soldiers; Denmark, 200 soldiers; Jordan, 500 soldiers. Mikhael Khodarenok, "Western Interest in Central Asia", Nezavisimoye Voennoye Obozseuniya, No. 10(2002), reproduced in English in *Dialogue*, Vol. 3, No. 4, April-June 2002, New Delhi.
64. *News from Russia*, Vol. 5 No. 12, 22 March, 2002, p. 10.
65. *The Statesman*, First Editorial, 8 November 2001.
66. See "Transcript of Press Briefing", Discover India, *www.medev.nic.in/news*, 17 July 2002.
67. *http://meaindia.nic.in/event/2002* Emphasis added.
68. My interview of Mr. S.K. Lamba on 25 December 2002 at his residence in New Delhi.

69. Interview of Yashwant Sinha, External Affairs Minister, to Vremya Novostie on 19 February 2003, ***http://meaindia.nic.in/interview***
70. Seminar by Carnegie Endowment for International Peace on 7 March 2003, ***http://www.carnegieendowment.org/events***
71. The data from Nidhi Narain, "Indian Aid to Afghanistan Post 9-11", *South Asia Politics*, pp. 30-33, November 2002, and from Statement on "India's Assistance to Afghanistan", 7 August 2002 ***http://meaindia.nic.in/sshome.htm***
72. *The Telegraph*, First Editorial, 23 November 2001.

72A. Cited in Preface in Hafeez Malik (ed.) "*The Roles of the US Russia and China in the New World Order*", Macmillan, London, 1997, P. xiii, emphasis added.

73. Morris Rossabi, "China seeks to Bolster its Economic Profile in Central Asia" 14 August, 2000, *eurasianet.org*
74. D. Trenin, Pro et Contra, 6 No. 1-2 (2001). *www.carnegie.ru/en/pubs/procontra*
75. K. Syroezhkin, in B. Rumer (ed.) *Central Asia: A Gathering Storm*? Aakar Books, New Delhi, (2003), p. 200.
76. Noteworthily, Russia's Deputy Foreign Minister Vyacheslav Trubnikov in his interview to Nezavisimaya Gazeta, on 12 May 2004, stated that Moscow opposed presence of all foreign forces, including the US as well as the Chinese in Central Asia and emphasized that Central Asia is a sphere of vital Russian interests. Cited in Stephen Blank, "Is the Shanghai Cooperative Organization Cracking?" *Central Asia-Caucasus Analyst*, 19 May 2004 *www.eurasianet.org*
77. *Hindustan Times*, 21 September 1994.

78. *Pioneer*, 19 July 2000.
79. D. Trenin in a Seminar on "Prospects for India-Russia Security Relations," hosted by Carnegie Endowment for International Peace, 7 March 2000 *http://www.carnegieendowmen.org/events*
80. Eric Sievers, *The Post-Soviet Decline of Central Asia: Sustainable Development and Comprehensive Capital, Routledge-Curzon, London*, p. 186.
81. *Ibid.*, p. 187.
82. Xibu di Kaifa (Urumqi, 2000), cited in K. Syroezhkin, *op. cit.*, p. 197.
83. Peter Ferdinand "The New Central Asia and China" in Peter Ferdinand (ed.) *The New Central Asia and Its Neighbours*, London, 1994, p. 103.
84. "China gives security assurance," B-Wire, cited in Z.Z. Khan, "Kazakhstan and Central Asia: regionial perspective," *Central Asia Survey*, Vol. 21, No. 2, June 2002, pp. 167-183.
85. *Ibid.*

Chapter 5

Conclusion: Making of A Relationship

Indo-Russian relations have an immediate context of Indo-Soviet relationship, tested over a span of more than forty years till the disintegration of the Soviet Union, which was developed within a different perspective of global configuration. The relevance of that relationship can hardly be dragged on to be linked to a new context, to a *new gestalt* of international relations. So, material grounds for a relationship, objectively related to the new pattern of global arrangements, are discussed to weigh the chances for a long-term relationship. A relationship, precisely, exceeds the average workable relations, it connotes stable relations *within a long-term perspective* that are sustainable on perceived objective grounds.

The Indo-Russian relationship has grown meaningfully against a new background: to shut out the US was the prime motivation for both the countries to make a relationship in the Cold War context, while to adjust themselves with the preponderance of the US in the post-Cold War context has been the principal compulsion for both, simultaneous with their urge to assert their respective national interests.

Russia

Resentments

To understand the depth of Russian resentment since mid-1990s regarding US policy postures, the key point has been Russians' belief that they have made enormous unilateral concessions since Gorbachev era, to the West for the sake of a new, rational and humane world order and a "Common European Home" to a point of having been duped. In Chapter One, it has been discussed that to convince the West of his sincerity, President Gorbachev had made major concessions.

Also, it has been explicated in chapter three how NATO's eastward expansion policy, NATO's military actions in Yugoslavia as well as the US support for the NMD project had hurt Russia's vital interests. In chapter Four, there is the point showing that US and Russia have a clash of interests in the post-Soviet space, in view of their conflicting geostrategic goals. Zbignew Brezezinski also pointed out that despite the Americans had launched the slogan of the "mature strategic partnership" between Washington and Moscow in the early 1990s, "Once differences (between Washington and Moscow) inevitably started to surface, the disproportion in political power, financial clout, technological innovation, and cultural appeal made the "mature strategic partnership" seem *hollow* – and it struck an increasing number of Russians *as deliberately designed to deceive Russia*."[1] The US policymakers were unable to decide whether the US should be more afraid of Russian weakness or Russian strength, whether the US policy should be directed toward gaining Russian cooperation or "containing and weakening Russia," as has been pointed out by Anatol Lieven.[2]

Cooperation

Suggestively, there has been the other side of the story-the drives of both countries to engage each other in tune with the post-Cold War environment. The highlights of bilateral cooperation have been: the 1993 US Friendship Act (Public Law 103-199) which stipulated re-examination of legislations that discriminated against Russia, conferring Most Favoured Nation status on Russia; the West's Coordinating Committee on Multilateral Export Controls (COCOM) of so-called dual-use technologies was superseded by the Universal Wassenaar Arrangement, under which, with Russia's participation, all decisions were to be based on consensus and Russia was included in the Group of 7 to make it G-8 in 1997 in Denver, when the US served as the chair of the Group; the Joint Statement on Common Security Challenges, signed by Presidents Boris Yeltsin and Bill Clinton on 2nd September 1998 which emphasized that the two countries are "natural partners" in advancing international peace and stability; In 2000, the bilateral trade volume stood at approximately $10.2 billion, and Russia's trade surplus reached $5.8 billion,[3] more than 35 per cent of all FDI in Russian economy comes from the US, mainly in the fuel and energy sector, particularly on Sakhalin.[4] President Putin emphasized, at the 5 October 2001 Joint Press Conference with President Bush in Shanghai, on the future of US-Russian relations, "in the century to come, our strategic priority is long-term partnership... that works toward the common goals of global development and progress."[5]

So, two opposite and simultaneous trends have been noticeably present in US-Russian relations: first, the US drive to marginalize Russia in the post-Soviet space and in Europe and the Russian drive to stall its marginalization with all its affordable means and second, to engage each other for reciprocal gains.

Another trend in Russian foreign policy orientations has been discerned in Chapters Three and Four: to reach out to other major powers to bring about a maneuverable space for itself in the context of its perception of being marginalized as well as to help establish a multipolar world order where other significant poles will be Russia, the EU, China, Japan and India. Significantly, Russia's foreign policy orientations towards Europe are balanced by its symbiotic relationship with the East, as noted in Chapter Three, and it strengthens Russia's position as a bridge across Eurasia. In its strive towards seeking a viable partner, which has vital interests in replacing the unipolar trend in international relations with a multipolar world order, Russia views India as a potential pole on grounds of its growing economic strength and has designated India as its "strategic partner" and has moved it to the top of the list of the most important countries with which it would maintain special relations.[6] Professor Yurlov emphasized on Indo-Russian international cooperation, that "must be a very important part of this (Russia's eastern) policy."[7]

India

Here, the concentration is on how India has coped with the challenge of building equations with the US during the decade. Indo-Soviet relations have been viewed in Chapter One in perspective, mainly in view of relative importance of Indo-US relations in the Cold War context of the bipolar international system. Indo-Russian relations in the post-Cold War environment cannot necessarily be of isolated growth but must be viewed in a proper perspective of the ascendance of the US as "the sole and, indeed, the first truly global power," as India had to adjust itself with a more *complex* and *competitive* environment, without the earlier leverage of stable political equations with one of the two superpowers.

J.N. Dixit, the-then Foreign Secretary, recalled a point made by Lawrence Eagleburger, the US acting Secretary of State during the opening session of bilateral talks in Washington in early February 1992, immediately after the end of the Cold War: "Both sides should predicate developing bilateral relations on positive lines while clearly acknowledging that there are some issues on which fundamental differences will remain constant between the US and India." J.N. Dixit retorted with clarifications that so far as the US did not "overinterpret or misinterpret" India's differences of opinion on basic issues like nuclear non-proliferation, transfer of "dual-use" technology and intellectual property rights and as far as "US policies did not *negatively* affect India's national security in all its dimensions," India would heartily subscribe to the *realistic* approach. This provided, in the words of J.N. Dixit, "overall terms of reference which governed Indo-US relations" despite change of governments in both countries during the decade.[8]

Studies of US strategic analysts on American interests in India and their recommendations to the US administration are significant materials to comprehend the fundamentals of US perception regarding India's place in the US geostrategic perspective. Their recommendations, however, were not often immediately followed by US administrations but they persisted as driving force to pursue US interests in India. Selig S. Harrison and Geoffrey Kemp in their Study Group's report of 1993 stated: "The Study Group's assessment is that India will gradually grow in economic and military power *whatever the United States does*... The United States should be guided by long-term as well as short-term considerations and should give a higher order of importance to India *than in the past*.... A *cooperative, or neutral*, Indian posture could be a critical factor for the United States in the event of American involvement in future conflicts in Southwest Asia and the Gulf... Looking to the east, an economically revitalized India with a military reach into the eastern Indian Ocean could have a significant impact on the Asian balance of power."[9]

But conflicting views, driven by conflicting interests of Washington and New Delhi, surfaced during the period 1992-98 on issues of Kashmir (as Robin Raphael, the US Assistant Secretary of State, described Kashmir as a "disputed territory" in March 1994 and President Clinton in his speech in the UN General Assembly in 1994 expressed, for the first time, his concerns over human rights in Kashmir), the unconditional and indefinite extension of the NPT (1995) and the endorsement of the Comprehensive Test Ban Treaty (1996) in the UN General Assembly.

The US sanctions on India on 13 May 1998 after the Pokhran-II, aggravated their differences. The US measures "included a halt to defense sales, export licenses for munitions, and military financing; denial of government credit and loan guarantees; US opposition to loans or technical assistance from international financial institutions like the World Bank and the International Monetary Fund; prohibition of most loans and credits from US banks; a hold on Export-Import Bank loan guarantees and credits for US exports to India; and termination or suspension of most assistance programmes."[10] A White House press release on 14 May 1998 estimated that the sanctions, taking into account pending and potential proposals, would amount to a damage of $20.7 billion.[11] India's 1998 nuclear tests signalled a major diplomatic failure for the US in that India had, in its act of defiance, undercut long-standing US efforts to bind it through the scrupulous construction of international regimes, such as the NPT, the CTBT and the MTCR.

The US role during the Kargil crisis was notable. The reason for the US involvement was, according to the first-hand account of the then Deputy Secretary of State, Strobe Talbott[12]: "The result (of non-involvement) could be an international free-for-all in which all the wrong outsiders would be looking for ways to score points against one another" as well as "the world was closer even than during the Cuban missile crisis to a nuclear war." The US role, in the context of the decades-long US sway over Pakistan, in ending the Kargil conflict was thus compacted: "the key sentence in the new document (the July 1999 Press statement of President Clinton and the visiting Pakistani Prime Minister Nawaz Sharif in Washington) was ours, not his, and it would nail the one thing we had to get out of the talks; 'The prime minister has agreed to take concrete and immediate steps for the restoration of the Line of Control." A significant change in Indo-US relations, which President Clinton's stand on the Kargil crisis indicated, was the US rejection of Pakistan's contention that the LOC was indeterminate, its assertion that Pakistan had crossed the LOC in Kargil, that the intruders had the full logistical support of the Pakistani army, and that the intruders consisted, at least in part, of Pakistani soldiers.

The initial US policy of pushing India by way of political isolation and economic sanctions after the Pokhran-II was, however, followed by strategic engagement as the-then US Deputy Secretary of State Strobe Talbott recalled in his memoirs that the dialogue between him and Jaswant Singh, the Indian Foreign Minister, was more than a dialogue, it was an engagement – "Both elements, conciliation and content, were present in what went on between Jaswant Singh and me."[13] However, the continued divergence in Indian and US nuclear perspectives was summed up in the Preamble to the Vision Statement, 2000, declaring: "The USA believes India should forego nuclear weapons. India believes that it needs to maintain a credible minimum nuclear deterrent in keeping with its own assessment of its security needs."[14]

US President Clinton's March 2000 visit to India highlighted the coming together of two "estranged democracies." During his visit, eleven bilateral business agreements were signed, totalling $1.4 billion,[15] which were followed by nine additional bilateral MoUs, valued at $ 3 billion.[16]

The US sanctions against India were lifted on 22 September 2001. A Memorandum of Justification, released by the White House, noted – "... it (the Justification) reflects a considered judgement that we are more likely to make progress on our nonproliferation agenda through a *cooperative relationship, in which sanctions are no longer an issue*."[17] Despite the proclamation of a cooperative relationship, the divergence in both countries' nuclear perspective was partly because both India and the US sought "to service divergent interests from inherently different levels of strength."[18]

Significantly, India upheld two US initiatives that were perceived to serve its national interests: India supported US President George Bush's National Missile Defence (NMD) plan. The respective viewpoints of India and Russia on NMD have been elaborately dwelt upon in Chapter Three. Second, the Indian Cabinet Committee on Security met on 14 September 2001 and decided to provide "all assistance required" including logistical help and a staging ground on Indian soil to help the "War on Terror." The Russian cooperation with the US during the "War on Terror" has been noted in Chapter Four. However, the US adoption of Pakistan as its frontline ally in its war on terror, the 13 December 2001 terrorist attack on Indian Parliament and the consequent mobilization in 2002 of Indian troops along its western border – "Operation Parakram" – widened the differences between the two countries in respective threat perceptions of the scourge of terrorism.

The dynamics of US – Russian relations and Indo-US relations have provided the context under which Indo-Russian relations have evolved. There is the need now to assess objectively the worth of the relationship in its related aspects: economic, political and defence.

The discussion in Chapter Two has pointed out that unlike in the Indo-Soviet relationship, the Indo-Russian economic relations are the weakest link in the chain: An account of the declining trend in the Russian economy and its subsequent recovery has been presented. A few indicators of the Indian economy during the decade are now referred: in 2001-02, India's GDP growth rate was 5.8 per cent, rate of agricultural production was 6.3 per cent and rate of industrial production was 2.7 per cent.[19] In foreign trade, India's exports grew from $22238 million in 1993-94 to $43999 million in 2001-02, while India's imports grew from $23306 million to $50654 million during the same period. Foreign direct investment stood at $3904 million in 2001-02 from $586 million in 1993-94 while foreign portfolio investment stood at $2021 million in 2001-02. Foreign exchange earnings during January-September 2002 were Rs. 9368 crores as against Rs. 10,740 crores during the corresponding period in 2001.[20] India's development expenditure as a percentage of GDP was 6.1 per cent in 2002-03, while military expenditure as a percentage of GDP was 3.9 per cent in 2002-03.[21] Two other strong points in Indian economy: while India's R&D expenditure as percentage of GDP was only 1.2 per cent in 2002-03, [in comparison with the US' (2.7%) and Japan's (3%)], yet the Indian Council of Scientific and Industrial Research (CSIR) was tied with number one position, alongwith Samsung of South Korea, as the major patent applicant in the top-50 list of the world, prepared in 2002 by the World Intellectual Property Organisation of Geneva. Another point is the emergence of a globally competitive Indian IT Sector, which is particularly significant as Dr. R.A. Mashelkar, the Director-General of the CSIR has pointed out that "tomorrow's wars will be fought in knowledge-markets with the new weapons of information and knowledge."[22] According to National Association for Software and Service Companies (NASSSCOM) estimates, the overall IT market in India has grown from $1.7 billion in 1994-95 to $16.5 billion in 2002-03, accounting for 3 per cent of India's GDP for the year[23] and India is in the process of becoming a hub for complex research and analytical process outsourcing for major global corporations like Bell Laboratory, Cisco Systems, IBM, Microsoft, GE, Samsung, Daimler-Chrysler etc.

Notably, these facts of the revival of Russian economy and the emergent strengths of the Indian economy have not yet been reflected in their bilateral economic relations. India's trade figures with Russia (in 2000-01 and 2001-02) may be placed against the trade figures with the US, and the EU, to illustrate this point:

In 2000-01, India's exports to Russia was worth Rs. 4054 crores, whereas it was worth Rs. 4,250,988.50 Lakhs with the US, India's imports, in that year, was worth Rs. 2344 crores from Russia, and of Rs. 13,77,386.88 Lakhs from the US In 2001, India's total trade with EU was worth Euro 25.02 billion.[24] In 2001-02, India's exports to Russia was worth Rs. 2787 crores and imports Rs. 2558 crores; while India's exports to the US, was worth Rs. 40,60,175.50 Lakhs and imports, Rs. 15,02,111.63 Lakhs in that year.[25]

Also, India has been increasingly involved in the global trade game of establishing Free Trade Agreements with various countries like with Sri Lanka (1998), and negotiations have been in process with the ASEAN, (Association of South-East Asian Nations), MERCOSUR, Syria, the South African Customs Union (SACU) and the SAARC (South Asian Association for Regional Cooperation). And, Russia has *not been a partner of India* in this global trade game. Despite these facts, the study in Chapter Two has noted that both the countries have *located* new grounds and have *activated* their bilateral cooperation in the economic sphere for a stable and sustainable relation within a long-term perspective.

In Chapter Three the bilateral political and defence relations have been analyzed, which are positively the support-base that stabilizes the relationship. In India's moments of crises, Russia upheld India's case singularly and unflinchingly. Russia was the key major country to sidetrack the apparent common front of the major powers, through its opposition to collective sanctions and political ostracization of India in the aftermath of Pokhran-II of 1998. Relatedly, though Russia has been persistent in its statements that India should sign the NPT and the CTBT, it has not insisted on India's adherence to them as a norm binding upon India, which might suggest a subtle form of coercion. During the Kargil crisis, Russia, set significantly, since the beginning of the conflict, the keynote of the Kargil crisis which subsequently tuned the global reactions and responses on the issue: unlike the western countries, Russia officially referred to Jammu and Kashmir as an "Indian State", denounced categorically Islamabad's action as "invasion" and explicitly referred to the Shimla Accord (1972) and the Lahore Declaration (1999) as the sole basis for resolving the problem. Russia was the staunchest supporter of India since the fight against terrorism "became everybody's war" and repeatedly equated America's fight against terrorism, post-II September, with both countries' decade-long efforts. When Pakistan threatened in mid-2002, to take its crisis with India (during "Operation Parakram") to the UN Security Council, Moscow communicated to New Delhi its readiness to use its veto in the UN if it came to that.

The significance of Indo-Russian defence relations needs to be viewed in perspective, keeping India's defence relations with other countries in their relative positions in terms of their scale and dimensions of defence cooperation.

From 1947-2001, the US provided $153 million in military assistance to India (94% of this amount was distributed from 1962-66), while neighbouring Pakistan received more than $3 billion in US military assistance during the same period.[26] The Indo-US Defence Policy Group, morribund since 1998, was revived in late 2001. In September 2001, the US lifted defence related sanctions clamped on India after Pokhran II. While joint training and military exercises and bilateral high-level visits became familiar evidences of Indo-US defence relations, the way both countries viewed defence sales was notable. Since 24 October 2002, exports of only those Major Defence Equipments (MDE) items above $14 million to India required Congressional notice, which put India at par with US Treaty allies like Japan and South Korea. In 2002, the US Congress approved the sale of eight (later four more sets were added) counter-battery radar sets or "Firefinder" radars worth more than $100 millions to India.[27] Also, the US State Department authorized Israel to sell the Phalcon airborne early warning system, jointly developed by the US and Israel, to India. Since 2001, the Indian government has been pressing the US to ease restrictions on the export of dual-use high-technology goods to India as well as to start civilian nuclear and space cooperation or the "Trinity" issues where "tangible evidence of a changed (Indo-US) relationship" awaits to be tested, as pointed out by Indian officials.

India has been discussing with the UK, since 2000, the procurement of and collaboration on advanced technologies, including spareparts for Jaguar aircrafts with the Indian IAF and for the Advanced Jet Trainer.[28]

India signed a defence cooperation pact with South Africa in 2000. India bought from South Africa 90 mine-protected armoured personnel carriers for around $12 million. South Africa has been the first country to enter into a joint venture with the Ordnance Factories Board of India for providing state-of-the-art manufacturing technology for the production of integrated weapons systems at Nalanda in Bihar.[29]

DRDO of India got the Green Pine radar system from Israel in 2001 for building an indigenous anti-missile defence capability. Also in 2001, the initial deal for the Israeli Barak anti-missile system worth $270 million was concluded. In late 2002, India concluded a $20 million agreement with IMI of Israel for over 3400 Tavor-21 5.56 mm. standard assault rifles and 175-200 Galil 7.62 mm Sniper rifles, in addition to varied night-vision and laser-range finding and targeting equipments. Israel also provided avionics and weapons systems for Russian SU-30 MKI fighters. Bharat Dynamics Limited (BDL) forged ties for licensed missile production with Rafael of Israel in 2002 for the spike missile systems for combat vehicles and ground forces.[30]

The India-France High Committee on defence production signed a framework agreement in June 2002 to provide India three diesel powered SSK Scorpene submarines to be built over 15 years at the Mazagaon dock. The deal has been awaiting approval of the Cabinet Committee on Security (CCS).[31]

Notably, this short study of India's defence relations with the above countries has excluded from its consideration, as has been in the case of Russia in Chapter Three, offers made by these countries but not realized by agreements or even MoUs for obvious reasons.

Also the context of India's defence relations with other countries highlights the unique advantages for India as a partner of the Military-Technical Cooperation (MTC) with Russia. Russian Defence Minister Sergei Ivanov, during Defence Minister George Fernandes' April 2002 Moscow visit, opined: "we have gone beyond the buyer-seller relationship in our military – technical cooperation for several years now and have undertaken projects that involve not only *technological* but also *scientific* collaboration", citing the examples of SU-30 MKI fighter plane and the Brahmos anti-ship missile.[32] Relatedly Alexei Federov, the President of the Irkutsk Aviation Industrial Association, in his interview to Sonia Trikha, made certain points clear: Sukhoi 30 MKK "for China is a different aircraft from a different company from the far east in Russia. It has different capabilities. The one (SU-30 MKI) for India is a much more advanced version .... we are not negotiating the same for China."[33] Federov, ahead of his departure for New Delhi to participate in the Indo-Russian Security Forum on April 23-24, 2002 told the Hindu: "Neither Russia nor India can compete on their own with four or five aerospace giants ..... Our aviation industries face the choice of either becoming appendices of western corporations or *joining* forces with each other to win a share of the aerospace market." So a joint project like the manufacture of a new multi-role (military-cum-passenger) transport plane, to be built on the basis of the Russian IL-214T medium-haul transport plane, was undertaken to make its maiden flight in five to six years.[34] He specified that Irkut, engaged in many countries of South-East Asia and the Asia-Pacific region, felt the impact of Russian-Indian synergic interaction: "I mean our participation in the Malaysian tender" in offering them the SU-MKM, basically a derivative of SU-MKI. Irkut was exploring the possibility of setting up a regional centre in India for integrated logistical support for SU-MKI. "*Convergence and mutual interpenetration* of Russian and Indian high -tech complexes must follow the chosen logic of further augmentation and expansion of cooperation between the leading aircraft manufacturing corporations (of both countries). The logic is fully in line with the political reference marks, outlined by the top management of both countries and the *realities* of strategic partnership."[35]

Notably, Alexander Vaskin of Indo-Russian Security Forum stated that "The Russian defence industry is capable of investing in India $600 to $700 million over the next three to four years.... As for technologies, the Russian contribution could be far more weighty, if, for example, the two countries go for the joint development of fifth-generation jet fighter or a fourth -generation tank on the basis of the Russian T-95 MBT."[36]

Pertinently, to demonstrate Russia's keenness to take the bilateral defence ties to new heights, President Putin passed a decree allowing India – the only exception – to deal directly with Russian defence equipment makers, bypassing Rosboronexport, the government owned arms marketing agency. India was allowed to export all kinds of defence equipments, manufactured under the Russian licence, to third countries, Russia retaining the veto power to decide the equipment items and the destination countries. Under a new dispensation, Russia agreed to commit to life-long supply of spares or to setting up facilities for their production in India and to allow Indian specialists access to technical documentation of the hardware sold to India.[37]

On the issue of dependability of the MIG series, due to frequent MIG crashes, Vladimir Barkovsky, Deputy General Designer of MiG Corporation, opined that "India buys low quality spareparts from Ukraine and East European countries. At times, it even buys spareparts that have outlived their utility, thus creating conditions for frequent crashes ... we have offered an upgradation programme for these aircrafts to India ..... Only Russia possesses the technology for prolonging the operational capabilities of these aircrafts."[38]

On the whole, the increasing share of high-end technologies in Russian defence exports to India, the progressive drive from licensed assembling of Russian -made weapons to joint development and production of weapon systems and mutual interpenetration of Russian and Indian high-tech complexes signify mutual trust in each other: "India's advantage as an MTC partner is that .... it is perceived as the most benign recipient of weapons, posing no threat whatsoever to Russia's own security concerns."[39] This has been substantiated by Russian Defence Minister Sergei Ivanov during George Fernandes' April 2002 Moscow visit: "Our countries trust each other so deeply that we can go in for joint design and production of weapons"[40] as well as by Prime Minister Vajpayee in his interview to ITAR-TASS on November 30, 2002: "we trust each other and therefore, our country has received technologies that other countries have not been given."[41]

We now focus on a unique aspect of the Indo-Russian relationship which the Central Asian Region provides for both the countries: Russia perceives the region as a platform to pull through its marginalization in the post-Soviet space; for India, the region offers an opportunity to come out of its sub-continental setting to a continental relevance. Coordinated efforts of both countries to combat the scourge of cross-border terrorism, religious extremism and forces of destabilization – that have portended an arc of instability from Pakistan through Afghanistan into Central Asia to impact massively on both countries' integrity, as well as to facilitate establishment of a democratic government in Afghanistan through bolstering the Northern Alliance vis-a-vis the Taliban, contribute significantly to Russia's positive perception of India's stabilizing role in the region. This has been reinforced by the absence of any sort of clash of interests for both in the region, a singular instance in the context of the virtual stampede of regional and global players jockeying for maximal access. A trilateral dimension has been imparted to a correlation among Russia, India and the Central Asian Republics (CARs), when the CARs correspond welcomingly to combat the scourge of cross-border terrorism, and to help install a democratic government in Afghanistan.

To comprehend essentially the making of the Indo-Russian relationship through the decade requires consideration of a few necessary points:

(i) Russia, despite its being the successor-state to the erstwhile Soviet Union, is one of the 15 Republics of the Commonwealth of Independent States (CIS), and is thus reduced in stature and in power-projection.

(ii) It is no longer a relationship between one of the two superpowers in a bipolar world and a leading Third World country as was evidenced in the Indo-Soviet relationship; it is a relationship between, at the most, a major power and a *growing* power, as India perceives itself or is perceived by powers of global influence -- for example, India is a Summit-Partner of the EU, and the only country outside the G-8 or P-5 (EU's other Summit Partners include the US, Russia, China, Japan and Canada), which is perceived to be a power, worthy of constant strategic dialogues;[42] France and India are engaged in a series of strategic dialogues since 1998; India and Japan agreed in 2000 on a "India-Japan Global Partnership for the 21st Century," based both on strategic convergences and economic complementarities.[43] And India is a Full Dialogue Partner of the ARF (ASEAN Regional Forum) since 1996 and a Summit-partner of the ASEAN since 2001.[44]

(iii) Necessarily, India is no longer an altogether recipient partner of the Indo-Russian relationship, it returns the same way: as it is shown in Chapter Two, India invests substantially in exploration of energy in Sakhalin-I in Russia and is a viable partner in joint R& D cooperation in science and technology; and in Chapter Three, it is noted India's active participation in joint R&D projects in defence-related matters.[45]

(iv) The maturity of the relationship is reflected in both countries' efforts to adjust their relations with the facts of Russia's reduced stature, its internal political and economic turmoils as well as to mould their relations meaningfully to be attuned to the new international environment. Article IX that provided the strategic angle to the 1971 Indo-Soviet Treaty in the Cold War context was thus expunged from the 1993 Indo-Russian Friendship Treaty, as it was found to be out of tune with the post-Cold War context. Notably, the term "Strategic" in the 2000 Strategic Partnership Declaration, as both countries have explained it, means *multifaceted* and *long-term* relations, shorn of any aggressive postures against any country.

The *commonness* in respective perceptions as well as "*interdependence*" of both to pursue their respective interests in general both bilaterally and in global matters are essentially the solid strength of the relationship. Relatedly, the former Soviet President Mikhail Gorbachev suggested, during the nascent stage of Indo-Russian relations, in a form of policy-prescription to the Russian policy-makers "who now plan and elaborate international political concepts for Russia" that, "...I think that Russia cannot conceive its global policy without taking into account and paying due attention to Russo-Indian relations, *the same way* as Soviet-Indian relations earlier."[46] The relationship has been further reinforced by the uniqueness of the relationship – the absence of any threat perceptions from each other, both historically and in foreseeable future. Pertinently, according to a public opinion poll, India elicited the *least negative* responses as an external threat by Russian respondents (4.8%), followed by Japan (9.2%), Israel (20.4%), China (21.1%) and Iraq (34.7%).[47] And findings from public opinion in an election survey showed that on a question, how the relationship of the US and of Russia with India were viewed-friend or enemy- 27.1 per cent of voters considered the US as friend, while 11.1 per cent considered it as enemy; 42.1 per cent of voters surveyed, considered Russia as friend while 1.4 per cent considered it as enemy.[48]

The strengths of the relationship include mutual trust that has stood the tests of time for fifty years, which include the Indo-Soviet relationship as well. Another is the factor of mutual accommodation, as was explicit when India adjusted to a higher rate in rupee-rouble exchange mechanism; or when Russia provided an increased number of cryogenic engines, as it failed to provide the related technology in totality; or when Russia took advantage of India's underfined nuclear status to supply Tarapur enriched uranium, itself being a recognized nuclear state. Relatedly, the *singular* advantage for both, which has contributed significantly to the ground-work for the relationship, has been the fact that no other country has ever been concerned to realize India's and Russia's problems and needs from their respective viewpoints, i.e., *understandability*, which each has communicated to the other.

Notes and References

1. Zbignew Brezezinski, *The Grand Chessboard: American Primacy and Its Geostrategic Imperatives*, Basic Books, New York, 1997, pp. 100-101, Emphasis added.

2. Anatol Lieven, "The Ham-Fisted Hegemon", *Current History*, 1999, p. 308.
3. Igor S. Ivanov, *op. cit.*, p. 116. See Chapter 3.
4. *Ibid.*
5. *Ibid.*, p. 118.
6. The National Security Council of the Russian Federation rates India's importance to Russia on par with that of the US and China. Presidential Decree 1300 dated 17 December 1997, reported in *RossiisKeije Vesti*,25 December 1997, cited I. Khripunov and A. Srivastava, *op. cit.* See Chapter 3.
7. F. Yurlov, *op. cit.*, See Chapter 3, pp. 56.
8. J.N. Dixit, *My South-Block Years, op. cit.*, p. 173. See Chapter 2. Emphasis added.
9. Selig S. Harrison – Geoffrey Kemp, *India and America After the Cold War: Report of the Carnegie Endowment Study Group on US – Indian Relations in a Changing International Environment*, The Carnegie Endowment for International Peace, 1993. pp. 26–27. Emphasis added.
10. Strobe Talbot, *Engaging India,: Diplomacy, Democracy and the Bomb*, Penguin Books India, New Delhi, 2004., n.4., p. 242.
11. Cited in Paromita Shastri and Sandipan Deb, "Now, Diffuse", *Outlook*, 25 May 1998.
12. Strobe Talbott, (2004), *op. cit.* See p. 157 and pp. 167-168.
13. Talbott, *Engaging India, op. cit.*,
14. Text is from *Hindu*, 22 March 2000.
15. *Times of India*, 23 March 2000.
16. *Asian Age*, 25 March 2000.
17. Cited in Talbott, *Engaging India, op. cit., p.* 213 emphasis added.
18. Ashley J. Tellis, *India's Emerging Nuclear Posture: Between Recessed Deterrent and Ready Arsenal*, OUP, New Delhi, 2001, p. 81.
19. *Economic Survey*, Government of India, 2004-05, in *Telegraph*, 26 February 2005.
20. *India: Economic Policy Update*, Vol. 3, No. 10, October 2002, CII.
21. I. Futehally – S. Bhatt, "The Cost of Conflict – India and Pakistan" Research Report by Strategic Foresight Group, *Businessworld* 23 February 2004.
22. R.A. Mashelkar, "Scientific Research Should Lead To Wealth Creation", *Business Today*, 18 January 2004.
23. Cited in, *ibid.*
24. Source: *www.meadev.nic.in*
25. Trade figures for Russia *www.meadev.nic.in* and for the US, *www.dgft.delhi.nic.in*
26. *Indian Defence Yearbook* 2004.
27. *Ibid.*
28. *Ibid.*

29. *Ibid.*
30. *Ibid.*
31. *Ibid.*
32. Vladimir Radyuhin, *Hindu*, 12 April 2002. Emphasis added.
33. *Indian Express*, 23 April 2002.
34. Vladimir Radyuhin, *Hindu*, 22 April 2002.
35. *Hindu*, 21 April 2002. Emphasis added.
36. *Hindu*, 18 February 2002.
37. *Indian Defence year book* 2002, p. 251–252.
38. *Hindustan Times*, 22 August 2001.
39. Igor Khripunov and Anupam Srivastava, *op. cit.* p. 248.
40. *Hindu*, 12 April 2002.
41. *Hindu*, 1 December 2002.
42. The EU has decided in 2004 to elevate India's status to a Strategic Partner.
43. *www.meadev.nic.in*
44. Notably, the 2003 National Security Strategy of the United States proclaimed: "... we start with a view of India as a growing world power with which we have common strategic interests," cited in Robert D. Blackwill, "US-India Defence Cooperation", Hindu, 13 May 2003 and in 2004 both sides have agreed on a Strategic Partnership (in technological issues).
45. During PM Vajpayee's Moscow visit in November 2003, India and Russia signed a MoU that provided for Russia's help to construct space-antennas and electric rocket-engines for ISRO's Moon Mission Chandrajan-1, and for India's participation in the upgradation of the Russian global space navigation system GLONASS and in joint fabrication and launching of navigation satellites. *Indian Defence Yearbook*, 2004.
46. M. Gorbachev's interview to Dev Murarka, "The Path Won", *Rethinking Russia*, *op. cit*, p. 278. See Chapter 1. Emphasis added
47. Report by the Russian Independent Institute of Social and National Problems, Moscow, January 1996, cited in Igor Khripunov-Anupam Srivastava, *op. cit.*, n. 37.
48. Data from the *Election Survey* conducted by the Centre for the Study of Developing Societies, New Delhi.

Annexure A

Moscow Declaration on the Protection of the Interests of Pluralistic States

The eve of the twenty-first century is witness to far-reaching historic changes which are destined to transform the world for the present and future generations.

The end of the Cold War has opened prospects for attaining global security and stability and has offered both opportunities and challenges for fruitful cooperation among States.

Internationally accepted standards of democracy and the rule of law are perceived by an increasing number of States as basic components of their political systems and a reliable guarantee for the promotion and protection of human rights.

Governments are becoming increasingly aware that economic reforms and integration into the world economy on the basis of equal rights and responsibilities are prerequisites for the progress of all States.

However, tension and violence still persist in the world. As ideological and other barriers to mutually beneficial cooperation are being overcome, new challenges to security and stability are emerging. In particular, there is a growing threat from the forces of aggressive nationalism, religious and political extremism, terrorism and separatism, which strike at the unity of pluralistic States.

India, and Russia, being among the largest multiethnic, multilingual and multireligious States, recognize their responsibility for opposing the threats to democracy and peace together with other members of the world community. They believe that the experience accumulated by them in governing their societies on the basis of their commitment to "unity in diversity", can make a valuable contribution in this respect. They are convinced that the guiding principles of every democratic society, such as equality, rule of law, observance of human rights, freedom of choice, and tolerance should be equally applicable to international relations. These must be based on respect for sovereignty, equality and territorial integrity of States, non-interference in their internal affairs and peaceful coexistence.

Exercising their right to self-determination, the peoples of India and Russia have established by law sovereign and free States. Throughout the territories of their respective countries the will of the people and the realization of their historic destiny are expressed through participation in the process of representative democracy.

The different religions that coexist in India and Russia enrich the spiritual values of societies and of world civilization. The right to profess, practice or promote any religion is guaranteed by the constitutions of the two countries and is characteristic of their everyday life. Claims to religious exclusivism are the threat to the exercise of that right and lead to extremism and intolerance both within States and internationally.

India and Russia are determined to protect the cultural and religious diversity of their societies from these dangers. They firmly declare that it is inadmissible to arouse interethnic and inter-religious hatred or to promote aggressive nationalism and religious fanaticism.

Both countries are convinced that destabilization of relations between ethnic or religious groups, efforts to forcibly displace them, ethnic cleansing and promotion of internal and transborder terrorism, motivated by vested interests, lead to annihilation of all the positive and constructive elements accumulated by mankind during the many thousands of years of its existence.

India and Russia are convinced that large multiethnic States bear a special responsibility for the destiny of hundreds of millions of people. They advocate unconditional observance of the principles of respect for territorial integrity and unity of the State as a key factor of viability of multiethnic States.

They reiterate their support for each other's territorial integrity as constituted by law and enshrined in their respective Constitution.

India welcomes the formation of the Commonwealth of Independent States (CIS), the various agreements on cooperation signed within that framework, including the Declaration on Respect for Sovereignty, Territorial Integrity and Inviolability of Frontiers of the States of the CIS of April 15, 1994. It appreciates Russia's efforts towards promoting the spirit of good neighbourliness and cooperation among States of the former USSR.

India understands Russia's concerns that all people residing in the territories of the former Soviet Union should have equal protection before law and safeguarding of their fundamental human rights as guaranteed in democratic societies.

Russia appreciates the efforts made by the Government and people of India to strengthen social harmony, promote development of the country, and preserve the territorial integrity and sovereignty of the country. It supports India's actions to create an atmosphere of confidence in South Asia and promote good neighbourliness and cooperation between the States of the region.

India and Russia agree to exchange experiences in nation building, including those which address the need for decentralization without impairing the integrity and unity of their States.

India and Russia believe that the successful development of multi-ethnic, multi-religious States promotes international peace and stability. They, therefore, urge other members of the international community, and international and regional organizations to respect the integrity of these States.

B. Yeltsin
President of the
Russian Federation
30 June 1994.

P.V. Narasimha Rao
Prime Minister of the
Republic of India

Annexure B

Declaration on Further Development and Intensification of Cooperation Between the Republic of India and the Russian Federation

The Republic of India and the Russian Federation, hereinafter referred to as the Sides;

Proceeding from the mutual desire of the peoples of the Republic of India and the Russian Federation to further strengthen their friendship and enhance their cooperation to mutual benefit;

Convinced that such cooperation corresponds to the fundamental long-term interests of both countries and strengthens global peace and security;

Determined to build on the positive legacy of bilateral relations between the two countries;

Emphasizing the fundamental and lasting importance of the Treaty of Friendship and Cooperation between the Republic of India and the Russian Federation;

Re-affirming their commitment to the aims and principles of the United Nations Charter;

Declare as follows:

The visit of the Prime Minister of India, Mr. P.V. Narasimha Rao to the Russian Federation from June 29 to July 2, 1994, the Russian-Indian talks, held in an atmosphere of traditional friendship and trust and the agreements signed thereafter, gave a strong impetus and new momentum to the development of bilateral relations between the two Sides and initiated a qualitatively new stage of their constructive interaction on a broad range of bilateral regional and international issues.

The Sides noted their broad identity of views on global and regional issues and reaffirmed their determination to continue their close cooperation in the international arena with a view to promoting the establishment of a just and equitable world order.

The Sides believe that international peace and security, adherence to democratic and secular values, observance of human rights and economic growth with social justice are essential prerequisites for sustainable economic development and enrichment of the intellectual, spiritual, cultural and social life of their peoples. They underline their commitment to deepening bilateral cooperation as well as cooperation with other countries sharing the same ideals in the interests of furthering the positive achievements of recent years, and in a joint search for ways of resolving contemporary problems.

The two have similar views regarding the important role of the United Nations Organization in furthering the cause of world peace and security. They noted with satisfaction the growing authority of the United Nations Organization and agreed to continue to promote strengthening, increasing the efficiency and further democratisation of this organization. The United Nations system should reflect the changing realities of the contemporary world to the fullest extent.

The Sides reiterated their fundamental commitment to all measures aimed at the complete and universal elimination of *weapons* of mass destruction. They agreed in particular to make every effort to facilitate the early conclusion of multilaterally negotiated comprehensive treaties on the universal ban of nuclear tests and cessation of production of fissile materials for weapons purposes.

The Sides noted with concern that new problems and conflicts have emerged in the world whose settlement requires greater attention and efforts by the international community. Aggressive nationalism, religious and political extremism, terrorism and separatism present a special threat to territorial integrity and unity of sovereign States and international peace and stability. Mindful of this, the Sides adopted the Moscow Declaration on Protection of Interests of Pluralistic States.

The Sides reiterated their deep interests in promoting peace and stability in the area between the border of the Republic of India and the Russian Federation. They expressed particular concern over the continuing sanguinary conflict in Afghanistan and its negative impact on the adjacent States and called for the speedy political settlement.

The Sides expressed their serious concern at the continuing tension on the Tajik-Afghan border. They reiterated the need to resolve the situation by political means and support the continuation of the inter-Tajik dialogue.

The Sides expressed their satisfaction with the general improvement of their relations with the countries of the Asia-Pacific Region and the development of consolidative processes therein. They noted the affinity of their approaches to the problems of the Asia-Pacific Region and favour the intensification of constructive interaction in settling existing conflicts and disputes in this region through peaceful means.

The Sides expressed their readiness to cooperate bilaterally and with all other States in combating terrorism supported from outside, subversive activities and international crime, which pose a serious threat to territorial integrity and the democratic and secular nature of their States and the human rights of their citizens.

Taking account of the present state and the prospects of their bilateral cooperation, the process of implementation of the agreements reached during the visit of the President of the Russian Federation to India in January 1993, the Sides agreed to concentrate their efforts in the following directions.

The Sides will utilize to the full extent the new opportunities which are emerging as a result of market-oriented changes and reforms in their economies in the directions of greater openness, competition and broad integration with the world economy.

The Sides will encourage cooperation between both public and private sector organizations in setting-up, modernising and reconstructing investment projects, the establishment of joint ventures as well as mutually beneficial investments in their territories. In accordance with their national legislation and international commitments, they will facilitate the creation of favourable organizational, fiscal and legal conditions for entrepreneurial and other forms of economic activity for each other's entities.

The Sides expressed their desire to further develop scientific and technological cooperation, especially in such high technology areas as utilization of nuclear energy for peaceful purposes, exploration and uses of outer space for peaceful purposes, joint research, development and designing of lasers and laser technologies, new generation passenger aircraft and information technologies. They agreed that there was need for expediting the industrial and commercial application of bilateral cooperation in high technology areas.

The Sides reaffirmed significance of the inter-governmental agreement of defence cooperation signed in New Delhi in January, 1993, and agreed to continue their efforts to further develop their military technical cooperation, including the establishment of joint production aimed, inter alia, at export to third countries. They reiterated that their military cooperation is not directed against any third party.

The Sides attached great importance to the further development of cooperation in human resource development and facilitating greater people-to-people contacts, particularly in the field of culture, education, art, information, tourism and sports. They will undertake concrete measures in these areas under the Cultural Exchange Programme signed in 1993 and other bilateral arrangements.

With the shared aim of providing for the dynamic and comprehensive development of their relations, the Sides signed Declaration on the Protection of the Interests of Pluralistic States and on the Further Development and Intensification of Cooperation between India and the Russian Federation, Agreements on Cooperation in the Exploration and Use of Outer Space for Peaceful Purposes, Science and Technology, Information Technology, Tourism, Protection of the Environment and Natural Resources, Memoranda on Cooperation in the Fields of Meteorology and Standardization, Metrology and Certification, Protocol on extending the Inter-Government Agreement of September 17, 1992, and the Indo-Russian aviation enterprise. They also declared their intention to conclude, as early as possible, Agreements on Promotion of Air Services and Merchant Shipping.

The results of the Indo-Russian Summit in Moscow once again confirmed the fruitful and constructive nature of the bilateral political dialogue at the highest level and the need to continue it on a regular basis. The continuation of this dialogue and bilateral and international interaction will promote multifaceted cooperation between the Republic of India and the Russian Federation, which contributes significantly to peace and stability in Asia and in the world.

Signed in Moscow on June 30, 1994 in two copies each in Hindi, Russian and English languages.

P.V. Narasimha Rao
Prime Minister of the
Republic of India

Boris N. Yeltsin
President of the
Russian Federation

30 June 1994

Annexure C

Indo-Russian Strategic Partnership for Enhanced Cooperation

The following is the text of the "Declaration on strategic partnership between India and Russia" signed here today by the Prime Minister, Mr. Atal Bihari Vajpayee, and the visiting Russian President, Mr. Vladimir Putin.

Proceeding from a desire to further consolidate their traditionally close and friendly ties to mutual benefit; drawing upon their rich and fruitful tradition of cooperation in various fields accumulated over half a century since their establishment of diplomatic relations; emphasizing the fundamental and lasting importance of the treaty of friendship and cooperation between the Republic of India and the Russian Federation of 28 January 1993 which was a continuation of the bilateral Treaty of Peace, Friendship and Cooperation of 9 August 1971, of the Declaration on the Further Development and Intensification of Cooperation between the Republic of India and the Russian Federation of 30 June 1994, and of the Moscow Declaration on the Protection of the Interests of Pluralistic States of 30 June 1994; convinced that the further comprehensive development of their bilateral ties would promote progress and prosperity in both states and the consolidation of positive trends in the world as a whole; seeking to impart a qualitatively new character and long-term perspective to their multi-faceted bilateral relations and to actively develop them in political, economic, trade, scientific, technological, cultural and other fields, in the years ahead and into the 21st century; proceeding from the conviction that it is necessary to build a multi-polar global structure based on sovereign equality of all states and peoples, democratic values and justice; confirming their adherence to the common ideals of peace, democracy, rule of law, human rights and fundamental freedoms, non-violence and secularism; recognising their special responsibility by virtue of being among the largest multi-ethnic, multi-lingual and multi-religious states; inspired by a desire to jointly contribute to the strengthening of international peace and security, the democratisation of international relations, as well as to the promotion of the establishment of a new, just and stable world order; reaffirming their commitment to the purpose and principles of the United Nations charter, declare as follows:

1. The sides hereby proclaim the establishment of relations of strategic partnership between them. Based on mutual understanding and long-term confidence in each other, this envisages the elevation of their multifaceted ties to an even higher and qualitative new level, while imparting them with a specially close and dynamic character, both in the bilateral field and in the international arena.
2. This strategic partnership between the sides is based upon the principles of sovereignty, equality and territorial integrity of states, non-interference in their internal affairs, mutual respect and mutual benefit.
3. Such a strategic partnership would include enhanced cooperation in the following fields:

   Political: Convening of annual summit level meetings; regular bilateral political and foreign office consultations on issues of mutual concern; closer cooperation at the United Nations, including its specialised agencies and institutions, at other international and regional fora; further intensifying their efforts aimed at strengthening international peace and security, general and complete disarmament, systematic and progressive efforts to reduce nuclear weapons globally, with the ultimate goal of eliminating these weapons, nuclear non-proliferation and the peaceful settlement of disputes; joint initiatives on key international and regional issues; informing each other of planned foreign policy initiatives in the international arena; non-participation in any military-political or other alliances or associations or armed conflict directed against the other side, or in any treaties, agreements or understandings infringing upon the independence, sovereignty, territorial integrity or national security interests of the other side.

Trade and Economy: Strengthening close cooperation within the framework of the Indo-Russian inter-governmental commission on trade, economic, scientific, technological and cultural cooperation, as well as other joint bodies of business and industry representatives, with a view to expanding trade and economic relations; deepening and diversifying cooperation in sectors such as metallurgy, fuel and energy, information technology, communications and transport, including merchant shipping and civil aviation; further development of cooperation in banking and finance, and improving credit and insurance facilities so as to promote bilateral trade; creating a favourable environment for mutual investments and guaranteeing their protection; simplifying customers and other procedures and promoting the removal of non-tariff barriers and gradual lowering of tariff barriers, establishing effective mechanisms for interaction between India and Russian entities with a view to achieving sustained expansion of bilateral trade in a long-term perspective; encouraging contacts between regions in both countries with a view to promoting trade and economic cooperation. Simplifying rules and procedures for travel by entrepreneurs and businessmen of both countries; further enhancing the quality and international competitiveness of their goods, by *inter alia*, promoting the joint development and sharing of the latest technologies; exploiting to mutual benefit the new opportunities arising out of the integration processes underway in the world economy; enhancing cooperation and coordination at international trade, economic and financial bodies; jointly exploring the possibilities of regional trading arrangements with third countries.

Defence: Consolidating defence and military-technical cooperation in a long-term perspective; deepening service-to-service cooperation.

Science and Technology: Promoting existing and new forms of cooperation in fundamental and applied scientific research, expanding the exchange of scientists and scientific information, establishing direct ties between scientific direct ties between scientific research/higher educational institutions. Cooperating in areas such as oceanology, agricultural sciences, medical sciences and biotechnology, environmentally clean technologies, meteorology, standardisation, metrology and certification of each other's products, jointly exploring the possibilities of commercial application of the results of scientific and technological research and development. Cooperating in the peaceful use of nuclear energy and the peaceful use of outer space.

Culture: Further promoting cultural cooperation and a wider exposure to each other's cultural heritage and achievements; activising contacts between peoples and organisations including in the fields of culture, education, mass media, youth and sports. Promoting tourist exchanges and cooperation between tourist organisations in both countries.

Other fields: Cooperation in the fight against international terrorism, separatism, organised crime and illegal trafficking in narcotics. Cooperating in rendering mutual legal assistance in civil and criminal matters and in matters relating to extradition, as well as in other related areas.

4. The strategic partnership between the sides is not directed against any other state or group of states, and does not need to create a military-political alliance.
5. Signed on 3 October 2000 at New Delhi in two originals each, in Hindi, Russian and English languages.

Annexure D

37th Munich Conference on Security Policy

[February 2-4, 2001]

Statement by Mr. Brajesh Mishra, National Security Advisor and Principal Secretary to the Prime Minister of India on India-Russia Relations

India-Russia relations have several remarkable characteristics. They have demonstrated a robust strength, withstanding major structural changes in both the countries. Indo-Soviet relations moved almost seamlessly into Indo-Russian relations, in spite of the post Cold War political and military realignments and the upheavals caused by the breakdown of our economic arrangements with the Soviet Union. We retained our mutuality of interests and shared perceptions even in these totally changed circumstances. There was, and remains, a national consensus in both countries on the fundamentals of our bilateral relations. As President Putin said in India in October last year, the two countries have never clashed even once nor has there ever been any serious dispute or contradiction between us.

A number of objective factors have shaped the congruence of outlook and shared concerns which have determined the course of India-Russia relations:

— History evolves-continuously and politics is ever volatile, but geography remains constant. There is a compelling geostrategic logic for close Indo-Russian relations, which has been clearly grasped by every leadership of both our countries, regardless of its political or economic ideology.

— The two countries have a common interest in the development of a multipolar world based on a cooperative security order. In fact, even in the bipolar construct of the Cold War, the development of India's relations with the Soviet Union was perhaps one of the first expressions of multipolarity.

— We do not share a border, but we do share neighbours and a number of security threats from across our borders. As President Putin pointed out in his address to the Indian Parliament in October last year, the same individuals, the same terrorist and extremist organizations are involved in terrorist acts from the Philippines to Kosovo, including in Jammu & Kashmir, Afghanistan and Chechnya. Sensitivity to each other's security concerns has been an integral part of our relations. We understand Russia's real security concerns in Europe, Central Asia and the Caucasus and about the destabilizing effects of undermining existing arms control and arms limitations treaties. We receive the same understanding from Russia on our concerns.

— Russia's "National Security Concept" of January 2000 and its "Foreign Policy Concept" of June 2000 enunciate a worldview similar to that of India. We share disquiet at insidious attempts to undermine sovereignty and to justify intervention in the name of human rights, to encourage protectionism in the guise of labour and environmental standards, and to impose alien sociocultural conditions in the name of globalization.

— Neither country perceives a threat from the strength of the other. In fact, each has a stake in the increased political and economic power of the other. Uniquely, the undercurrent of competition or suspicion, often evident in relations between two equal partners in such close geographical proximity, is totally absent in the Indo-Russian equation. Russia's public and unequivocal support for India's permanent membership of the UN Security Council is only one illustration of this.

— The increasing political and economic importance of Asia has created a new security matrix in which both India and Russia have crucial and complementary interests. Asia does not have an institutional security framework like that in Europe. Any Asian security framework can be sustained only with strong inputs from India and Russia. The importance of Indo-Russian relations for a stable security order in Asia is enhanced by the fact that both countries have separately been steadily strengthening their bilateral relations with other major powers – USA, EU, China, Japan, as well as Iran and Central Asian, ASEAN, and West Asian countries. This web of bilateral relations helps us to promote a cooperative security order rooted in pluralism.

— Over 500 years ago, a Russian traveller, Afanasy Nikitin, became the first recorded European to set foot on Indian soil, over 25 years before Vasco da Gama. He travelled along the land and sea route, which we today call the North-South transport corridor. In September last year, India and Russia signed an agreement on developing this corridor to promote bilateral trade and other exchanges by reducing transport and transit costs. A cursory glance at a Eurasian map would show that this corridor has more than an economic significance.

— As two large and modernizing economies, we have similar perspectives on the pace and direction of the globalization process. We have the complementarities to exploit the opportunities created by economic liberalization and technology diffusion to our mutual advantage.

Our close bilateral relations are serviced by intensive and sustained dialogue at all levels. In implementation of the decision on annual summit meetings, our Prime Minister will be going to Moscow later this year. Regular exchanges are maintained between Foreign Ministries, Defence Ministries and our National Security Councils.

It is no secret that the two countries have had substantial military-technical cooperation over many decades. A significant proportion of the military equipment of our three armed services is of Russian (or Soviet) manufacture. In recent years, our defence relations have moved from a mere buyer-seller nexus towards joint research, development and manufacture.

We place special emphasis on cooperation in the energy sector. This is a crucial element in our goal of energy security. Indian companies hope to enter the Russian oil industry through investments in Sakhalin. It is the same objective that drives our cooperation in nuclear power. Russia is collaborating in the construction of 2 × 1000 MW nuclear power plant in Kudankulam in Southern India.

We acknowledge the underachievement in our bilateral trade, which has an annual turnover of only about US $1.6 billion. Much of our trade is through the rupee repayment track by which India repays the rouble debts of the Soviet Union days. [Incidentally, among the countries with debts to the former Soviet Union, India is the only one to have reached agreement with Russia, fully addressing the debts]. The financial and banking crisis in Russia in 1998, and the slowdown in our economy due to the Asian crisis had some impact on our trade, but we have put them behind us. We are shifting gradually from our traditional areas of economic interaction like power, steel, coal and pharmaceuticals to areas like space, information technology, robotics and oil exploration.

Of course, I am not saying that we do not have our differences. But we recognise and manage them with mutual understanding and without rancour. We have our separate views on nuclear proliferation. During his visit to India, President Putin expressed the hope that India would continue to move toward a non-proliferation regime, taking into account its national interests. Unlike other nuclear powers, Russia did not impose economic sanctions or participate in indiscriminate technology denial regimes after India's nuclear tests. This would have simply had the effect of throwing out the baby of our flourishing civilian economic and technological cooperation along with the bath water of proliferation concerns, which were, in any event, unfounded. Russia also refrained from lecturing, hectoring, posturing or offering gratuitous advice on the validity of our security concerns and on how we should address them. I think this demonstrated the maturity and depth in our relationship.

It is this mature understanding of the mutuality of interests that inspired our Declaration on Strategic Partnership, signed during President Putin's recent visit to India. Strategic partnership is not a military alliance, not is it directed against any third country or group of countries. It is a long-term perspective on bilateral relations, based both on geostrategic realities and economic opportunities. It is a declaration of our solidarity in the emerging political, economic and security scenario of the new millennium.

Annexure E

Moscow Declaration between India and the Russian Federation on International Terrorism

Moscow, November 06, 2001

India and the Russian Federation affirm that international terrorism is a threat to peace and security, a grave violation of human rights and a crime against humanity. The struggle against international terrorism has become one of the priority tasks of the world community. This evil can be vanquished only by combining the efforts of all States.

Whatever be the motive of their perpetration – political, ideological, philosophical, racial, ethnic, religious or any other, terrorist acts are unjustifiable.

India and the Russian Federation support the adoption on the basis of international law of decisive measures against all States, individuals, and entities which render support, harbour, finance, instigate or train terrorists or promotion terrorism. It is essential that all States, without exception, should pay particular attention to the prevention of access of terrorists and extremist organisations and groups to financial resources on the basis of international law.

In multi-ethnic and democratic countries such as India and the Russian Federation, violent actions being prepetrated under the slogan of self-determination, in reality represent acts of terrorism which in most cases have strong international links. In addition, all acts and methods and practices of terrorism constitute a grave violation of the purposes and the principles of the United Nations, jeopardise friendly relations amongst States and are aimed at destruction of human rights, fundamental freedoms and democratic basis of society. Multi-ethnic and democratic societies are especially vulnerable to acts of terrorism which are an attack against the values and freedoms enshrined in such societies.

Fully resolved to developing cooperation in the struggle against new challenges in international terrorism including in the nuclear, chemical, biological, space, cybernetics and other spheres, both Sides noted the presence of close nexus between terrorism and illegal trafficking in narcotics, trade in arms and organised crime and pointed to the significance of the need for close interaction at the bilateral, as also at the multilateral level in combating these challenges to international stability and security.

India and the Russian Federation are closely following the development of the situation in and around Afghanistan and emphasise the necessity to avert the spilling over of the conflict beyond the boundaries of one region, to prevent further extension of terrorism. The Sides accorded highest priority to the continuation of effective interaction on Afghanistan in the framework of the Indo-Russian Joint Working Group on Afghanistan established between the two countries in October 2000.

India and the Russian Federation reaffirmed the central role of the United Nations in the efforts of the international community in the struggle against terrorism. They agreed that such a struggle must be conducted on the basis of international law including the United Nations Charter. In this connection the Sides called for early completion of negotiations under U.N. auspices on the draft Comprehensive Convention on International Terrorism and the Convention for the suppression of acts of Nuclear Terrorism. Adoption of these Conventions would assist in strengthening the international legal basis for effectively combating the global menace of terrorism.

Signed on 6th November 2001 at Moscow in two originals, each in Hindi, Russian and English languages.

Prime Minister of the Republic of India	President of the Russian Federation Moscow

6th November 2001.

Annexure F

Delhi Declaration on Further Consolidation of Strategic Partnership between the Republic of India and the Russian Federation

New Delhi, December 04, 2002

The Republic of India and the Russian Federation,

- relying on long-standing traditions of friendship and good-neighbourliness;
- recalling the Treaty of Friendship and Cooperation between the Republic of India and the Russian Federation of 28 January 1993 and the Declaration on Strategic Partnership between the Republic of India and the Russian Federation of 5 October 2000;
- proceeding from the fact that the strategic partnership between India and Russia is founded on the complementarity of national interests and geopolitical priorities of the two countries;
- determined to elevate their strategic partnership to an even higher and qualitatively new level in both bilateral and international arenas;
- recognizing respect for national sovereignty, territorial integrity, plurality, diversity and tolerance as the cornerstone of a stable and enduring multi-polar world;
- recognizing also their unique role and responsibility as multi-ethnic and pluralistic States in contributing to a stable world order, as envisaged in the United Nations Millennium Declaration of 8 September 2000 and the Moscow Declaration by the Republic of India and the Russian Federation of 30 June 1994 on the Protection of Interests of Pluralistic States, and in contributing to peace, stability and prosperity in Asia and all over the world;

- determined to counter new challenges and threats to security – primarily international terrorism – through mechanisms of bilateral and multilateral cooperation;

hereby declare:

Our strategic partnership provides a solid framework for long-term and all-round development of relations. Mutual security, development and prosperity of our peoples are core objectives of this partnership. It also contributes to countering global challenges and threats and promoting strategic stability at the international level.

The established practice of holding annual meetings at summit level as well as at Ministerial and working levels, and exchanges between Parliamentary, judicial and other constitutional bodies would be further intensified. There would be particular emphasis on deepening the economic content of bilateral relations. People to people contacts would be strengthened through an expanding network of ties between the two societies.

Internationally accepted standards of democracy and the rule of law, as enshrined in our respective Constitutions, are basic components of our political systems. They are reliable guarantees for a pluralistic political, social and economic framework and for the promotion and protection of the aspirations of our peoples for human rights, life with dignity, and freedom from want and fear. These are standards which shall also guide our relations with other countries. As large multiethnic and pluralistic states, we are convinced of our special responsibility to combat and bring to an end challenges posed to our unique attributes, including our territorial integrity, by forces of terrorism, extremism and separatism.

We reiterate our support for each other's territorial integrity and respect for each other's sovereignty, enshrined in our respective Constitutions. Neither side shall take any actions which might threaten or impair the security of the other. Both sides shall be guided by this principle in determining their security and defence policies as well as in military technical cooperation with third countries.

Bilateral cooperation as well as cooperation with other countries would be further enhanced to meet the various challenges of globalization, in particular the mitigation of its negative manifestations. Globalization and national identity represent complementary components of world order. Recognition of and respect for diversity is a necessary precondition for human progress, and an essential component of the Dialogue between Civilizations.

Enduring ties of friendship, trust and confidence and commonality of interests confer on India and Russia a unique capability to contribute to the evolution of a new world order, which would be stable, secure, equitable and sustainable and will be based on the respect for the principles of the UN Charter and international law. To fulfill this vision, both sides would endeavour to strengthen relevant international institutions and mechanisms. Both countries reaffirm that now more than ever before there is a need for the international community to commit itself to the UN and multi-lateralism.

Both countries favour strengthening of UN's central role in promoting international security in a multi-polar world. They stand for enhancing the efficiency of the UN and its Security Council and making them more reflective of the contemporary geo-political and economic realities and rendering them more representative of the interests of the vast majority of the UN members by completing the process of rationally reforming the Organisation based on the broadest consensus of its member-states. In this context, Russia reaffirms its support to India as a strong and appropriate candidate for permanent membership in an expanded United Nations Security Council.

We take note of the outcome of the World Summit on Sustainable Development at Johannesburg and in this context, welcome the reaffirmation of the Rio principles. Taking note of the importance attached to the issue of climate change by both the countries, we welcome the results of the Eighth Conference of Parties to the United Nations Framework Convention on Climate Change hosted by India in October-November 2002 and the initiative of the President of the Russian Federation to convene in Moscow in Autumn 2003 the World Conference on Climate Change.

Both the countries reiterate their commitment to work towards a new cooperative security order that recognizes the legitimate security interests of all countries and promotes global peace and stability at lower levels of armaments, and strengthens non-proliferation and disarmament goals. India and Russia are convinced that the promotion of the disarmament process, including reduction and eventual elimination of nuclear weapons, is one of the most important components of security both in Asia and in the world at large.

We call for early start of multilateral talks aimed at preparing a comprehensive arrangement on non-deployment of weapons in outer space, non-use or threat of use of force in respect of space based objects and preserving the use of space for full range of cooperative, peaceful and developmental activities.

Situation in our common neighbourhood – Afghanistan and Central Asia – is of vital security interest to both the countries. We feel that there is a need to continuously assess the evolving Afghan situation and intend to continue and expand the close cooperation on Afghanistan. We welcome the successful implementation of the Bonn Agreement and extend full support to the Transitional Administration, aimed at promoting national reconciliation, reconstruction of Afghan economy and rebuilding the Afghan institutions, including indigenous security structures, which are important for countering and defeating internal and external threats to Afghanistan's security. India and Russia agree to cooperate closely in the reconstruction efforts in Afghanistan and agreed that these should be driven by Afghan priorities. We underline the need for the United Nations and the international community to remain engaged for ensuring the revival of Afghanistan as a sovereign and independent state, free from terrorism, drugs and external interference. Both sides have a vital interest in maintaining security, stability and a secular order in the Central Asian region.

We call for containment of the spiral of violence in the Middle East and resumption, in good faith, of the negotiations towards establishment of a just and durable peace on the basis of UN Security Council Resolutions 242 (1967), 338 (1973) and 1397 (2002).

Both the countries support the continuation of political and diplomatic efforts to fully implement all the United Nations Security Council Resolutions on Iraq.

India and Russia have been victims of terrorism and, as democratic and open societies, have been vulnerable to the threats posed by globalization of terror, including new manifestations of linkage between terrorism and weapons of mass destruction. Terrorism constitutes a gross violation of human rights, particularly the most fundamental right – the right to life – and is a crime against humanity. India and Russia firmly condemn all acts of terrorism wherever they may occur and whatever may be their motivation. Terrorism cannot be justified on any grounds and must be condemned unambiguously wherever it exists. Both the countries strongly condemn those who support terrorism or finance, train, harbour or support terrorists. States that aid abet or shelter terrorists are as guilty of the acts of terrorism as their perpetrators.

We are fully determined to strengthen our cooperation in the fight against terrorism, separatism and extremism, and the support these phenomena receive from organized crime and illicit arms and drugs trafficking. Both the countries regard these as global threats, which can be effectively countered only through collective, comprehensive, determined and sustained efforts of the international community. The fight against terrorism must not admit of any double standards and should also target the financial and other sources of support to terrorism. Both the countries reaffirm the relevance of the Moscow Declaration by the Republic of India and the Russian Federation on International Terrorism of 6 November 2001. In this regard, they also stress the paramount importance of strict implementation of UN Security Council Resolutions on the fight against terrorism, in particular Resolution 1373, and universal antiterrorist conventions which create the basic framework for national, regional and international obligations and cooperation of the international community in combating terrorism, in accordance with the UN Charter. India and Russia remain fully committed to implement this Resolution and call for an early agreement on, and entry into force of, the Comprehensive Convention on International Terrorism and the Convention for the Suppression of Acts of Nuclear Terrorism.

As victims of terrorism having its roots in our common neighbourhood, we have a particular interest in putting an end to this common threat through preventive and deterrent measures nationally and bilaterally. The two countries agree to enhance bilateral cooperation in order to combat terrorism, including in the context of the cooperation under the aegis of the Joint Working Group on Afghanistan and the Group on terrorism set up by the National Security Council of India and the Security Council of the Russian Federation. The agreement to set up an Indo-Russian Joint Working Group on Counter-terrorism will further strengthen our cooperation in this sphere. Both sides recognize that factors influencing global energy production and supplies constituted an element of vital national interest and would be the subject of regular bilateral discussions through relevant mechanisms. India and Russia would strengthen cooperation in all areas of the energy sector taking into account the needs of sustainable development and environmental protection.

The Republic of India and the Russian Federation are convinced that this Declaration will widen and strengthen the framework of the existing cooperation in different areas and will contribute to consolidation of our strategic partnership.

Prime Minister of The Republic of India	President of The Russian Federation

Bibliography

Unpublished Sources

Interviews

A.K. Chanda, Shipping Corporation of India, Kolkata, July 2000.

Brahma Chellaney, Centre for Policy Research, and a Member of National Security Advisory Board, (NSAB), New Delhi, 11 December, 2002.

Dr. Jayantanuja Bandyopadhyay, Emeritus Professor, Department of International Reklations, Jadavpur University, Kolkata, 3 March, 2003.

Honourable President APJ Abdul Kalam, his letter dated 12 September, 2003.

Honourable (former) Prime Minister PV Narasimha Rao, his letter dated January 2003.

J.N. Dixit, former Foreign Secretary, New Delhi, 17 December, 2002.

Jasjit Singh, Air-Commodore, former Director of Institute of Defence Studies and Analyses and a Member of NSAB, New Delhi, 12 December, 2002.

K. Subrahmanyam, former Director of IDSA, and the Convenor of NSAB, New Delhi, 7 December, 2002.

Manojit Dasgupta, Additional Secretary of Indian Tea Association, Kolkata, July, 2000.

N.N. Vohra, Former Defence Secretary, New Delhi, 26 December, 2002.

Pradip Gooptu, Deputy Secretary, Bengal Chamber of Commerce, Kolkata, July, 2000.

Pranab Mukherjee, ex-Minister in Indira Gandhi and Narsimha Rao Cabinet, Kolkata, 14 November, 2002.

Prof. Felix N. Yurlov, Head of Modern Studies Department of Institute of Oriental Studies, Russian Academy of Sciences, Kolkata, 31 March, 2004.

Prof. N.K. Chandra, Indian Institute of Management, Kolkata, 8 May, 2003.

S.K. Lamba, former Ambassador to Russia, New Delhi, 25 December, 2002.

Sarit Patra, Indian Tea Association, Kolkata, July, 2000.

Sarit Roy, Indian Jute Manufacturers' Association, Kolkata, July, 2000.

Unpublished Ph.D. Dissertations

D'Mello, Bernard C., *Foreign Collaboration in the Public Sector Steel Industry*, (Indian Institute of Management, Kolkata, 1986).

Mohanti, Kharavela, *Indo-Soviet Relations – Indira Gandhi Era* (Utkal University, 1995).

Internet Materials

Alibekov, Ibrahim, "India set to expand presence in Central Asia", *www.eurasianet.org*

Asia 2025, *http://www.rockfordinsitute.org/news*

Bilateral Relations between India and the Russian Federation >*http://meadev.nic.in/foreign/newrussia.htm*

Blagov, Sergei, "Post-Soviet diplomacy faces check of Asian realities" >*http://www.atimes.com/c-asia*.

Blank, Stephen, "American Bases in the Former Soviet Union?" *www.cacianalyst.org*.

——, "Is the Shaghai Cooperative Organization Cracking?" *www.cacianalyst.org*.

Chabotarev, Andrei, *Kazakhstan, NATO and Russia*, Eurasia Insight, *www.eurasianet.org*.

Cohen, Ariel, "Central Asians Launch Another Regional Association" *www.cacianalyst.org*

Cutler, Robert M., "Russia Slouches towards Central Asia", *www.cacianalyst.org*.

Dailey, Erika, "Government and International Responses to Human Rights Abuses at Tajikistan, >*www.eurasianet.org*

Dixit, JN "Vajpayee in Russia and Central Asia: Meaningful revival of equations", *http:news.indiamart.com/news_analysis/vajpayee_in_ russia*.

Embassy of the Russian Federation in India, *www.india.mid.ru*

India's external trade >*www.dgft.delhi.nic.in* and *http://meadev.nic.in/foreign.newrussia*

International Narcotics Control Strategy Report > *www.state.gov/g/int/rls/nrcrp*.

Interview of External Affairs Minister Yashwant Sinha with Vremya Novostie >*http:meaindia.nic.in/interview/2003*

Interviews of the Russian President Vladimir Putin and Indian Defence Minister George Fernandes >*www.india_today.com*

Inside Central Asia, BBC Worldwide Monitoring, >*www.monitor.bbc.co.uk*

Interfax News >*www.interfax_new.com*

Joint Statement on Russia-EU Energy Dialogue, *www.Kremlin.ru.article*

Joint Statements and Joint Declarations >*http://meadev.nic.in*

Joint Vision 2020, *http://www.dtic.mil/ju2020*

Kazi, Aftab, "India and the politics of the Trans-Afghan Gas Pipeline", *www.cacianalyst.org*

Lieven, Anatol "GUUAM: What is it and what is it for ? Eurasia Insight, *www.eurasianet.org*

Mir, Hamid, "Afghanistan's 'pipeline policy'" *http://rediff.com/news/2002*.

President Putin's visit to India December 3-5, 2002, >*http:meaindia.nic.in/event.*
Proet Contra >*www.carnegie.ru/en/pubs/procontra*
RFE/RL Research Reports >*www.rferl.org*
Rossabi, Morris, "China Seeks to Bolster its Economic Profile in Central Asia", *www.eurasianet.org*
Russian Daily News, *www.mte.gov.ru*
Sirotin, A., "Narkotiki is Afghanisatana", Chika No. 1(17), 2002 *www.chayka.org.article*
Technical data on weapons systems >*www.defenceindia.com* and *www.globalsecurity.org/military/world/russia*
The Outline of Russia's Strategy for Energy Development toward 2020. *www.nte.gov.ru/official/strategy.energy.*
Torbakov, Igor "Re-examining Old Concepts about the Caucasus and Central Asia," Eurasia Insight, *www.eurasianet.org*
Torbakov, Igor, "GUUAM's Potential to Play Role In Anti-Terrorism Appears Limited," Eurasia Insight, *www.eurasianet.org/2004.*
US Government Fact Sheet >*http://www.state.gov/p/eur/rls*
US Government Aid > *www.info.usaid.gov/pubs*
UNDP Reports >*www.undp.org*
Washington Files >*http://usinfo.state.gov/products/washfile.*
Wishnick, Elizabeth, "India Walks Central Asian Tightrope," *http://www.isu.ethz.ch/news.*
www.iranexport.com
www.ap.com, *www.timesofindia.com*
www.indianembassy.org.special/cabinet/primeminister

Published Sources

Government Documents

India

Annual Reports of Ministry of Commerce, 1998-2000.
Annual Reports of Ministry of Defence, 1990-91–2003-04.
Annual Reports of Ministry of External Affairs, 1990-91–2003-04.
Annual Reports of Reserve Bank of India, 1997-1998, 1998-1999.
Economic Survey, Government of India, 1985-86, 1998-2000.
Final Report of the Market Study for Indian products in Russian market commissioned by Indian Trade Promotion Organisation, 2000.
India's views on the Afghan Situation, Ministry of External Affairs, New Delhi, December 1980.
Payment Procedures: Exports to Russian Federation, Reserve Bank of India, December 1995.
Statistics of the Foreign Trade of India by Countries (Vol. I-II), DGCIS 1990-91–2000-2001.

Russia

Backgrounder, Information Department, USSR Embassy, New Delhi, 1986.
Military Doctrine of the Russian Federation, 2000.
National Security Concept of the Russian Federation, 1997.
National Security Concept of the Russian Federation, 2000.
President Boris Yeltsin's Address to Russian Diplomats, International Affairs, Vol. 44, No. 3, 1998.

USA

Fisher, Benjamin B., *At Cold War's End: US Intelligence on the Soviet Union and Eastern Europe 1989-91*, Central Intelligence Agency, Washington, 1999.

Non-Governmental Reports and Papers

India

Annual Summary of Jute and Gunny Statistics, Indian Jute Manufacturers' Association, 1998.
Dixit, J.N., *Future Conflict, Clash of Civilisations -- Validity of Huntington's Thesis and The Security Challenges of This Paradigm to India*, USI National Security Paper, No. 15, USI, New Delhi, 1998.
Growth Through Partnership – Doing Business with CIS, Theme Paper, Gulshan Sachdeva, 2002.
India: Economic Policy Update, Vol. 3, No. 10, October 2002, Confederation of Indian Industry.
India-Russia: The Road Ahead, Confederation of Indian Industry, New Delhi, October 2000.
India-Russia Economic Partnership, Background Paper, Confederation of Indian Industry, New Delhi, October 1995.
Industrial Mission to Central Asia, A Report, Confederation of Indian Industry, March 1993.
Issues of Tea Production and Export Scenario, Indian Tea Association, 2000.
Pant NK, *Light Combat Aircraft: Unduly Long Wait*, IPCS Article No. 257, September 1999. *http:www.ipcs.org/issues/articles*
Russian-Indian Relations, Annexure III-IV, CII, 2000.
Stobdan, P. *The Afghan Conflict and India*, Delhi Papers 6, IDSA, New Delhi, 1998.
Vasudevan, Hari. *Origins of Regime Diversity in Contemporary Russia: "Revolution" and "transition" in Central Eurasia, 1988-1992*, Peace Studies Research, Europe-Eurasia Series No. 4, Calcutta University, 1997.
Warikoo, K. (ed.). *Afghanistan Factor in Central and South Asian Politics*, Occasional Paper No. 1, Himalayan Research and Cultural Foundation, New Delhi, 1994.

USA

Allison, Graham T. – Carter Ashton B. (ed.), *Cooperative Denuclearization: From Pledges to Deeds*, CSIA Studies Paper, Harvard University, Cambridge, 1993.

Garnett, Sherman – Rahr, Alexander – Watanabe, Koji. *The New Central Asia: In Search of Stability*, A Report to the Trilateral Commission, New York, Paris, Tokyo, October 2000.

Harrison, Seligs, – Kemp, Geoffrey. *India and America: After the Cold War*, Report of the Carnegie Endowment Study Group on US -- Indian Relations in a Changing International Environment, Carnegie Endowment for International Peace, Washington, 1993.

Harrison, Selig S., *India and the United States: The First Fifty years*, India Abroad Centre for Political Awareness, Occasional Paper, November 1997.

Hass, Richarch N. and Rose, Gideon, *A New US Policy Toward India and Pakistan*, Report of An Independent Task Force, sponsored by The Council on Foreign Relations Washington, 1997.

Nunn, Sam, *Calming the Ferghana Valley: Development and Dialogue in the Heart of Central Asia*, Report of the Ferghana Valley Working Group of the Centre for Preventive Action, 1999.

The Nuclear Blackmarket, Task Force Report, Global Organized Crime Project, Centre for Strategic and International Studies, Washington, 1996.

Resources and Economic Cooperation in the Caspian and Black Sea Region and Security in South-Western Europe, eMISS Paper, Institute for Social and Political Studies, Sofia, 1999.

Yearbooks

Agence France Presse (AFP) Report

Armaments Disarmament and International Security, SIPRI, OUP.

Asian Recorder, New Delhi

Current Digest of Post-Soviet Press

Current Digest of Soviet Press

Foreign Broadcast Information Service Report, US.

Indian Defence Yearbook, Natraj Publishers, New Delhi.

Keesing's Record of World Events

Royal United Services Institute and Brassey's Defence Yearbook, The Royal United Services Institute for Defence Studies, London.

Short-Wave Broadcast Report, British Broadcasting Service.

SP's Military Yearbook, Guide Publications, New Delhi.

Statistical Yearbook, Confederation of Indian Industries, New Delhi.

Newspapers

India

Amirta Bazar Patrika (Kolkata)
Patriot (New Delhi)
The Asian Age (Kolkata)
The Economic Times (Mumbai)
The Hindu (Chennai)
The Hindustan Times (New Delhi)
The Statesman (Kolkata)
The Telegraph (Kolkata)
The Times of India (Mumbai)

Russia and Central Asia

Pravda, Nezavisimaya Gazeta, Moscow News, News from Russia
Times of Central Asia

Britain

The Guardian
The Independent

The USA

Los Angeles Times
New York Times
The Washington Post

China

Beijing Review

Seminar Papers

Building a New Asia: Problems and Prospects of Regional and Pan Asian Cooperation for Security and Development, Maulana Abdul Kalam Azad Institute of Asian Studies, Kolkata, 29-31 March 2004.

Disintegration of the Soviet Union and Its Impact Upon the International Political System with Special reference to South Asian Security, Seminar Paper No. 15, USI, New Delhi, 1993.

Foreign and Defence Policies for India in the 1990s, Seminar Paper No. 13, United Services Institute (USI), New Delhi, 1990.

India and Russia: Towards Partnership, Round Table Discussion, Centre for Russian, Central Asian and East European Studies, Jawaharlal Nehru University, 2000.

Nuclear India, Centre for Advanced Strategic Studies, Pune, 26-27 February, 1999.

Prospects for India-Russia Security Relations, Proceedings on *www.carnegieendowment.org/events.*

The Afghanistan Crisis: Problems and Prospects of Peace, Himalayan Research and Cultural Foundation – Indian Council of Social Science Research, New Delhi, 19-21 November 2000.

The Changing Pattern of India's Relations With America, Fourth SL. Kirloskar Memorial Lecture by Dr. Abid Hussein, Centre for Advanced Strategic Studies, Pune, July 1998.

Memoirs

Baker, James A., *The Politics of Diplomacy: Revolution, War and Peace, 1989-1992*, G.P. Putnam's Sons, New York, 1995.

Bowles, Chester, *Promises to keep: My years in Public Life*, Harper and Row, New York, 1971.

Bush, George and Scowcroft, Brent., *A World Transformed*, Knopf (distributed by Random House), New York, 1998.

Dixit, J.N., *My South Block Years: Memoirs of a Foreign Secretary*, UBS Publishers, New Delhi, 1996.

Dobrynin, Anatoly, *In Confidence: Moscow's Ambassador to Six Cold War Presidents*, Random House/Times Books, New York, 1995.

Galbraith, John Kenneth, *"Ambassador's Journal,"* Houghton Miffin, Boston, 1971.

Ivanov, Igor, "*New Russian Diplomacy*", Olma-Press, Moscow, 2001.

Kalam, A.P.J., *Wings of Fire*, Universities Press (India) Limited, Hyderabad, 1999.

Kaul, T.N., *Diplomacy in Peace and War*; Vikas Publishing House, New Delhi, 1979.

Kissinger, Henry, *White House Years*, Little Brown, Boston, 1971.

Shevardnadze, Eduard, *The Future Belongs To Freedom*, Sinclair-Stevenson Ltd., U.K., 1991.

Talbott, Strobe and Mikhael R. Beschloss, *At the Highest Levels: The Inside Story of the End of the Cold War*, Little, Brown and Company, Boston, 1993.

Talbott, Strobe, *The Russia Hand: A Memoir of Presidential Diplomacy*, Random House, New York, 2000.

——, *Engaging India: Diplomacy, Democracy and the Bomb*, Brookings Institute, Washington, 2004.

Yeltsin, Boris, *The View From the Kremlin*, Harper Collins, London, 1994.

——, *Midnight Diaries*, Public Affairs, New York, 2000.

Books

Allison, Roy, *The Soviet Union and the Strategy of Non-Alignment in the Third World*, Cambridge University Press, Cambridge, 1988.

Allison, Roy-Bluth, Christopher (ed.), *Security Dilemmas in Russia and Eurasia*, RIIA, London, 1998.

Anderson, John, *International Politics of Central Asia*, Manchester University Press, New York, 1997.

Arbatov, Alexie-Chayes, A. (ed.), *Managing Conflict in the Former Soviet Union: Russian and American Perspective*, MIT Press, Cambridge, Massachusetts, 1997.

Arnett, Eric, *Military Capacity and the Risk of War: China, India, Pakistan and Iran*, Oxford University Press, SIPRI, 1997.

Aslund, Anders,, *Gorbachev's Struggle for Economic Reform*, Pinter Publishers, London, 1989.

——, *The Post-Soviet Economy: Soviet and Western Perspective*, St. Martin's Press, New York, 1992.

——, *Building Capitalism: The Transformation of the Former Soviet Bloc*, Cambridge University Press, 2002.

Baev Pavel K., *The Russian Army In A Time of Troubles*, Sage Publications, London-New Delhi, 1996.

Bakshi, Jyotsna, *Russia and India: From Ideology to Geopolitics 1947-1998*, Dev Publications, New Delhi, 1999.

——, *Russia–China Relation: Relevance for India*, Shipra Publications, New Delhi, 2004.

Balababushevich V.V. – Prasad Bimla (ed.), *India and the Soviet Union: A Symposium*, People's Publishing House, New Delhi.

Banerjee, Arun K. (ed.), *Integration, Disintegration and World Order*, School of International Relations and Strategic Studies, Jadavpur University, 1995.

——, *Security Issues in South Asia: Domestic and External Sources of Threats of Security*, Minerva Associates (Publications), Kolkata, 1998.

Banerjee, Dipankar, *Security in the New World Order: An Indo-French Dialogue*, IDSA, New Delhi, 1994.

Banerjee, Dipankar (ed.), *Security Studies in South Asia: Change and Challenges*, Manohar Publications, New Delhi, 2000.

Banerjee, Jyotirmoy, *India in Soviet Global Strategy: A Conceptual Strategy*, Minerva Associates (Publications), Kolkata, 1977.

Banuazizi Ali-Weiner Myron (ed.), *The New Geopolitics of Central Asia and Its Borderlands*, Indiana University Press, Bloomington, 1994.

Barnet, Richard, J., *The Alliance: America-Europe-Japan Makers of the Postwar World*, Simon and Schuster, New York, 1983.

Beloff, Max (ed.), *Beyond the Soviet Union: The Fragmentation of Power*, Ashgate Publishing, England, 1997.

Bertsch Garry – Srivastava A. – Gehlaut S. (ed.), *Emerging India: US Strategic Relations with the World's Largest Democracy*, Routledge, New York, 1999.

Blank, Stephen, *Challenging the New World Order: The Arms Transfer Policies of the Russian Republic*, Strategic Studies Institute, US Army War College, 1993.

Brezezinski, Zbignew, *The Grand Chessboard: American Primacy and Its Geostrategic Imperatives*, Basic Books, New York, 1997.

Brown, Archie-Lilia Shevtsova (ed.), *Gorbachev, Yeltsin, and Putin: Political Leadership in Russia's Transition*, Carnegie Endowment for International Peace, Washington D.C., 2001.

Busyzynski, L., *Russian Foreign Policy after the Cold War*; Praeger, London, 1996.

Byrnes, Robert F., *After Brezhnev: Sources of Soviet Conduct in the 1980s*, Indiana University Press, Bloomington, 1983.

Cassen, Robert (ed.), *Soviet Interests in the Third World*, Sage Publications, London, New Delhi, 1986.

Chakraborty, Bhaskar (ed.), *Exploring Regional Security: South and Central Asia*, KP Bagchi, Kolkata, 2003.

Chellaney, Brahma (ed.), *Securing India's Future in the New Millennium*, Orient Longman, New Delhi, 1999.

Chenoy, Anuradha M., *The Making of New Russia*, Har-Anand, New Delhi, 2001.

Chopra, Pran, *India's Second Liberation*, MIT Press, Cambridge, 1974.

Chopra, V.D. (ed.), *Indo-Russian Relations: Prospects, Problems and Russia Today*, Kalpaz Publications, New Delhi, 2001.

——, *New Trends in Indo-Russian Relations*, Kalpaz Publications, New Delhi, 2003.

Chowdhury, GW, *India, Pakistan, Bangladesh and the Major Powers: Politics of a Divided Subcontinent*, Free Press, New York, 1975.

Chufrin, Gennady (ed.), *Russia and Asia: The Emerging Security Agenda*, OUP, 1999.

Cohen, Stephen F., *Failed Crusade: America and the Tragedy of Post-Communist Russia*, WW Norton, London, New York, 2000.

Cohen, Stephen P., *India: Emerging Power*, Oxford University Press, New Delhi, 2001.

Conley, Jerome M., *Indo-Russian Military and Nuclear Cooperation: Lessons and Options for US Policy in South Asia*, Lexington Books, New York, 2001.

Cummings, Sally N (ed.), *Oil, Transition and Security in Central Asia*, Routledge – Curzon, London, New York, 2003.

Damodaran A.K. – Bajpai, US, *Indian Foreign Policy: The Indira Gandhi Years*, Radiant Publishers, New Delhi, 1990.

Dasgupta, J.B. *Islamic Fundamentalism and India*, Hope India Publications, Gurgaon, 2002.

Dawisha, A. – Dawisha, K. (ed.), *The Making of Foreign Policy In Russia and the New States of Eurasia*, ME Sharpe, London, New York, 1995.

Donaldson, Robert H. (ed.), *The Soviet Union in the Third World: Successes and Failures*, Westview Press, Boulder, 1981.

Duncan, Peter J.S., *The Soviet Union and India*, RIIA, Routledge, London, New York, 1989.

Dunlop, John B., *The Rise of Russia and The Fall of the Soviet Empire*, Princeton University Press, USA, 1993.

Ferdinand, Peter (ed.), *The New Central Asia and Its Neighbours*, Pinter Publishers, London, 1994.

Fuller, Graham E. – Lesser Ian (ed.), *A Sense of Siege: The Geopolitics of Islam and the West*, Westview Press, Boulder, 1995.

Ganguly, Sumit, *The Origins of War in South Asia: The Indo-Pakistani Conflicts since 1947*, Westview Press, Boulder, 1986.

Goebel, K. (ed.), *International Seminar on Nuclear War and Planetary Emergencies*, World Scientific Publishing Co., London/New York, 1988.

Gopal, S. *Jawaharlal Nehru, A Biography*, Vol. 2, Oxford University Press, New Delhi, 1979.

Gopal, Surendra (ed.), *India and Central Asia: Cultural, Economic and Political Links*, Shipra, New Delhi, 2001.

Gorbachev, Mikhail, *Toward a Better World*, Richarson and Stairman, New York, 1987.

——, *Perestroika: New Thinking for Our Country and the World*, Harper and Row, New York, 1998.

Gorodetsky, Gabriel (ed.), *Soviet Foreign Policy 1917-91: A Retrospective*, Frank Cass, London, Portland, 1994.

Gould, Harold A – Ganguly Sumit (ed.), *The Hope and the Reality: US-Indian Relations from Roosevelt to Reagan*, Westview Press, San Francisco, 1992.

Haghayeghi, Mehrdad, *Islam and Politics in Central Asia*, St. Martin's Press, New York, 1996.

Haksar P.N. – Chopra, V.D. (ed.), *Studies in Indo-Soviet Relations*, Patriot Publishers, New Delhi, 1991.

Hane, Donald G., *Terrorism: The Newest Face of Warfare*, Pergamon – Brassey's International Defence Publisher's Inc., London, Washington, 1989.

Hiro, Dilip, *Between Marx and Muhammed: The Changing Face of Central Asia*, Harper Collins, London, 1994.

Hogan, Michael J. *The End of the Cold War: Its Meaning and Implications*, Cambridge University Press, Cambridge, 1992.

Horn Robert C., *Soviet–Indian Relations: Issues and Influence*, Praeger Publications, USA, 1982.

Huntington, Samuel, *The Third Wave: Democratization in the Late 20th Century*, University of Oklahoma Press, Norman, 1991.

Imam, Zafar, *Ideology and Reality in Soviet Policy in Asia*, Kalyani Publishers, New Delhi, 1975.

——, *Towards A Model Relationship: A Study of Soviet Treaties with India and Other Third World Countries*, ABC Publishing House, New Delhi, 1983.

Jackson, Nicole J., *Russian Foreign Policy and the CIS: Theories, debates and actions*, Routledge, London – New York, 2003.

Jain, B.M. *India and the United States 1961-1963*, Radiant, New Delhi, 1987.

Jonson, Lena, *Russia and Central Asia: A New Web of Relations*, Royal Institute of International Affairs, London 1998.

Joshi, Nirmala (ed.), *Central Asia: The Great Game Replayed An Indian Perspective*, New Century Publications, New Delhi, 2003.

Kanoria, J.P., *Business With New Russia*, Published by the author, Kolkata, 1993.

Kapur, Ashok – ML Sondhi, *US and India: Changing Strategic Parameters*, Manak Publications, New Delhi, 2002.

Kartha, Tara, *Tools of Terror: Light Weapons and India's Security*, Knowledgeworld, New Delhi, 1999.

Kaul, T.N. (ed.), *Indo-Soviet Relations: Prospects and Problems*, Patriot, New Delhi, 1991.

——, *India and the New World Order*, Gyan Publishing House, New Delhi, 2000.

Keddie, Nikki R – Gasiorowski, Mark J. (ed.) *Neither East, Nor West: Iran, the Soviet Union and the United States*, Yale University Press, London, New Haven, 1990.

Klein, Lawrence R. – Pomer Marshall (ed.), *The New Russia: Transition Gone Awry*, Stanford University Press, Stanford, 2000.

Kleveman, Lutz, *The New Great Game: Blood and Oil in Central Asia*, Atlantic Books, 2003.

Kux, Dennis, *India and the United States: Estranged Democracies 1941-1991*, National Defence University Press, 1993.

Lester, Jeremy, *Modern Tsars and Princes: The Strategy for Hegemony in Russia*, Verso, London, New York, 1995.

Lieven, Anatol, *Chechnya: Tombstone of Russian Power*, Yale University Press, London, New Haven, 1998.

Magnus, R.H. – Naby, Eden, *Afghanistan: Mullah, Marx and Mujahid*, Harper-Collins, India, 1998.

Majumdar, Anindyo J. (ed.), *Nuclear India Into the New Millennium*, Lancer's Books, New Delhi, 2000.

Malcom, Neil (ed.), *Russia and Europe: End to Confrontation*, Pinter Publishers, London, 1994.

Malik, Hafeez, (ed.), *Central Asia: Its Strategic Importance and Future Prospects*, Macmillan, London, 1994.

——, *Soviet – Pakistan Relations and Post-Soviet Dynamics (1947-92)*, Macmillan, London, 1994.

——, *The Roles of the US, Russia and China in the New World Order*, Macmillan, London, 1997.

Mandelbaum, Michael, (ed.), *Central Asia and the World*, Council on Foreign Relations, New York, 1994.

——, (ed.), *The New Russian Foreign Policy*, Council on Foreign Relations, New York, 1998.

——, *The Ideas that Conquered the World*, Public Affairs, USA, 2002.

Mann, Poonam, *India's Foreign Policy in the Post Cold War Era*, Harman Publishing House, New Delhi, 2000.

Mansingh, Surjeet, *India's Search for Power: Indira Gandhi's Foreign Policy 1966-1982*, Sage Publications, New Delhi, 1984.

McFaul, M., *Russia's Unfinished Revolution: Political Change from Gorbachev to Putin*, Cornell University Press, London – Ithaca, 2001.

Mcnamara, Robert, *Out of the Cold: new thinking for American foreign and defense policy in the 21st Century*, Simon and Schuster, New York, 1989.

Medvedev, Roy – Chiesa G., *Time of Change*, Pantheon Books, New York, 1989.

Mehrotra, Santosh, *India and the Soviet Union: Trade and Technology Transfer*, Oxford University Press, New Delhi, 1991.

Mellovl, John W. (ed.), *India: A Rising Middle Power*, Westview Press, Boulder, 1979.

Menon, KPS, *The Flying Troika*, London University Press, London, 1963.

Menon, Rajan, *Soviet Power and the Third World*, Yale University Press, London – New Haven, 1986.

Menon, R. – Fedorov, Y. – Nodia, G. (ed.), *Russia, the Caucasus and Central Asia: The 21st Century Security Environment*, ME Sharpe, New York, 1999.

Menon, R. – Ebel, R. (ed.), *Energy and Conflict in Central Asia and the Caucasus*, Rowman and Littlefield, Lanham, 2000.

Mishra, Om Prakash – Ghosh, Sucheta (ed.), *Terrorism and Low Intensity Conflict in South Asian Region*, Manak Publications, New Delhi, 2003.

Mozaffari, M. (ed.), *Security Politics in the CIS: The Southern Belt*, Macmillan, London, 1997.

Nayar, B – Paul, T.V., *India in the World Order: Searching for Major Power Status*, Cambridge University Press, Cambridge, 2003.

Nayar, Baldev Raj, *American Geopolitics and India*, South Asia Books, Columbia MO, 1976.

Nayyar, D. (ed.), *Economic Relations between Socialist Countries and the Third World*, Macmillan, London, 1977.

Nehru, Jawaharlal, *India and the World*, Allen and Unwin, 1937.

Nogee, Joseph L. – Mitchell, RJ, *Russian Politics: The Struggle For A New Order*, Allyn and Bacon, London-Boston, 1997.

Nolan, Peter, *China's Rise, Russia's Fall: Politics, Economics and Planning in the Transition from Stalinism*, Macmillan, London, 1995.

Olcott, Martha Brill, *Central Asia's New States*, US Institute of Peace Studies Press, Washington, 1996.

Oliker, Olga – Szayna T. (ed.), *Faultlines of Conflict in Central Asia and the South Caucasus: Implications for the US Army*, RAND Corporation, USA, 2003.

Palat, Madhavan K. – Sen, Geeti (ed.), *Rethinking Russia*, UBS Publishers, New Delhi, 1994.

Palat, Madhavan K., *Ideological Choices in Post-Soviet Russia*, Delhi Policy Group, New Delhi, 1997.

Pierre, A.J., *The Global Politics of Arms Sales*, Princeton University Press, Princeton, 1982.

Prasad, B.P., *Indo-Soviet Relation 1947-1972*, Allied Publishers, New Delhi, 1973.

Racioppi, Linda, *Soviet Policy Towards South Asia*, Cambridge University Press, Cambridge, 1994.

Rahr, Alexander – Krause Joachim, *Russia's New Foreign Policy*, Deutsche Gessellschaft Fur Auswartige Politike, Bonn, 1995.

Rajamohan, C., *Crossing the Rubicon: The Shaping of India's New Foreign Policy*, Viking, New Delhi, 2003.

Rasgotra M. – Chopra V.D. (ed.), *India's Relations with Russia and China: A New Phase*, Gyan Publishing House, 1997.

Rashid, Ahmed, *The Resurgence of Central Asia: Islam or Nationalism*, Oxford University Press, London, 1994.

——, *Taliban: Islam, Oil and the New Great Game in Central Asia*, Yale University Press, New Haven, 2000.

——, *Jihad: The Rise of Militant Islam in Central Asia*, Orient Longman, New Delhi, 2002.

Roy, J.K. (ed.), *Asia Annual 2000*, MAKAIAS, Kolkata, 2000.

Roy, Olivier, *The New Central Asia: The Creation of Nations*, I.B. Tauris, London-New York, 2000.

Roy, Ramashray (ed.), *The Federal Experience: India and Russia*, Shipra Publications, New Delhi, 2003.

Rubenstein, A.Z. (ed.), *Soviet and Chinese Influence in the Third World*, Praeger Publications, New Delhi, 1975.

Rubenstein A.Z. – Smolansky, O.P. (ed.), *Regional Power Rivalries in the New Eurasia*, ME Sharpe, London – New York, 1995.

Rumer, Boris (ed.), *Central Asia in Transition: Dilemmas of Political and Economic Development*, ME Sharpe, New York, 1996.

Rumer, Boris – Zhukov, S. (ed.), *Central Asia: The Challenges of Independence* (ME Sharpe) Aakar Books, New Delhi, 2003.

Rumer, Boris (ed.), *Central Asia: A Gathering Storm ?* (ME Sharpe), Aakar Books, New Delhi, 2003.

Santhanam K. – Sreedhar (ed.), *Jihadis in Jammu and Kashmir: A Portrait Gallery*, IDSA, New Delhi, 2003.

Santhanam K. – Dwivedi R. (ed.), *India and Central Asia: Advancing the Common Interest*, Anamaya Publishers, New Delhi, 2004.

Schweiger, Peter, *Victory – The Reagan Administration's Secret Strategy that Hastened the Collapse of the Soviet Union*, Atlantic Monthly Press, New York, 1994.

Schweitzer Y. – Shay S., *The Globalization of Terror*, Viva Books, New Delhi, 2004.

Sen, Samir K., *Military Technology and Defence Industrialization: The Indian Experience*, Manas Publications, New Delhi, 2000.

Sengupta, Bhabani, *The USSR in Asia: An Interpretational Study of Soviet – Asian Relations*, Young Asia Publications, New Delhi, 1980.

Shamsuddin – Sarkar, Bhaswati (ed.), *Geopolitics and Energy Resources in Central Asian and Caspian Sea Region*, Lancer's Books, New Delhi, 2000.

——, (ed.), *India and Russia: Towards Strategic Partnership*, Lancer's Books, New Delhi, 2001.

——, (ed.), *Afghanistan and Central Asia in the New Great Game*, Lancer's Books, New Delhi, 2003.

Sharma, R.K. (ed.), *Indo-Soviet Cooperation and India's Economic Development*, Allied Publishers, New Delhi, 1982.

Sharma, S.D. (ed.), *Studies in Indo-Soviet Cooperation*, Lancer International, New Delhi, 1981.

Shaw, Dennis J.B., *Russia in the Modern World*, Blackwell Publishers, UK, 1999.

Shearman, Peter (ed.), *Russia's Foreign Policy Since 1990*, Westview Press, Boulder-Oxford, 1995.

Shevchenko, Arkadi N., *Breaking with Moscow*, Alfred A. Knopf, New York, 1985.

Shleifer, Andrei – Treisman, Daniel, *Without A Map: Political Tactics and Economic Reform in Russia*, MIT Press, Cambridge, 2000.

Sievers, Eric W., *The Post-Soviet Decline of Central Asia: Sustainable Development and Comprehensive Capital*, Routledge – Curzon, London – New York, 2003.

Singh Mahavir (ed.), *Eurasian Vision*, Anamika Publishers, New Delhi, 2003.

——, (ed.), *India and Tajikistan: Revitalising A Traditional Relationship*, Anamika Publishers, 2003.

——, (ed.), *International Terrorism and Religious Extremism: Challenges to Central and South Asia*, Anamika Publishers, New Delhi, 2004.

Smith, Chris, *India's Ad Hoc Arsenal: Direction or Drift in Defence Policy*, OUP, New York, 1994.

Solzhenitsyn, Aleksandr, *The Russian Question At the End of the 20th Century*, Harvill Press, London, 1994.

Sreedhar, *Taliban and the Afghan Turmoil: The Role of USA, Pakistan, Iran and China*, Himalayan Books, New Delhi, 1997.

Tellis, Ashley, *India's Emerging Nuclear Posture: Between Recessed Deterrent and Ready Arsenal*, OUP, New Delhi, 2001.

Thomas, Raju G.C., *Indian Security Policy*, Princeton University Press, Princeton, 1986.

Thomas, Raju – Gupta, Amit (ed.), *India's Nuclear Security*, Vistaar, Publications, New Delhi, 2000.

Trenin, Dmitri (ed.), *Russia in World Arms Trade: The Strategic, Political and Economic Dimensions*, Carnegie Endowment for International Peace, 1996.

Trenin, Dmitri – Coppieters, B. (ed.), *Commonwealth and Independence in Post-Soviet Eurasia*, Frank Cass, London, 1998.

Trofimenko, Henry, *Russian National Interests and the Current Crisis in Russia*, Ashgate Publishing, England & USA, 1999.

Truscott, Peter, *Russia First: Breaking with the West*, I.B. Tauris, London – New York, 1997.

Warikoo, K. (ed.), *The Afghanistan Crisis: Issues and Perspectives*, Bhavana Books and Prints, New Delhi, 2002.

Articles

Adomeit, Hannes, "Russia as a 'great power' in world affairs: images and reality", *International Affairs*, 71.1, 1995.

Akbarzadeh, Shahram, "India and Pakistan's geostrategic rivalry in Central Asia", *Contemporary South Asia*, June 2003.

Akcali, Pinar, "Islam as a 'common bond' in Central Asia: Islamic Renaissance Party and the Afghan mujahidin", *Central Asian Survey*, 17(2), 1998.

Alam, Mohammad Munir, "Central Asian Republics' Quest for Security Since Independence," *Contemporary Central Asia*, Vol. IV, No. 3, 2000.

Allison, Roy, "Strategic reassertion in Russia's Central Asia Policy," *International Affairs* (London), Vol. 80, No. 2, March 2004.

Altan, Turker, "An Exhausted Environmental Legacy", *Eurasian Studies*, Vol. 2, No. 1, Spring 1995.

Arbatov, AG, "Russia's Foreign Policy Alternatives," *International Security*, Vol. 18, No. 2, Fall 1993.

Aslund, Anders, "Gorbachev, Perestroyka and Economic Crisis", *Problems of Communism*, January-April 1991.

——, "Russia's Collapse", *Foreign Affairs*, September-October, 1999.

Asian Defence Journal, January 1993.

Atanesian, Artur. "Terrorism, Its Roots and Threats: Current Trends Analyzed", *Central Asia and the Caucasus*, 6(24), 2003.

Bakshi, Jyotsna, "Russia, India and the Central Asia Republics: Geopolitical Convergence," *Strategic Analysis*, August 1996.

——, "India in Russia's Strategic Thinking," *Strategic Analysis*, January 1998.

——, "Russia-China Military Technical Cooperation: Implications for India," *Strategic Analysis*, July 2000.

——, "Russia's National Security Concepts and Military Doctrines: Continuity and Change", *Strategic Analysis*, October 2000.

Banerjee, Jyotirmoy, "Indo-Russian Relations: The Cryogenic Rocket Deal", *Jadavpur Journal of International Relations*, Vol. 1, 1995.

Basu, Baidya Bikash, "Putin's visit and Future of Indo-Russian Cooperation", *Strategic Analysis*, December 2000.

——, "Reforms in Russian Defence Industry: Problems and Prospects", *Strategic Analysis*, Vol. 23, No. 10, January 2000.

——, "Trends in Russian Arms Export", *Strategic Analysis*, February 2000.

Basu, Kaushik, "Structural Reform in India 1991-93: Experience and Agenda", *Economic and Political Weekly*, 27 November, 1993.

Becker, Abraham S., "Russia and Caspian Oil: Moscow Loses Control," *Post-Soviet Affairs*, 16(2), 2000.

Bedi, Rahul "India and Central Asia", *Frontline*, 14-27 September 2002.

——, "Mixed Fortunes for India's Defence Industrial Revolution", *Jane's International Defence Review*, May 1999.

Blank, Stephen, "Central Asia, South Asia and Asian Security," *Eurasian Studies*, Vol. 2, No. 3, Fall 1995.

Bogaturov, A. "The Eurasian support of the World Stability", *International Affairs* (Moscow), February 1993.

Bowles, Chester, "America and Russia in India", *Foreign Affairs*, July 1971.

Budhraj, Vijoy Sen, "Moscow and the Birth of Bangladesh," *Asian Survey*, May 1972.

Businessworld, 14 July, 2003.

Chandra, Amiya, "Turkmen-India Cooperation for Peace and Development," *Strategic Analysis*, December 1996.

Chandra, Nirmal Kumar, "Russia's Sinking Economy: External Dimensions," *Economic and Political Weekly*, 15 May 1993.

——, "India's Rouble Debt and Depreciating Rouble," *Economic and Political Weekly*, 3-10 July, 1993.

——, "*Dimensions of Social and Economic Crisis in Russia Today*," *Economic and Political Weekly*, 11 May 1996.

——, "India in the 1990s: The Impact of Globalisation", *China Report*, January-March 2002.

Chiesa, Gieulietto, "The 28th Congress of the CPSU," *Problems of Communism*, July-August 1990.

Chung, Chien-peng, "China's 'War on Terror'", *Foreign Affairs*, July-August 2002.

Clairmont, F., "Yeltsin: The Death Rattle," *Economic and Political Weekly*, 18 May 1996.

Contemporary Central Asia, Vol. III, No. 1, 1999.

Cohen, Ariel, "The 'New Great Game': Pipeline Politics in Eurasia," *Eurasian Studies*, 3(1), Spring 1996.

Croissant, Cynthia M. – Croissant, Michael P., "The Caspian Sea Status Dispute: Context and Implications", *Eurasian Studies*, 3(4), Winter 1996/97.

Dash, PL, "Caspian Debate and Route Options for Energy Transportation", *India Quarterly*, January-June 2003.

——, "Indo-Russian Relations", *Economic and Political Weekly*, 18 January 2003.

Davis, Anthony, "Foreign Combatants in Afghanistan," *Jane's Intelligence Review*, Vol. 5, No. 7, July 1993.

——, "Xinjiang Learns to live with resurgent Islam", *Jane's Intelligence Review*, Vol. 8, No. 9, September 1996.

Dorian, James P. – Wigdortz, B., "Central Asia and Xinjiang, China: Emerging Energy, Economic and Ethnic Relations," *Central Asian Survey*, 16(4), 1997.

Effendi, Yahiya, "The Emerging Central Asian Security Framework and Its Implications For the Southern RIM States", *Central Asia*, No. 35, Winter 1994.

Enders, Walters. – Sandler, Todd, "Patterns of Transnational Terrorism, 1970-1999: Alternative Time-Series Estimates", *International Studies Quarterly*, No. 46, 2002.

Fialkovsky, Andrei, "We Rejoice at Your Achievements," *New Times*, No. 4, January 1981.

Frontline, 23 April 2004.

Futehally, I. – Bhatt, S., "The Cost of Conflict – India and Pakistan", *Businessworld*, 23 February 2004.

Gaddis, John Lewis, "History, Grand Strategy and NATO Enlargement." *Survival*, Spring 1998.

Ghosh, Jayati, "India's Structural Adjustment As Assessment in Comparative Asian Context, *Economic and Political Weekly*, 17-24 May 1997.

Gidadhubli, RG, "Perestroika and Soviet Economic Relations with Developing Countries: India, a Test Case," *Economic and Political Weekly*, 29 July 1989.

——, "Russia's Economic Relations with Asia", *Economic and Political Weekly*, 17 June 1995.

——, "Growing Regional Economic Disparities in Russia", *Economic and Political Weekly*, 17 August 1996.

Gobarev, Victor, "Russia-NATO Relations after the Kosovo Crisis: Strategic Implications", *Journal of Slavic Studies*, reproduced in *Strategic Digest*, February 2000.

Goetz, Roland, "Political Spheres of Interest in the Southern Caucasus and Central Asia," *Aussenpolitik*, 3/97.

Grossouvre, Henri De, "Paris, Berlin, Moscow: Prospects for Eurasian Cooperation," *World Affairs*, Vol. 8, No. 1, January-March 2004.

Hale, Henry E-Taagepera R., "Russia: Consolidation or Collapse?", *Europe-Asia Studies*, Vol. 54, No. 7, 2002.

Hansen, Flemming – Splidsboel, "Past and Future Meet: Alaksandr Gorchakov and Russian Foreign Policy," *Europe-Asia Studies*, Vol. 54, No. 3, 2002.

Hanson, Philip, "The Russian Economic Recovery: Do Four Years of Growth Tell Us that the Fundamentals have changed ?", *Europe-Asia Studies*, Vol. 55, No. 3, 2003.

Hayden, William, "*Seeds of Unrest: The Political Genesis of the Conflict in Chechnya*", *The Fletcher Forum of World Affairs*, Vol. 24, 1, Spring 2000.

Heisbourg, Francois, "A New Security Landscape: the End of the Post-Cold War Era", *Asia-Pacific Review*, Vol. 10, No. 1, 2003.

Hoehmann, Hans-Hermann – Meier Christian, "Russia, 'Summit of the Eight' and International Economic Organisations", *Ossenpolitik*, 4/97.

Hollen, Christopher, Van, "The Tilt Policy Revisited: Nixon-Kissinger Geopolitics and South Asia", *Asian Survey*, April 1980.

Hunter, Shireen T., "The Muslim Republics of the Former Soviet Union: Policy Challenges for the United States," *The Washington Quarterly*, Summer 1992.

Hunter, Tom, "Russia's mafiyas: the new revolution", *Jane's Intelligence Review*, Vol. 9, No. 6, June 1997.

Huntington, Samuel P., "The Clash of Civilisations," *Foreign Affairs*, Vol. 75, No. 3, May-June 1996.

Hyman, Anthony, "Turkestan and Pan-Turkism Revisited", *Central Asian Survey*, 16(3), 1997.

ICCCI Newsletters, February and March 2000.

Jaffe, Amy Myers – Manning, Robert A., "The Shocks of a World of Cheap Oil", *Foreign Affairs*, January – February 2000.

Jaya Shekhar, "CIS: Economic Reintegration or Disintegration?" *Economic and Political Weekly*, 18 September 1993.

Kadakin, AM, "Indo-Russian Relations", *Journal of Indian Ocean Studies*, Vol. 9, No. 3, December 2001.

Kalam, A.P.J. Abdul, "Igniting India's Mind", *The Week*, 28 December 2003.

Kalicki, Jan H. "Caspian Energy at the Crossroads," *Foreign Affairs*, Vol. 80, No. 5, September-October 2001.

Kamenev, Sergey, "Turkmenistan: Energy Policy and Energy Projects", *Central Asia and the Caucasus*, 4(22), 2003.

Kamet, RE – Biregerson SM, "The Domestic Foreign Policy Linkage in Russian Politics: Nationalist Influences on Russian Foreign Policy", *Communist and Post-Communist Studies*, Vol. 30, No. 4, December 1997.

Kamp, Heinz Karl, "The NATO-Russia Founding Act: Trojan Horse or Milestone of Reconciliation ?", *Aussenpolitik*, 4/97.

Kanwar, Sunil, "Rupee-Rouble Agreement: Was It a Sell-Out ?", *Economic and Political Weekly*, 13 March 1993.

Karayianni, Marika S. "Russia's Foreign Policy for Central Asia Passes Through Energy Agreements", *Central Asia and the Caucasus*, 4(22), 2003.

Karniol, Robert, "Russian Industry Hunts Out a Future for Itself," Jane's Defence Weekly, 1 March 2000.

Kastl, Joerg, "European Security Without Russia ?", *Aussenpolitik*, 1/97.

Kaushik, Devendra, "India and Central Asia: Renewing A Traditional Relationship", *South Asia Survey*, July-December 1998.

——, "Central Asia: Changing Geo-Political Alignment in the Aftermath of 11 September," *Dialogue*, Vol. 3, No. 4, April-June, 2002.

Khodarenok, Mikhael, "Western Interest in Central Asia", *Dialogue*, Vol. 3, No. 4, April-June 2002.

Khripunov, I., – Mathews Mary M. "Russia's Oil and Gas Interest Group and its Foreign Policy Agenda", *Problems of Post-Communism*, Vol. 43, No. 3, May/June 1996.

Khusainov, Bulat – Turkeeva, Kulyash, "Kazakhstan's Energy Potential Today and Tomorrow", *Central Asia and the Caucasus*, No. 4(22), 2003.

Klevemann, Lutz, "Oil and the New Great Game," *The Nation*, February 2004.

Kohli, Sanjib, "Indo-Russian Economic and Commercial Engagement", *Business Messenger*, December 2002.

Komissina, Irina, "India: Cooperation With the Central Asian Countries in Regional Security," *Central Asia and the Caucasus*, 6(24), 2003.

Kozyrev, Andrei, "What Foreign Policy Russia Should Pursue", *International Affairs* (Moscow), February 1993.

Kramer Mark. "The Armies of the Post-Soviet States", *Current History*, October 1992.

Kuchins, Andrew C. "Explaining Mr. Putin: Russia's New Nuclear Diplomacy", *Arms Control Today*, October 2002.

Kumar, B.B. "Central Asia: The Indian Links", *Dialogue*, Vol. 3, No. 4, April-June 2002.

Kux, Stephen, "Soviet Federalism," *Problems of Communism*, March-April 1990.

Kuzmin, Nikolai, "Central Asia After the Operation in Afghanistan," *Central Asia and the Caucasus*, 1(19), 2003.

Legvold, Robert, "Russia's Unformed Foreign Policy", *Foreign Affairs*, September-October 2001.

Lieven, Anatol, "Ham-Fisted Hegemon: The Clinton Administration and Russia", *Current History*, October 1999.

——, "Through a Distorted Lens: Chechnya and Western Media", *Current History*, October 2000.

Lounev, Sergei, "Russia and India: Political Cooperation in the Sphere of Global, Regional and Bilateral Relations," *China Report*, 38:1, 2002.

Maass, Citha D., "The Afghanistan conflict: external involvement", *Central Asian Survey*, 18(1), 1999.

Mahmood, Tahmina, "Pakistan and Central Asia", *Eurasian Studies*, Vol. 3, No. 4, 1996/97.

Maley, William, "The 'War against Terrorism' in South Asia", *Contemporary South Asia*, 12(2), 2003.

Mandelbaum, Michael, "The Case Against NATO Expansion," *Current History*, March 1998.

Mann, Poonam, "Fighting Terrorism: India and Central Asia", *Strategic Analysis*, February 2001.

Marantz, Paul, "Russia's Foreign Policy During Yeltsin's Second Term", *Communist and Post-Communist Studies*, Vol. 30, No. 4, 1997.

Mashelkar, RA, "Scientific Research Should Lead To Wealth Creation", *Business Today*, 18 January 2004.

Melet, Yasmin, "China's Political and Economic Relations with Kazakhstan and Kyrgyzstan," *Central Asian Survey*, 17(2), 1992.

Menon, Rajan – Fuller, Graham, "Russia's Ruinous Chechen War", *Foreign Affairs*, March-April 2000.

Menon, Rajan – Barkey, Henry J., "The Transformation of Central Asia: Implications for Regional and International Security", *Survival*, Vol. 14, No. 3, Winter 1992-93.

Miller, D. – Perovic J. – Wenger A., "The New Approach to Russian Security in the context of the Programme for Change", *Aussenpolitik*, 1/98.

Minasian, Sergei, "CIS: Building a Collective Security System," *Central Asia and the Caucasus*, No. 1(19), 2003.

Misra, Amalendu, "Shanghai 5 and the emerging alliance in Central Asia: the closed society and its enemies", *Central Asian Survey*, 20(3), 2001.

Mohanty, Arun, "55 years to Indo-Russian Diplomatic Relations," *Business Messenger*, June 2002.

Mukherjee, Dilip, "Indo-Soviet Economic Ties", *Problems of Communism*, January-February 1987.

Nagaraj, R. "What Has Happened since 1991 ?", *Economic and Political Weekly*, 8 November 1997.

Narain, Nidhi, "Indian Aid to Afghanistan Post 9-11", *South Asia Politics*, November 2002.

Narayanswamy, Ramnath, "Soviet Economy: What Transition to What Market?" *Economic and Political Weekly*, 5 October 1991.

Neumann, Iver B. "European Identity, EU Expansion and the Integration/ Exclusion Nexus," *Alternatives*, 23, 1998.

Nikolaev, A., "Indo-Russian Cooperation in the 21st Century", *Indian Defence Review*, 17(1), January-March 2002.

Niyazi, Aziz, "Tajikistan: Its Hydropower Resources and the Problems of Their Use," *Central Asia and the Caucasus*, No. 4(22), 2003.

Odom, William E. "Russia's Several Seats at the Table," *International Affairs*, 74.4, 1998.

Olcott, Martha Brill, *Central Asia Monitor*, No. 5: 24.28, 1992.

Palat, Madhavan K., "Eurasianism As An Ideology For Russia's Future", *Economic and Political Weekly*, 18 December 1993.

Pozduyakov, Elgiz, "Russia is a Great Power", *International Affairs*, Moscow, Vol. 39, No. 1, 1993.

Prakash, Shri, "India-Uzbekistan Relations During the 1990s and Future Prospects," *Contemporary Central Asia*, Vol. V, No. 1, 2001.

Preiger, David – Maliarchuk, I. – Grinkevich T., "Pipelines for Caspian Oil," *Central Asia and the Caucasus*, No. 4(22), 2003.

Puri, Madan Mohan, "Central Asian Geopolitics: the Indian View." *Central Asian Survey*, 16(2), 1997.

Rajan, M.S. "The Tashkent Declaration: Retrospect and Prospect," *International Studies*, Vol. 8, No. 1-2, July-October 1966.

Rashid, Ahmed, "The Taliban: Exporting Extremism", *Foreign Affairs*, 78(6), November-December 1999.

Rose, Leo E., "The Superpowers in South Asia: A Geostrategic Analysis," *Orbis*, Summer 1978.

Roy, Arundhati, "Indo-Russian Military Ties in the Post-Cold War Period: Some Observations," *Jadavpur Journal of International Relations*, Vol. 2, 1996.

Roy, Denny, "Current Sino-US Relations in Strategic Perspective", *Contemporary South East Asia*, Vol. 20, No. 3, December 1998.

Roy, Meena Singh, "Russia and Central Asia: Problems and Prospects", *Strategic Analysis*, Vol. XXV, No. 3, June 2001.

——, "India-Kazakhstan: Emerging Ties", *Strategic Analysis*, January-March 2002.

Salitsky, Alexandr, "China, India, Russia: Why A Strategic Triangle", *World Affairs*, 5(1), January-March 2001.

Sautman, Barry, "The Devil to Pay: The 1989 Debate and the Intellectual Origins of Yeltsin's 'Soft Authoritarianism'", *Communist and Post-Communist Studies*, Vol. 28, No. 1, 1995.

Savara Sharapova, "The US – Western Europe-Russia Triangle and Central Asia", *Central Asia and the Caucasus*, 1(19), 2003.

Saxena, Hari Mohan, "Scientific and Technological Cooperation Between India and Russia," *Business Messenger*, December 2002.

Segal, Gerald, "Does China Matter?" *Foreign Affairs*, September-October 1999.

Sen, Pronab, "Growth and Instability of Indian Exports to the USSR," *Economic and Political Weekly*, April 1989.

——, "Rupee-Rouble Exchange Rate", *Economic and Political Weekly*, 24 March 1993.

Sethi, Manpreet, "Indo-Russian Nuclear Cooperation: Opportunities and Challenges", *Strategic Analysis*, Vol. XXIV, No. 9, 2000.

Shakoor, Abdul, "Central Asia: The US Interest-perception and its Security Policies," *Eurasian Studies*, Vol. 2, No. 2, Summer 1995.

Shastri, Paromita – Deb, Sandipan, "Now, Diffuse", *Outlook*, 25 May 1998.

Sherlock, Thomas, "Politics and History under Gorbachev", *Problems of Communism*, May-August 1988.

Shlapentokh, Dmitry V. "Eurasianism: Past and Present", *Communist and Post-Communist Studies*, Vol. 39, No. 2, 1997.

Shub, Anatol, "The Fourth Russian Revolution: Historical Perspectives", *Problems of Communism*, November-December 1991.

Simon, Gerhard, "Russia's Identity and International Politics," *Aussenpolitik*, 3/97.

Singh, Anita Inder, "India's Relations with Russia and Central Asia", *International Affairs*, Vol. 71(1), 1995.

Singh, Jasjit, "Post-Cold War Security Situation in Southern Asia", *Strategic Analysis*, April 1994.

Singh, Uma, "The Afghanistan Crisis and Its Impact on South Asia,", *Himalayan and Central Asian Studies*, 1(2), July-September 1997.

Stobdan, P., "Regional Issues in Central Asia: Implications for South Asia", *South Asia Survey*, No. 2, July-December 1998.

Subrahmanyam, K. "Nuclear India in Global Politics", *World Affairs: The Journal of International Issues*, reproduced in *Strategic Digest*, September 1998.

——, "Self-Reliant Defence and Indian Industry", *Strategic Analysis*, Vol. XXIV, No. 7, October 2000.

Sulaiman, Sadia, "Role of Central Asia in War Against Global Terrorism: Futuristic Appraisal," *Strategic Studies* (Islamabad), Vol. XXII, No. 2, Summer 2002.

Tarock, Adam, "Iran's Policy in Central Asia", *Central Asian Survey*, 16(2), 1997.

Tazmini, Ghoncheh, "The Islamic revival in Central Asia: a potent force or a misconception ?", *Central Asian Survey*, 20(1), 2001.

"The Geopolitics of Caspian Oil", *Jane's Intelligence Review*, Vol. XII, No. 7, July 2000.

Tolipov, Farkhod, "Nationalism as a geopolitical phenomenon: the Central Asian Case," *Central Asian Survey*, 20(2), 2001.

Tomberg, Igor, "Energy Policy in the Countries of Central Asia and the Caucasus", *Central Asia and the Caucasus*, No. 4(22), 2003.

Trofimov, Dmitry, "Russia and the United States in Central Asia: Problems, Prospects and Interests," *Central Asia and the Caucasus*, 1(19), 2003.

Tsepkalo, Valery V. "The Remaking of Eurasia," *Foreign Affairs*, 77(2), March/April 1998.

Ulam, Adam B. "Looking At the Past: The Unraveling of the Soviet Union", *Current History*, October 1992.

Vasudevan, Hari, "Russia's Presidency", *Economic and Political Weekly*, 18 December 1993.

Warikoo, K., "Islamist Mercenaries and Terrorism in Kashmir," *Himalayan and Central Asian Studies*, Vol. 2, No. 2, April-June 1998.

Winrow, Gareth M., "Turkey and ECO", *Himalayan and Central Asian Studies*, April-June 1998.

Withington, Thomas, "The Other Allies: Russia, India and Afghanistan's United Front", *Current History*, January 2002.

Wolosky, Lee S. "Putin's Plutocrat Problems", *Foreign Affairs*, March-April 2000.

Yujun, Feng – Xiao Xing – Dong, Li, "Russia's New Energy Diplomacy and Its Impact," *Contemporary International Relations* (Beijing), Vol. 12, No. 10, October 2002.

Yurlov, Felix N. "Russia: Problems of Security in the Post-Cold War World," *World Affairs*, Vol. 4, No. 2, April-June 2000.

Zagorsky, A., "The Commonwealth: One Year On", *International Affairs* (Moscow), February 1993.

Zardykhan, Zharmukhamed, "Kazakhstan and Central Asia: regional perspectives", *Central Asian Survey*, 21(2), June 2002.

Index